*Cues: Theatre Training & Projects
from Classroom to Stage*

CUES

THEATRE TRAINING & PROJECTS
from Classroom to Stage

TALIA PURA

J. GORDON SHILLINGFORD
PUBLISHING INC

Cover design by Relish New Brand Experience
Author photo by Image 2

We acknowledge the financial assistance of the Manitoba Arts Council
and The Canada Council for the Arts for our publishing program.
Printed and bound in Canada on 100% post-consumer recycled paper.

J. Gordon Shillingford Publishing Inc.
P.O. Box 86, RPO Corydon Avenue
Winnipeg, MB R3M 3S3
Canada

LIBRARY AND ARCHIVES CANADA CATALOGUING IN PUBLICATION

Pura, Talia, author
        Cues : theatre training and projects from classroom to stage /
Talia Pura.

Companion to: Stages: creative ideas for teaching drama.
ISBN 978-1-897289-93-8 (pbk.)

        1. Theater--Study and teaching. 2. Acting--Study and teaching.
I. Title.

PN1701.P87 2013 Suppl.   792.071   C2013-906489-3

for
John B. Wiebe
who taught me about
setting goals, planning strategies
and the value of hard work

Dad, this one is for you

ACKNOWLEDGEMENTS

This book would never have been written without a myriad of people providing interest, insight and support. First, I thank all the students that I have taught, spanning more than 25 years, from high schools in Fort Richmond, St. Vital, North Kildonan to the University of Winnipeg, Department of Education. Then, there are all the educators and directors that have challenged and inspired me, especially John Hirsch, Carol Rosenfeld, Mort Ransen, Tibor Fehergyhazi, Rosemary Dunsmore, William B. Davis, Matthew Harrison, Tomson Highway and Guy Maddin. Thank you as well to Gordon Shillingford, for publishing this book. Lastly, there is my family, thank you Adrian, Alexia, Noelani and Bill, my inspiration, my rock, and the provider of my best ideas.

TABLE OF CONTENTS

INTRODUCTION

In 2002, I wrote **STAGES: Creative Ideas for Teaching Drama**. It was filled with all the accumulated material I had developed while teaching high school drama. I wrote it for my pre-service educators; to give them a tool to take into their own classrooms. In writing its revised second edition, I acknowledged that there was so much more to be said on the subject. Since leaving the high school classroom in 1999, I have not only taught university students, I have also conducted numerous workshops for adolescents, educators, actors and beginning directors. Along the way, I kept writing plays, acting on stage and in films, making my own films, and producing my own dramas. When it was time to publish the second edition, I knew that it couldn't be just one book. **STAGES** is for the classroom, teaching drama and using it across the curriculum. This book is for those who want to take the experience further. Everything here could stay in the classroom, but it could also be used in preparing for the stage. It's for new directors that are looking for guidance in working with new actors, either in their schools or in a wider community. There are so many things to think about if you are the one in charge of a project. This is an attempt to break it all down into manageable pieces. Then, there are the creative projects, the real fun of guiding actors through the creation and production of their own work. I have found so much satisfaction in working with diverse groups of people who prepared pieces for the stage, or used the exercises for their own sake, to guide their exploration and understanding of issues that were important to them.

I hope that you will use this book as a springboard for your own creative journey of discovery in the theatrical arts.

PART I
CLASSROOM TRAINING

An actor begins by training the instruments needed for the stage: the voice, the body, and the imagination. Through the fun of improvisations and the discoveries made in the activities used to prepare scenes and monologues, comes an understanding of how to use these instruments to effectively portray a character on the stage.

VOICE

Voice training should be part of every actor's development. Student actors may not see it as the most fun part of the process, but with the use of tongue twisters, interactive activities and poetry that the group can relate to, it can be as enjoyable as it is useful. It is important for actors to use their voices safely, working on breath control and voice projection in order to develop an effective stage voice without strain or damage to this important instrument.

VOICE PRODUCTION

Voice production can be broken down into four stages.

1. Respiration   2. Phonation   3. Resonation   4. Articulation

RESPIRATION

This is the process by which air reaches the vocal folds. A well-controlled voice begins in the diaphragm, the web-like membrane of muscle and sinew attached to the lower rib cage, which separates the thorax from the abdomen. When air is expelled, the diaphragm slowly relaxes. As we inhale, the diaphragm can contract, pushing against the abdomen, raising the rib cage as air fills the lungs. As we exhale, the diaphragm can be used to control the flow of air, giving our voices support.

Method: Find the diaphragm by standing up straight and placing fingertips on the bottom of the rib cage, then drawing a line across the body. Place a hand on the stomach covering this line, during the following exercises:

1. Say, "Ha, ha, ha, ha, ha." Feel the diaphragm jump and the hand move at each sound. This is the diaphragm working to push the air from the lungs. Repeat the sounds without the hand jumping against the stomach. This is a weak voice, unsupported by the diaphragm. Say, "Hello, how are you? Hurry up," and other phrases, feeling the diaphragm move. It will be most obvious on an H sound.

2. Lie on the floor, facing the ceiling. Place a hand on the diaphragm, inhale to a count of twenty, and then exhale to the same count. Feel the diaphragm rise on the inhales and lower on the exhales. Release the air to the sound of AHH, as slowly as possible, finding a spot on the ceiling on which to focus the sound.

It is important to fill the lungs with air to ensure sufficient breath to speak clearly. Keep shoulders down and relaxed. Raising shoulders does nothing to increase lung capacity.

PHONATION

This is the passage of the air from the lungs, through the vibrating vocal folds within the larynx and out of the mouth and nose. It is very important to relax the throat as the air passes through. There is a tendency to raise the pitch when trying to increase the volume, thereby tightening the vocal folds and causing the voice to strain. This is both unpleasant to listen to and damages the folds, leading to a sore, scratchy throat by the end of a performance. Any increase in volume must be supported by the diaphragm; not forced through a tightening of the throat.

Method: Stand, feet shoulder width apart, arms dropped loosely at the sides. Relax.

1. Drop the head forward, releasing all tension in the neck. Let it drop from side to side. Drop it backwards, opening the mouth. Roll head from side to side. Avoid rolling through the back, as it crunches the cartilage at the back of the neck.

2. Drop the head forward, followed by the shoulders and back, finally drop forward from the waist, on an exhale. In this position, shake the head and shoulders to ensure a total release of tension. Then slowly roll back up, one vertebra at a time, with the head being the last to fall back into place in an upright position. The inhale continues as the arms reach above the head. The exhale triggers a repetition of the exercise.

RESONATION

Without resonation, the sounds made by the vibrating vocal folds would scarcely be audible. The slight vibration of air in the back of the throat, mouth and sometimes the nose accentuate the sound already begun in the larynx. It is in these resonating chambers that sounds are selectively amplified to become the sounds we hear. The more open the resonating chambers, the stronger and clearer the sound. This is why a vowel sound carries better than a consonant.

Method: Stand; feet shoulder width apart, arms dropped loosely at the sides. Relax.

1. Open your mouth wide and yawn, stretching the arms overhead; the ultimate throat-relaxing exercise. Now, keeping that same open feeling in the throat, release a slow sustained AHH sound.

2. Starting at a mid-range, comfortable pitch, perform this exercise using all of the vowel sounds, rising one note with each repetition. A-E-I-O-U. Hold each sound for a moment before going on to the next one. Maintain an open throat as the pitch rises.

3. Instead of simple vowel sounds, repeat the sounds:

    UN GA YA YA LA LA MA MA

ARTICULATION

The vibrating air in the resonating chambers is modified by the tongue, lips, teeth, soft palate and jaw to become the sounds that we recognize as words. There are many articulation drills, such as tongue twisters, to encourage the proper use of these tools in forming words clearly.

Method: Stand; feet shoulder width apart, arms dropped loosely at the sides. Relax.

1. **Peanut butter:** Pretend to have a mouthful of peanut butter. Use the tongue to clear it out of first one cheek, then the other and around the front of the teeth.

2. **Brrr:** Relax the lips and allow them to vibrate, blowing air out on a BRRRRR sound. Now allow the tongue to relax and vibrate, RRRRRR. Add the letter B to produce the sounds, BREEEEE and BRAAAA, smiling widely.

3. **Shh/Sss:** Smile widely and produce the sound SSSSSSS. Purse the lips to create the sound SHHHHH. Go from one to the other quickly.

4. **ABC:** Say the alphabet as quickly and clearly as possible. As a breath control exercise, repeat the alphabet three times in one breath.

5. **Tongue Twisters:** Keeping the jaw and neck relaxed, repeat these tongue twisters as many times as possible in one breath. Keep the volume and strength of the voice constant until the end of the breath. Support from the diaphragm.

> The lips, the teeth, the tip of the tongue
>
> Little Laura Lynn loves liquorice lollipops and lemonade
>
> Bobby borrowed Barry's baseball bat
>
> Six sickly salmon swam swiftly sideways
>
> Herman Hubert Humphries hobbled haltingly home

BREATH CONTROL

Breath must be controlled and released slowly. The sound produced should be as strong at the end of the phrase as it is at the beginning.

Method: Read the following samples, controlling the amount of breath released on each line.

1. Repeat each line five times in one breath.
   - ☐ Round and round
     Round and round the rugged rocks
     Round and round the rugged rocks the ragged rascal ran
   - ☐ Bring the butter
     Bring the butter to the baker
     Bring the butter to the baker to be baked
     Bring the butter to the baker to be baked into the bread

□ Sit with Shelly
Sit with Shelly and Sammy
Sit with Shelly and Sammy Smithers
Sit with Shelly and Sammy Smithers and slip
Sit with Shelly and Sammy Smithers and slip some salt
into their soup

□ Did you dance?
Did you dance with Danny?
Did you dance with Danny the dragon?
Did you dance with Danny the dragon in the dungeon?
Did you dance with Danny the dragon in the dungeon
dining on dandelions?
Did you dance with Danny the dragon in the dungeon
dining on dandelions dumbly in the dark?

2. Limericks can be used in the same way, slowly for articulation and quickly for breath control. Try to use only one
breath per limerick.

□ There was a young lady of Niger,
who smiled as she rode on a Tiger.
They returned from the ride
with the lady inside
and a smile on the face of the tiger.

□ There was an old man with a beard,
who said, "It is just as I feared,
two owls and a hen,
four larks and a wren
have just built a home in my beard."

□ There was a young man of Japan,
who wrote verses that no one could scan.
When they told him twas so,
he replied, "Yes, I know,
but I like to get as many words in the last line as I
possibly can."

□ There was a young man of Quebec
who stood in the snow to his neck.
When they said, "Are you frizz?"
He replied, "Yes, I is,
but we don't call this cold in Quebec."

□ There was a an old man of Nantucket,
who kept all of his gold in a bucket,
till his daughter named Nan

ran away with a man,
and as for the bucket, Nantucket.

☐ There was a young fellow named Dave
whose parents told him to behave.
But he played his guitar
making sounds most bizarre
and created an outlandish new wave.

3. Repeat the following lyrics from Gilbert and Sullivan. Try to keep the articulation very clean and say as much of the passage as possible in one breath.

from: **The Mikado** by W.S. Gilbert of *Gilbert and Sullivan*

To sit in sullen silence in a dull, dark dock
In a pestilential prison with a life-long lock
Awaiting the sensation of a short sharp shock
From a cheap and chippy chopper on a big black block.

To sit in solemn silence in a dull, dark dock,
In a pestilential prison, with a life-long lock,
Awaiting the sensation of a short, sharp shock,
From a cheap and chippy chopper on a big black block!

A dull, dark dock, a life-long lock,
A short, sharp shock, a big black block!
To sit in solemn silence in a pestilential prison,
And awaiting the sensation
From a cheap and chippy chopper on a big black block!

from: **Princess Ida** by W.S. Gilbert of *Gilbert and Sullivan*
For a month to dwell
In a dungeon cell;
Growing thin and wizen
In a solitary prison,
Is a poor look out
For a soldier stout,
Who is longing for the rattle
Of a complicated battle
For the rum-tum-tum
Of the military drum,
And the guns that go boom ! boom !

ELEMENTS OF EFFECTIVE SPEECH

After working on breath control and articulation, there are other elements of speech to focus on that will improve the quality of a stage voice. It's not enough for the voice to simply be heard. In order to keep the listener interested in the words, the voice must not be monotonous or boring. It must have variety. This may be achieved by the speaker simply being interested in what he is saying and conveying this to his audience, but there are also technical ways of bringing variety to the voice. This is achieved by varying:

Pitch – Emphasis – Tone – Tempo/pauses – Volume – Rhythm

Pitch: This refers to the highs and lows of the voice. The speaker should stay within a comfortable range, in order to sound natural. Pitch will vary naturally if the speaker follows the intent of a word or phrase.

Method: Repeat the following words and phrases aloud, reflecting the intention in brackets:

- Hello   (do I know you?)
  Hello   (I haven't seen you in ages)
  Hello   (I'm glad that I haven't seen you in ages)
  Hello   (I have something to sell you)
- I'm leaving now   (I love you and I'll be right back)
  I'm leaving now   (I don't ever want to come back)
  I'm leaving now   (Because you hurt my feelings)
  I'm leaving now   (I'm pretending to leave so I can eavesdrop)
- May I have that?   (It's mine and you took it)
  May I have that?   (I can't believe you'd let me keep it)
  May I have that?   (I can't believe you were giving it to HER)
  May I have that?   (It's ugly and I don't really want it)

Use the alphabet in place of words, allowing the pitch to imply meaning:

- **Give a speech.** Say only the letters of the alphabet and let the real text play in your head. Choose a topic you feel passionate about. For example: Your favourite piece of music. The saddest movie you ever saw. The most fun you ever had on a vacation.

- **Hold a conversation.** Use only the alphabet. In pairs, one person picks up the next letter when it is his turn to speak, or one partner can repeat letters until he feels he has made his point. For example: Talk about the weather. Bring up the money your friend owes you. Decide which movie to go and see. Have a pointless argument.

Emphasis: This is finding the important words in a sentence to stress to convey meaning and intent or to create interest.

Method: Read these paragraphs, making their meanings absolutely clear:

- I will go to see Will, if you will come with me. Will will make us dinner, if we will bring Will the dessert. Will will read his Uncle William's will after dinner.

- Now see here! I hear that Harold and Melissa will be here within the hour, if our calculations are correct. There's a reason for their present to remain here for the present. I'll be sure to present it to them after the party winds down. That is, if the winds on the patio aren't too strong. I wound up Harold's wound, but as he was already an invalid, his insurance is invalid. Unfortunately, he got too close to the box's lid to close it safely, and he and Melissa had quite a row in the rowboat. She had to subject him to some strong language, as the box was the subject of the investigation. He pounded on the lid a number of times, and his fist got number and number. Finally, she shed a tear at the tear in her dress and is trying to lead him here. If only they would get the lead out!

Reading Shakespeare can be a challenge (see the Language section of INTRODUCING SHAKESPEARE). It is always important to emphasis those words which will bring out the meaning of the phrases most clearly.

> **Phoebe**   *As You Like It* – Act III scene 5
> I would not be thy executioner,
> I fly thee, for I would not injure thee:
> Thou tell'st me there is murder in mine eye;
> 'Tis pretty, sure, and very probable,
> That eyes, that are the frail'st and softest things,
> Who shut their coward gates on atomies,
> Should be called tyrants, butchers, murderers!
> Now I do frown on thee with all my heart,
> And if mine eyes can wound, now let them kill thee,
> Now counterfeit to swoon, why now fall down,
> Or if thou canst not, O, for shame, for shame,
> Lie not, to say mine eyes are murderers!
> Now show the wound mine eye hath made in thee,
> Scratch thee but with a pin, and there remains
> Some scar of it; lean upon a rush,

The cicatrice and capable impressure
Thy palm some moment keeps; but now mine eyes,
Which I have darted at thee, hurt thee not,
Nor I am sure there is no force in eyes
That can do hurt.

When using emphasis to create interest, choose the words that will catch the listener's ear and help you create a picture with your words. Read this poem, drawing out long vowel sounds. Of course, the other elements of speech – pitch, tone, tempo and volume – will also make the reading more effective.

Daffodils
by William Wordsworth

I wandered lonely as a cloud
That floats on high o'er vales and hills,
When all at once I saw a crowd,
A host, of golden Daffodils;
Beside the lake, beneath the trees,
Fluttering and dancing in the breeze.

Continuous as the stars that shine
And twinkle on the Milky Way,
They stretched in never-ending line
Along the margin of the bay:
Ten thousand saw I at a glance,
Tossing their heads in sprightly dance.

The waves beside them danced, but they
Out-did the sparkling waves with glee:
A poet could not but be gay,
In such a jocund company:
I gazed—and gazed—but little thought
What wealth the show to me had brought:

For oft, when on my couch I lie
In vacant or in pensive mood,
They flash upon that inward eye
Which is the bliss of solitude;
And then my heart with pleasure fills,
And dances with the Daffodils.

Tone: This refers to the mood the speaker wishes to create for the listener. She might darken or lighten her voice, depending on the effect she wishes to have on her audience. Find the author's attitude towards the subject and let that dictate the tone.

Method: Read this poem, deciding on an attitude for each stanza. Have fun with it. This poem makes use of repetition. Whenever a word or phrase is repeated, find a new attitude for it each time. The easiest way of showing this is to emphasize a different word in each repetition. This will change the intonation of the line and vary its meaning slightly.

I Can't Think What He Sees In Her
— A. P. Herbert

Jealousy's an awful thing and foreign to my nature:
I'd punish it by law if I was in the Legislature.
One can't have all of anyone, and wanting it is mean,
But still, there is a limit, and I speak of Miss Duveen.

I'm not a jealous woman,
    But I can't see what he sees in her,
      I can't see what he sees in her,
        I can't see what he sees in her!

If she was something striking
I could understand the liking,
And I wouldn't have a word to say to that:
But I can't see why he's fond
Of that objectionable blonde—
That fluffy little, stuffy little, flashy little, trashy little,
creepy-crawly, music-hally, horrid little CAT!

I wouldn't say a word against the girl—be sure of that;
It's not the creature's fault she has the manners of a rat.
Her dresses may be dowdy, but her hair is always new,
And if she squints a little bit—well, many people do.

I'm not a jealous woman,
    But I can't see what he sees in her,
      I can't see what he sees in her,
        I can't see what he sees in her!

He's absolutely free—
There's no bitterness in me,
Though an ordinary woman would explode:
I'd only like to know
What he sees in such a crow,
As that insinuating, calculating, irritating, titivating,
sleepy little, creepy little, sticky little TOAD.

Tempo/pauses: When the tempo is varied the interest of the audience is maintained. It also varies according to the mood of the piece. A pause before a word heightens its importance. A pause after a word or phrase gives the audience time to think about its significance.

Method: Read the following paragraphs, pausing where appropriate for effect.

- Always remember, if you want people to realize the importance of the words you are saying, you cannot spit them all out at the same time. You must take all the time their importance requires. Sometimes, it may be necessary to even stop... and wait for your audience to grasp the meaning of your words.

- You may also use pauses for dramatic effect. When you know that something is out there in the black night, you want to pause, because you don't want your listener to find out too quickly what it is. You'll want to speak slowly as well, to build suspense. But then—once you have revealed that you are being chased by the world's largest living monster, you may want to speak very fast, in short choppy sentences, every breath coming out in short, little gasps, to indicate to your audience just how frightened you really are.

Volume: The voice will naturally increase in volume to emphatically make a point and soften to create a warm loving mood. The volume of the voice must also be appropriate for the size of the audience and the distance it is away from the speaker.

Method: Repeat the following sentences twice, the first time in anger, the second time in a warm welcoming tone.

- Take that thing out of the box.
- I told you that I would be coming at 4:00.
- You always say stuff like that.
- Come over here right now.
- I can't help feeling like that.
- What do you want me to say?
- I can't believe you said that.

Place a student five steps away from the group. Have the speaker repeat a limerick, give instructions on making his favourite sandwich, or deliver any material he is familiar with. Instruct him to speak loudly enough for the group to hear him comfortably. After a few sentences, have him move away from the group another five steps and continue speaking. Repeat this process until he is as far away from the group as the space will allow. His volume should increase to accommodate the distance that he is from his audience. The quality of voice used should remain rich and grounded in the diaphragm, not pushed from the throat. The tone should remain conversational.

Rhythm: When reading a piece of pose, or free-form verse, the reader decides on the rhythm he will adopt. If he wishes to relax his audience, his tone will be soothing and his rhythm fairly regular, with few changes that would surprise them. However, if it is his intent to shock, motivate, inspire or excite his audience, his rhythm will go through many changes, constantly challenging his audience to keep up with him.

There is another facet of rhythm when reading poetry that needs to be addressed. Many pieces of classical poetry and some modern poems, especially those written for children, are written in an iambic meter. This means that every other syllable is accented. Unless reading with small children, to read an iambic poem with a strong emphasis on every other syllable isn't very compelling. The previous five ways of creating interest in a reading will be completely lost. The audience will not pay attention to the words; they will simply hear the rhythm. As iambic meter closely follows the natural cadence of English speech, it will always be there in the background. If it is stressed, it will take over and become the only thing heard.

The first step in ignoring this rhythm is to look at the punctuation of the piece, rather than stopping at the end of every line whether the thought continues on to the next line or not. Significant pauses are only taken at a period, or in the middle of a line if needed for effect or emphasis. Then, pitch, tone, tempo and volume can be explored and applied to the poem. Emphasis is especially important, in order to stress the words that are significant to the meaning of the poem and to create interest, rather than simply because of their position in the line.

Method: The following poem has been written in an iambic meter. Read it aloud, trying not to fall into its rhythm.

Progress
by Alfred Lord Tennyson

As we surpass our fathers' skill,
Our sons will shame our own;

A thousand things are hidden still,
And not a hundred known.

And had some prophet spoken true
Of all we shall achieve,
The wonders were so wildly new,
That no man would believe.

Meanwhile, my brothers, work, and wield
The forces of to-day,
And plough the Present like a field,
And garner all you may!

You, what the cultured surface grows,
Dispense with careful hands;
Deep under deep for ever goes,
Heaven our heaven expands.

Of course, there may be times when the rhythm of a poem is stressed very effectively, if only for short intervals as a contrast to the rest of the poem. In other applications, such as poetry with a rap beat, it would be appropriate to maintain the intended rhythm.

USING POETRY

CHORAL SPEAKING

Poems are very useful in demonstrating the techniques needed to develop a strong stage voice. In performing a piece of Readers Theatre or Collage Collective, poetry could play a role, but as its own art form, it has been largely forgotten. It does have a place, however, in acting as a bridge between speech work and theatre. Find poems that the group loves and try choral speaking: collectively reciting a poem with the lines divided between individual, small group and unison voices.

Method: The following poem is fun for any age group. It could be done as a choral speech choir; however, it could really come alive with pantomime, students creating the monster with their bodies, as well as their voices.

Jabberwocky
from *Through the Looking-Glass* by Lewis Carroll

'Twas brillig, and the slithy toves
Did gyre and gimble in the wabe:
All mimsy were the borogoves,
And the mome raths outgrabe.
"Beware the Jabberwock, my son!

The jaws that bite, the claws that catch!
Beware the Jubjub bird, and shun
The frumious Bandersnatch!"
He took the vorpal sword in hand:
Long time the manxome foe he sought—
So rested he by the Tumtum tree,
And stood awhile in thought.
And as in uffish thought he stood,
The Jabberwock, with eyes of flame,
Came whiffling through the tulgey wood,
And burbled as it came!
One, two! One two! And through and through
The vorpal blade went snicker-snack!
He left it dead, and with its head
He went galumphing back.
"And hast thou slain the Jabberwock?
Come to my arms, my beamish boy!
O frabjous day! Callooh! Callay!"
He chortled in his joy.
'Twas brillig, and the slithy toves
Did gyre and gimble in the wabe:
All mimsy were the borogoves,
And the mome raths outgrabe.

POETRY AS MONOLOGUE STUDY

Using poetry as a monologue is difficult. It isn't comfortable to
use it conversationally because the language is unnatural.
Using naturalistic dialogue is easier to fake, because it is like
real life. Poetry makes the actor more exposed. Each word is
specifically chosen and can't be wasted.

Method: Students each chose a poem to perform for the group.
The speaker must decide who the poem is addressed to. If it is
an individual, put a person on stage with her to stand in for
that individual. Encourage the speaker to really use the words
of the poem to tell the story. Play the thought and stay with
each word in turn, moment by moment. Make each choice
very specific. Every word, every gesture is trying to change the
audience in some way. The poems of William Blake are a good
place to start for this exercise.

A Poison Tree
I was angry with my friend:
I told my wrath, my wrath did end.

I was angry with my foe:
I told it not, my wrath did grow.

And I watered it in fears,
Night and morning with my tears;
And I sunned it with smiles,
And with soft deceitful wiles.

And it grew both day and night,
Till it bore an apple bright.
And my foe beheld it shine.
And he knew that it was mine,

And into my garden stole
When the night had veiled the pole;
In the morning glad I see
My foe outstretched beneath the tree.

LITANY

Poetry can flow very naturally into litany, which in turn can be used to introduce the concept of rituals. This would lead the group to the project on creating an Ancient Ritual. The rhythms and repetition of this invocation are a suitable introduction to ritual.

Method: Students are divided into groups of six to eight participants. They are given fifteen minutes to plan and rehearse this litany. Movement patterns could be incorporated, as well as simple instruments to create a repetitive rhythm.

A Litany for the Moon

LEADER:	RESPONSE:
Great Spirit of the night, hear our cry	Hear our cry
Oh moon, rise, rise up on high	Let it rise up
Fill the darkness with your light	Let it rise up
Great Spirit of the night, hear our cry	Hear our cry
Rise up in your fullness	Let it rise up
Gather the stars in the heavens	Gather them up
Bring forth the beasts for our hunt	Bring them forth
Let them be seen in the night	Let them be seen
Give us strength for the hunt	Give us strength
Guide our path in this journey	Guide our path
Oh moon, rise, rise up on high	Let it rise up
Great Spirit of the night, hear our cry	Hear our cry
Hear our cry	Hear our cry

RADIO PLAYS

As a voice project, radio plays will take students in another direction, rather than only using voice exercises as a means of training actors for the stage, or having it flow into the physical applications of litany and ancient rituals. As radio is an audio medium, the voice is the only instrument needed. Radio plays are also a great introduction to script writing. They help develop skills in writing dialogue and allow for a great deal of creativity. With no staging requirements, plays can be set in any location with unlimited action. Students can also experiment with sounds and vocal characterizations.

Method:

1. Play excerpts of classic and modern radio plays, which are readily available online.

2. Discuss the different genres. Horror, soap operas (the origin of the term is from radio, where early sponsors of daytime continuing dramas were soap companies), action adventure, cliff hanger serials, 'whodunnit' (detective), etc. Talk about how most types of shows we see on television today originated in radio. Until televisions became common in the 1950s, families would gather around the radio, listening to their favourite programs. This is why TV took over so many of the genres. They knew what people would want to watch.

3. Groups of five or six students are formed. Gender balance the groups for variety in voice pitches and tones.

4. Hand out the requirements of the assignment and discuss them.

5. Each group begins work with brainstorming for genre and story line.

6. Dialogues and situations are improvised, then scripted.

7. Sound effects are planned, with a means to achieve them found and rehearsed.

8. Groups rehearse completed plays.

9. Groups are given the means to record their plays.

10. Plays are aired for the whole group to enjoy and offer feedback.

Sample Radio Play assignment

Requirements:

- The play should be between five and ten minutes in length.
- Each actor must play a minimum of two characters. Consider accents and other means of changing your voice.
- It must have a beginning, middle and end (no talk, reality or game shows).
- The play may contain old-fashioned short commercials, an announcer and station identification breaks (filling no more than one quarter of the total time).
- Characters may be human, animal or inanimate objects, or a mixture of all three.
- The play must contain a minimum of ten sound effects, from a minimum of six different sources. For example: 3 sets of footsteps, 1 door slam, 2 bells, 1 horse galloping, 1 gun shot, 2 phones ringing. All sound effects must be made live, vocally or with objects, not taken from a recorded library of sound effects.
- The play can be 'shot to edit'; recorded in sequence, to save on editing time.
- The play should be of a recognizable genre.

Evaluation could take the group process into account, as well as the fulfillment of the requirements, creativity and voice characterizations.

Variation #1. Cartoons: The play could be written as a cartoon, with all cartoon voices. All sound effects are vocalized. This project takes much less time and is a good alternative to a full radio play. Students could take their inspiration from a comic script, putting known characters into a new situation. Discourage them from taking their inspiration from a TV cartoon. They will be tempted to follow an already existing story line, and imitate the voices. Students could work in pairs or trios. Instead of recording these plays, the scripts could be read to the class, with students turning their backs on the performers in order to only hear them.

TABLEAUX

Tableau: "a frozen moment in time," like a photograph that stops an action in progress, or is carefully constructed, like an illustration or painting. It can also be viewed as a statue, as it is being created from human bodies, which can be sculpted like lumps of clay to represent something literally or abstractly. The companion book, **STAGES: Creative Ideas for Teaching Drama**, has an extensive chapter on using tableaux in creative drama. Here, they are described in a more abstract manner, which is then translated into physical form to be utilized in presentational projects (see Collage Collectives).

DESIGN CONCEPTS THROUGH TABLEAUX

Using pair and small group tableaux exercises is a very effective way of teaching basic design elements, which will become important when tableaux become part of the stage pictures created for presentations. They are also fun to explore for team building, which is a good way to begin the work on a new project.

Elements of design demonstrated through tableaux:

- Balance – literal and visual
- Symmetry and asymmetry – formal versus informal
- Line – static versus dynamic
- Mass – positive and negative space

BALANCE – LITERAL

Literal balance refers to students in a tableau supporting each other physically.

Method: Working with a partner, students create tableaux in which

- one student balances the other – dependent
- both students need each other for balance – inter-dependent

Students show their tableaux. Ask the group to identify some aspects that they have in common. What you will find is that most inter-dependent tableaux will be symmetrical, with one student in a mirror image pose of the other. Dependent tableaux are most likely to be asymmetrical. Ask students to explore moving across the room while maintaining the balanced positions.

Hint: Once the project is further along, and various tableaux have been created and chosen to be part of the final project, have the groups go back to the concept of dependent and inter-dependent tableaux, to see if some of their tableaux could incorporate literal balance as an element. How would it subtly change or enhance the meaning of a certain tableau to add that aspect, or to also have the tableau move or shift on stage?

BALANCE – VISUAL

Visual balance refers to the stage picture as a whole; what the audience sees. Even if the scene is full of action, it should always be considered.

The stage area can be viewed as a seesaw. If there is equal weight on both sides, it is balanced. Weight consists of people, set pieces and anything providing mass. Lighting can also contribute to weight. There are times when the seesaw should be unbalanced: when someone is being overpowered (an employee sitting on a small chair and the boss behind a huge desk), or in danger (one person alone against a gang in a back alley). Visual balance is an important element to consider in conveying mood and meaning.

Method: In groups of eight, all but two of the group members form an interconnected tableau, creating a large mass, while the remaining two group members form another tableau on the other side of the stage. Show these stage pictures to the larger group, to demonstrate what the audience sees when looking at this imbalance. What happens to the power structure? Is there a way for the pair on one side to claim the power in this situation? What would have to happen for that to shift? Ask them to try various tactics, with the audience responding to the results and offering feedback. Ask students to create storylines that support the tableaux they create. Remind students that visual balance is one more element to keep in mind when using tableaux to create stage pictures in their projects.

SYMMETRY AND ASYMMETRY

Symmetry: The same on both sides of an imaginary centerline through the tableau.
Asymmetry: Lack of symmetry. Different on each side.

Method: In small groups of six to eight, students create:

- symmetrical tableaux
- asymmetrical tableaux

Have students view other groups' tableaux and asses whether the tableau has a formal or informal, relaxed feeling to it. Guide them to discover that symmetrical tableaux tend to appear more formal, while an asymmetrical tableau will suggest an informal, casual feeling. Help the students explore what this means for future work by discovering when they would appropriately use a more formal tableau and when an asymmetrical pose would demonstrate what they were trying to portray.

FAMILY PORTRAITS

This exercise helps students understand how to use symmetry and asymmetry to plan a tableau for maximum effect.

Method: Small groups of students form family portraits.

- Students create a posed portrait of a family that is very upper crust and proper, where family members don't communicate on anything but a formal level (symmetry).

- Students create a posed family portrait of a rural family, who is casual, warm and relaxed with each other, having their pictures taken outdoors (asymmetry).

After each group has formed their own family portrait, it is useful to look at each one and discuss the choices made. What will be discovered is that when a casual, relaxed family was portrayed, the group was likely to have used an asymmetrical tableau, with family members in poses of their own choosing. In the portrait of a very formal family, it is likely that the group chose a more symmetrical tableau.

Once this concept is understood, have each group form their own family portraits. The family types can be picked from a deck of cards containing various possibilities, or each group can decide this for itself. The game might also be to use famous families that are well known to the group. Once they have formed the tableau, the rest of the groups try to guess the identity of the family.

Sample families: circus family – politician's family – banker's family – mortician's family – ghost family – royal family – hillbilly family – explorer's family

LINE

Just as a work of visual art can be described in terms of its line, so too can a tableau be planned to use line as an effective element in conveying meaning.

Method: Discuss whether a symmetrical tableau or an asymmetrical tableau will be better able to convey the feeling of movement. Which one looks more likely to burst into action? Demonstrate this theory by asking the students to form a tableau of:

- ☐ A newspaper photograph of one head of government meeting a head of state from another country.
- ☐ A photograph taken at a baseball game as the batter going for a home run is struck out at home base.

■ Students view each other's tableaux and discuss them in terms of dynamic action versus static non-action. Diagonal lines suggest movement. Horizontal and vertical lines appear more grounded and immobile. Multiple levels add interest to any tableau. These lines are created not only with limbs shooting out at interesting angles, or staying close to the body, but also by the composition as a whole. Multiple levels allow for more variations, as the line continues from person to person, sometimes creating dramatic swoops or arcs between people.

STATIC VERSUS DYNAMIC TABLEAUX

This exercise continues the exploration of what line does to the mood of a tableau.

Method: Have students form groups of five to seven players and ask them to plan and form various tableaux on a variety of themes. Each will act as an illustration of a static, formal tableau or an active, dynamic tableau. As with the Family Portraits, a discussion can follow to establish what was discovered.

Sample static tableaux:
A meeting of the heads of state of two different countries
An award ceremony with a public figure
A lecture given by a distinguished guest in an auditorium
A graduation ceremony

Sample dynamic tableaux:
A team sport as a point is being scored
A group of clowns performing in a circus
A group of children in a playground
A group of actors getting ready for a performance
A team that has just won an important game

Have students view each other's tableaux and discuss them in terms of dynamic action versus static non-action. Discuss when to appropriately use each of them.

MASS

A person's body has mass. It can be seen and touched. It is, therefore, positive space. The area around a person can then be described as negative space.

Method: Students explore how they can create shapes of negative space with their own bodies (one hand on a hip forms a triangle, etc.). They can also use the floor or a wall as positive space and create shapes in relationship to a flat surface. Then, have students form groups of six. Each player takes a turn as the sculptor, moulding the rest of the group into a tableau that contains lots of large shapes of negative space. The artist crawls through the completed sculpture, exploring the negative spaces.

Once participants are aware of the concept of positive and negative space, they can use it in future tableaux work, exploring when dense masses of positive space best convey their message, and when negative space is preferable. Talk about the feelings that are generated from the participants themselves, and by the audience viewing them.

MULTILEVEL TABLEAUX

In this exercise students learn about creating interesting tableaux by having people pose at various heights, or levels. They will also discover when they would choose to keep everyone at the same level.

Method: In groups of five to seven players, ask students to create a variety of tableaux, one at a time, with all groups working on the same theme. Students view other groups' tableaux and talk about what they find interesting about each one. Guide them to discover that when a tableau has more than one level, it creates interest for the viewer. Ask them to consider using multiple levels in all of their tableaux, unless they specifically choose not to. Talk about times when a tableau might appropriately be formed with everyone on the same level; for example, when trying to show equality, in a tableau depicting friendship or world peace.

Students create new tableaux in which they consider using multilevel poses, having some students low to the floor, others at a medium height, and others as high as possible.

Sample themes:
A photograph representing the moment of highest excitement at:

A rock concert	A sporting event
A family discussion	In a video game
An action movie	A hike in the woods
A trip to the zoo	A performance in a circus
The finish line of a marathon	

A statue representing the concept of:

World hunger	Circle of friendship
Peace of mind	Human understanding
Forgiveness	Revenge is a dish best served cold
Contentment	Where there is a will, there is a way
The realities of war	Make your own luck

FOCUS

This exercise allows students to discover that they can tell the audience where to look.

Method: In groups of five to seven players, have students create tableaux in which one person is more important than the rest of the group. As a context, they could be setting up the pose for a movie poster, with a major actor as the star. Allow each group to show its tableau before talking about how they made that person the obvious star of the group.

Lead the group to discover that several factors were employed in directing focus.

- Prominent position: the star was placed in the center, or at the front of the tableau, or at a higher position than the rest of the group.

- Stage focus: the rest of the group, or most of it, was likely looking at the star. The audience will look at whatever the actors on stage are looking at.

- Line: the lines of the bodies, or the arms of the other players, were likely positioned in such a way as to draw attention to the star's face. The line of the group might also have encircled or created an arch around the star, or pointed to the star, or led the viewers' eyes there in some other way.

Students' awareness of the design elements used in creating tableaux will assist them in making their tableaux more effective as they use them in future exercises. They will have an understanding of how to best use tableaux to portray an idea or relationship. At all times, in refining the tableaux that they spontaneously create, being aware of how the elements of design affect their stage pictures will ensure that the audience is effectively reading whatever they wish to communicate to them.

MOVEMENT

Movement is an important component of every actor's training. It can also greatly enhance the effectiveness of a piece of devised theatre. While actors would certainly benefit from formal dance instruction, complex dance steps aren't necessarily needed for effectively training the body to move. Creative movement can also free the actor of physical inhibitions and create body awareness.

GET MOVING: A VOCABULARY

Using the basic forms of locomotion and stillness can create a vocabulary of movement for all students.

Method: Put on some music and ask students to explore these various forms of locomotion and balances. Creating a series of short pieces of music of various styles and tempos will allow students to discover how the same form of movement can change drastically to fit different musical styles. Call out directions for the movements you are looking for, starting with the walks. Once they have been fully explored, go on to the various other forms. The entire vocabulary doesn't have to be taught in one session. It can be brought back and developed further at any point of the training. Encourage students to move freely and spontaneously through the space. There is no need for circles or lines. Students should remain aware of their proximity to others in the space, but otherwise move anywhere at all. Also encourage exploration of all the ways in which your directions can be interpreted and expressed. There is never a single right way of moving within any category. The students could imitate different animals in their movements, or could be given any other images and stories to work with that will encourage further movement exploration within the categories of locomotion.

Walks – Runs – Skips – Hops – Jumps – Leaps – Turns
Balances – Kicks – Crawls – Rolls – Falls

- **WALKS** – may be executed in various ways
  - ☐ Directions – forward, backward, sideways
  - ☐ Levels – high on the balls of the feet, low with legs bent at the knee, or medium, as in a normal walk
  - ☐ Tempos – slow, moderate, fast (run)
  - ☐ Foot orientation – lead with toe or heel
  - ☐ Various arm positions and isolations
- **RUNS** – may be executed in various ways
  - ☐ Directions
  - ☐ Levels
  - ☐ Tempos
  - ☐ Foot orientation – flat footed or on balls of feet
  - ☐ Variations:
    - Prance – small steps, pointed toes
    - Jazz run – long, low, smooth steps, toes drag slightly, pass through lunge position
    - Large to small steps – change from one to the other
- **SKIPS** – step, hop on same leg
  - ☐ Add hop after several skips to change feet
  - ☐ Vary direction – side, front, back
- **HOPS** – one foot to same foot
  - ☐ Various positions of the free leg
  - ☐ Various positions of the arms and body
- **JUMPS** – two feet to two feet
  - ☐ Straight jump – legs straighten in the air, bend knees on landing
  - ☐ Tuck jump – knees bend and tuck up in the air, bend knees on landing
- **LEAPS** – one foot to other foot
  - ☐ Cat leap – bent knees change in the air
  - ☐ Hitch kick – straight legs, kick forward and change in the air
  - ☐ Split leap - legs extend, one forward, one back
- **TURNS**
  - ☐ Pivot 1/2 turn – one foot front, up on balls of feet, turn body 180 degrees, lower heels

- Pivot 1/1 turn = two 1/2 turns, or, swing back leg across front, pivot body
- Push turn (step pivot), like you are opening curtains across a window, then turning away from the window
- Full turn up on the ball of one foot
- Jump turns – tuck, straight, pike
- Leap turns – cat leaps: legs bend and change in the air during turn, then step out

■ BALANCES
- One foot balance, other leg extended straight or bent
- Lunge – weight on bent leg, other straight on floor
- Endless other creative possibilities:
  - balance on body parts – butt, hands, lying on side, squat, crouch, etc.
  - move from one balance point to another

■ KICKS – forward, backwards, sideways
- legs bent or straight
- toes pointed or flexed
- various arm positions
- "kick-ball-change" – kick leg forward, swing it back and step on it, transferring weight from one foot to the other and back again

■ CRAWLS
- Use animal images to encourage ways of crawling on "all fours"
- Use snake images to encourage ways of slithering on floor

■ ROLLS
- Log (side) rolls, forward and backward shoulder rolls. Look to the side, to ensure rolling on a shoulder, not straight down the spine.

■ FALLS
- Falls: side, back, forward – ways of getting down to the floor and back up again. This can be done naturally, but it is the one category where it is a good idea to teach an actual technique, to ensure students' safety. It is important to practice these techniques until they become natural, and can be used without planning or thought. The techniques for the falls are included in the chapter on Stage Combat.

STAND BACK UP

If including falls in a movement sequence, there must also be a way of getting back up. Encourage students to explore many ways of doing this, and consider teaching this method of getting up from one knee.

Method: Sitting on the floor, both knees are bent, as if to sit cross-legged, except that the foot of the top leg is placed flat on the floor in front of you. As you reach forward with your arms (or use them to push off of the floor, if necessary), push off with the knee on the floor, transferring your bodyweight to the standing leg. Rise on that leg, into a standing position. With practice, this will happen in one fluid motion without the use of hands.

USING THE MOVEMENT VOCABULARY

TEMPOS

This exercise explores how to determine the tempo of movements, as tempo is an important element to vary in creative movement.

Method: Students run around in the space as fast as they can. Call this speed number ten. Now ask them to run in slow motion, still moving forward, but as slowly as humanly possible. Call this speed number one. Now suggest a medium run, and call it number five. Call various numbers in between one and ten, to have the students explore how they feel various speeds can be represented. Challenge them to explore the subtle difference between numbers; a six and a seven or eight, for example.

RUNNING STOP

This is the beginning of exploring how to combine various forms of movement and stillness.

Method: Students run as fast as they can, number ten, and then stop instantly on your command (or whistle, tambourine or clap). Experiment with running a little more slowly sideways or backwards and stopping instantly. Repeat with the intent of freezing in an interesting tableau when stopping.

COMBINATIONS

This is the beginning of choreography, allowing students to experience that it is possible to create patterns, and repeat them.

Method: Students combine various elements from the different forms of movement and stillness. Once they have devised a combination, have them practice it several times and then teach it to a partner or small group.

Variation #1. Students find a way of combining each other's patterns, giving the pair or group a short performance piece to share with the class.

Sample combinations:

- two forms of walking, one balance, one hop, and a fall
- running, one leap, two kicks, three walking steps, two turns
- any walks, two different jumps, a fall, a crawl, a roll, two turns and a run

ADD FOUR

Also to begin dance choreography, this exercise works with beats of music, and alternates between partners.

Method: One partner begins a four-beat (count) movement. The other partner repeats it and adds another four-beat movement of her own. They take turns until they have an entire movement sequence sixteen to twenty beats in length. Partners can then share them with the class. Various styles of music can be played to inspire the movement.

EMOTIONAL WALKS

This exercise explores how to express states of mind physically.

Method: Students walk about the space in neutral; a relaxed posture, arms swinging at their sides, chin up, medium stride. Call this walk a five. Now ask them to imagine that they are walking down the street to something that they have really been looking forward to. They have just heard the best news and feel absolutely on top of the world. Call this number ten. As they continue to walk, ask them to go back to number five, neutral, to number ten, the best. Make sure that their whole bodies are expressing this number, so that it isn't just about the tempo. Ask them to use every number in between to very subtly go from one to the other, as you call out the numbers in the scale. What changes occur in their movements and tempo and the way in which they carry themselves as they feel better and better? After holding the number ten walk for a minute, bring them slowly back down to number five. Tell them that they have just heard some bad news that put their state of mind down to a four. Ask them to show that with their bodies. How does that affect the speed at which they walk, how they carry their heads and swing their arms? Talk them down to a number one, slowly, in stages, exploring what number three and number two look like before getting to the lowest state of mind, and how it affects their movements. Play with the numbers, as they try to recreate the walks associated with the various stages.

Variation #1. Once they have established movement patterns for the various stages, they can use them as characterizations in improvisations. The group could be counted off into two groups, numbered A and B. As they all mingle and make eye contact with each other, instruct group A to be one number on the scale, and group B to become another. Ask them to speak to someone near them, creating a scenario to explain their personal states of mind. Give the entire group a neutral setting, like a city street, explaining that they have run into this other person by chance. In the course of the exercise, have them find a new partner frequently, so that at times they will interact with someone at the same number as themselves, and at other times, they will encounter someone of a contrasting number. Switch the numbers for the groups at will, allowing everyone a chance to interact with others as various numbers.

MUSICAL INFLUENCES

Music can also assist in the physical development of characters.

Method: Playing various styles and tempos of music, have actors move around the space, interpreting the music as they wish. Instrumental music works best for this exercise, as lyrics will automatically influence the listener. Instrumental music also has more shifts in tempo and variety in themes than most pop songs. As they move, offer side coaching. Does the music make them feel happy or sad, vulnerable or strong, energized or relaxed? How are they moving because of the music? Ask them to simply walk. How does the music affect how they walk? Ask them to start to pretend that they are someone else, as a result of this music. Are they older or younger than themselves? What kind of occupation has this character chosen? Have them walk to work as this character. Is the character looking forward to her day, or dreading it? Have them walk home from work. What are they looking forward to doing after work? Keeping the music as their inspiration, encourage them to make decisions for the character. Who is home when they get there, or are they alone? Have them move into pantomiming their actions once they arrive home. This could become a solo pantomime piece, fitting this particular piece of music. If the group is ready, the short pieces might be performed for each other. Repeat the exercise with a new piece of music and a new story to explore.

Variation #1. After exploring the music for themselves, invite them to acknowledge each other's presence, and exchange a few words with whomever they encounter. What is the state of mind that the music suggests to each individual? It is likely to be similar, but not the same for any two people. As they speak, encourage them to keep developing the specific character inspired by this piece of music.

Variation #2. After exploring various pieces of music as a specific character in each, encourage them all to pick the character he or she enjoyed the most. Without music, have them spend time with partners, interacting as their two favourite characters until they develop a scene. As the characters are not necessarily from the same round of the activity, the scene will not be done with music. The music does not define the action of the scene, just the characters. The scene could be rehearsed and played for class.

MUSICAL PANTOMIME

While a particular piece of music can define a character, it can also define the actions of a scene, which is then populated with various characters.

Method: Have students relax in a comfortable position on the floor, while various short pieces of instrumental music are played. Ask them to close their eyes and, as they listen to the music, imagine that it is the soundtrack for a movie, in which they are individually the stars. After a minute or so of music, ask them to share where they were, what they were doing, and how that changed with the changes in the music. Once a few students have shared, play another, contrasting piece of music. After several short pieces and more sharing of individuals' movie stories, play the music on which the actual project will be based. Something between two and a half to three minutes works well. Look for an interesting piece with lots of changes in dynamics. Ballet pieces, like Tchaikovsky's *Swan Lake*, work very well, as do many movie soundtracks, or medleys of soundtracks. Once it has been played, do not ask them to share their stories. Instead, begin the project.

1. Divide the actors into groups of five to eight students each.
2. Have them share the story ideas from their first listening of the music with each other and pick one, or a combination of several, to develop further.
3. Play the music again, to allow them to talk through how their story will fit the soundtrack. Remind them that they need to account for changes in the music with changes in the action of their narrative.
4. Play the music as many times as they'd like to rehearse, in order to make their pantomime as specific as possible. Their actions should incorporate not only the changes in dynamics of the music, but also the mood or tone and tempo. The story might be very small and detailed, with finely articulated mimed objects and facial expressions, or a sweeping tale of grandeur, with larger-than-life characters; princesses and sword fights and dragons. It is up to the group to interpret the music and bring their story to life.
5. When all the groups are ready, each preforms its pantomime for the class. Costumes, props and set pieces may be added.

Variation #1. As part of a unit on mask work, white face or character masks may be used. The use of masks tends to help the students make their movements more stylized and clearer. Care must be taken to use open body positions in order to share with the audience. In order to relate to the character, the audience needs to see an actor's masked face full frontal, showing their eyes, at all times. Using masks in a presentation can be of value to students on several levels. In addition to teaching them the skill of effectively using the mask technique, the masks also add a layer of comfort for the new performer, as her face is not visible to the audience. This can be helpful in performing for a large group of their peers. They are able to tell their stories without feeling exposed.

Variation #2. Instead of using pantomime to tell the story, it could be done as an extended Fluid Tableau, with the story unfolding in a series of tableaux, with characters breaking the group tableau one at a time and moving to a new place in the story and freezing again, allowing someone else to break and respond to the new position of the first person. This is repeated until the music ends and the story is told.

Musical Pantomime can be an effective addition to a piece of Devised Theatre.

CHOREOGRAPHY

There are many different ways to work out the choreography for a musical number, but here are a few that may work for you and your cast:

- Find stage pictures (positions on the stage) that the dancers will move into, then create specific steps for them to perform while they are there, before moving into a new picture. The musical beats can be counted, or certain cues can be listened for in the music that tell the dancers when to change positions or pictures. The steps themselves can be very simple. It is the changes in the pictures that will create most of the movement and interest. This works well for non-dancers.

- Set the steps, teach them to everyone, then vary the patterns they are done in. The beats of the music are counted, with the movements matching the beats. The same basic steps can be used over and over again by different combinations of dancers, in different patterns and directions, creating different stage pictures.

- If the musical number has lyrics, set the movements and stage positions to the lyrical phrases. Guard against literally interpreting the lyrics through pantomime, but do allow them to suggest appropriate movements. Some of the choreography might be based on activities that are suggested by the lyrics or storyline. The activities can be done in stylized movements, rather than using actual dance steps.

Hints:

- It is easier to work with an even numbers of dancers, if you have a choice.

- Find different possible combinations of dancers to move in and out of. For example, pairs, trios, groups of four or five.

- The choreography can be kept very simple, mostly walks or held positions with interesting arm changes.

- Try not to leave a dancer in a held pose for more than eight counts.

- If the dancers begin the number on stage, start and end it in strong stage positions. Vary the way dancers enter and exit the stage and match it to the musical style.

- If working with mostly non-dancers, consider featuring an individual (or pair) with ability and keep the background movements for the group very simple.

- It is easier for a group to look good when in a tight formation, instead of spread out over the whole stage, where they will be more exposed individually.

- If working with inexperienced dancers, the more the merrier. It may seem easier to pick just a few participants who can move a little, but it may look better if the stage is full of bodies doing fairly simple movement than a few lonely people doing something only marginally more interesting. Also, there is strength in numbers. Working in a large group will give all of the participants the courage and confidence to take risks and move without discomfort or embarrassment. Keep them in tight groups for much of the time, changing patterns (positions on stage) fairly frequently.

- You can always use the "New York City rush" – eight counts – to have everyone get to a new formation.

- Movements can be done in cannon, meaning that a single dancer (or several dancers), creates an action that ends in a held position, and is recreated by others along the line, in a wave action. That will use more musical beats than if everyone did that same action simultaneously.

- Use the movement vocabulary with the choreography exercises, Add Four, and Combinations to discover dance steps that can be added together to form the choreography of a dance number.

CHOREOGRAPHY – PATTERNS:

Dancers can create movement patterns by changing their positions on the stage. They perform some movements in one position before moving into another. This is more interesting than keeping dancers in one single position for the entire number, but do create some movements in each position selected, so that dancers are not simply running through various positions on the stage for the entire piece. The following stage positions are a start in exploring all of the possible configurations that can be found for the dancers in order to create patterns on the stage.

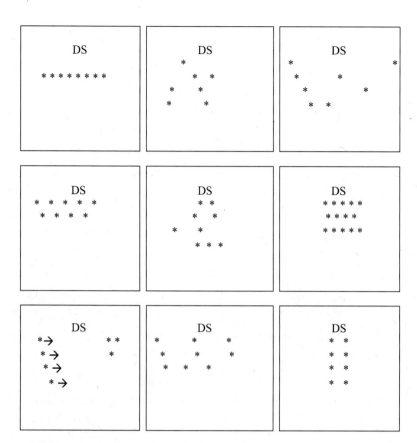

STAGE COMBAT

Nothing can truly replace learning stage combat from a qualified instructor, in a face-to-face class setting. However, it should be possible to perform these introductory moves safely and effectively after reading these guidelines with care and attention. It is possible that a play being considered for production will require some fight scenes. This chapter will provide the resource needed to choreograph an effective sequence. Stage combat is also fun and builds confidence in physical prowess.

SAFETY

- Stage combat should never be improvised. All movements are planned.
- Stage combat should not be confused with "play wrestling".

- Before a specific movement is executed, it is communicated between partners, then marked, then practiced in slow motion, before being done for real.
- All moves are only ever done using 60 – 70% energy. If full energy is used, control during the movement may be lost, resulting in missed targets, or worse, injury. 70% is plenty of energy for the audience to believe in the reality of the move.
- Rings, bracelets and other jewellery should be removed to prevent injury to the victim, and neck chains and long earrings to prevent them from being caught and broken.

TERMS

- **Move:** The name for the actions that are executed in stage combat, such as punches, kicks, falls, etc.
- **Cover:** The reactions or actions of the attacker and/or the victim that make the move look real to the audience.
- **The Knap:** The sound made in order to have the move appear real to the audience.
- **Cage:** The protective position of the body, lying on the floor or against a wall, in which one knee is bent, allowing the thigh and calf of the leg to touch the surface, but not the torso. Hands touch, but arms are bent up and away from the surface.
- **Mark:** A verb, meaning to walk (and sometimes talk) through a move without using any energy or actually performing the move.
- **Timer:** Performing the actions involved in the preparation phase of a move, at appropriate energy, but then stopping short before doing the move. This could be done to work out the number and spacing of steps needed to get into the correct position for a move.
- **To "sell" the move:** The "acting" that the players do to make the audience believe that the move and the resulting pain are real. For believability, the following points also apply:
  - □ 50% of the believability of the move comes from the technique employed in its performance. The other 50% comes from the realistic reaction of the victim. If the technique of the execution is perfect, but the victim doesn't show any pain, the believability is gone. If the technique is sloppy, no amount of "acting" on the part of the victim will make the move believable. It takes both parties to be fully invested in the moment to sell the move.

☐ For most moves, the most effective view for the audience, in terms of believability, is behind the victim. So, place the victim's back to the audience whenever possible.

Note: These moves are meant for portraying a physical fight on stage. The techniques used in film are different, and not addressed here.

WARM-UPS

The body needs to be warmed up before a session of stage combat is taught. Any physical warm-ups to get the blood flowing will work, such as those presented in the companion book, **STAGES: Creative Ideas for Teaching Drama**. After some gentle cardio, the following specific stretches and balance exercises would also be effective.

Arms:

- Standing with feet shoulder width apart, circle each arm, in turn, forwards and backwards.

- Standing with feet shoulder width apart, lean forward slightly, bend knees, and place one hand on the same side knee, for support. Create small circles in front of body with free hand. Repeat to count of eight. Repeat on other side. Repeat standing, with large circles in front of body, eight counts in each direction, with each arm in turn.

- Clasp hands in front of torso. Circle both hands, as a unit, to warm up wrists. Repeat to count of eight in each direction.

Shoulders:

- Standing with feet shoulder width apart and arms at sides, raise shoulders and drop them forward, palms facing backwards. Lift shoulders again and drop them backwards, palms facing forward. Repeat to a count of eight.

- Repeat this movement eight times with arms about 30 degrees away from the body, and again with arms at 90 degrees to the body.

- Circle shoulders forwards and backwards, eight counts in each direction.

- Bring elbows together in front of torso, pushing shoulders down. With hands facing each other, slowly raise them, keeping elbows together and shoulders down.

- Stretch one arm across the front of the body, cradling it in the opposite arm. Gently pull the outstretched arm. Repeat with opposite arm.
- Bring arms up to sides at 90 degrees. Bend elbows to raise hands. Push shoulders down and pinch shoulder blades towards the back. Gently lower hands until palms are 90 degrees to the floor. Repeat to count of eight.
- Clasp hands behind back and lean forward, stretching arms overhead, reaching hands forward.

Lunges:
- Step forward on one foot into a deep lunge. Ensure that the front knee lines up with the front foot, and does not extend past it. Keep hips square to the front. Various body and arm positions can be used:

  Hands on the floor on each side of the front leg, body forward

  Hands on hips, or reaching forward or sideways, body upright

  Back leg stretched straight, with toes on floor, knee off floor

  Back leg bent, knee on the floor, hips pushed forward

  Rock from straight back leg to straight front leg, hands on floor
- Step back into lunge, lower torso towards the floor, pushing hips forward, both legs bent.
- Step into side lunge, lower torso to one side over bent knee, butt close to floor. Shift weight onto other foot, repeating torso position. Repeat to count of eight.

Squats:
- Standing with feet shoulder width apart, lower torso, sticking butt out, leaning forward as if to sit on a chair. Hold when thighs are parallel to the floor. Arms swing forward on squat. Repeat to count of eight.
- Advanced variations: Hands in prayer position on front of chest, lower butt to floor, straighten only until thighs are parallel to floor and repeat.

  Hands touch floor between feet in deep squat. Straighten legs. Hands remain on floor between reps.

  Rise up on balls of feet. Squat to thighs parallel to floor.

Stay on balls of feet throughout reps. Arms swing forward on squat.

Place one foot across opposite thigh. Squat on one leg. Arms reach forward during squat.

Step sideways into deep squat. Bring feet together to stand. Repeat to opposite side.

Turn feet slightly to outside. Squat, leaving heels on floor and torso upright, arms out to the sides. Keep knees over toes (ballet plié in second position).

Balances:

- Standing with feet together, hands together overhead, close eyes. This demonstrates how much easier it is to balance with visual cues and focus on a static point in the distance. Practise eyes closed for longer periods each session to improve balance. Try it on one foot. This is usually more successful on the dominant side. Try it on both sides.

- Place one foot on the inside of the opposite thigh. Hands touch overhead. Hold position. Try with eyes closed.

- Try static balances in twisted positions, first on two feet, then on one foot or other body part. Talk about what is needed for optimum balance:

  A wide stance

  Arms out for counterbalance

  Center of gravity lowered (bend knees)

  Eyes focused on object

  Core muscles contracted

Demonstrate the optimum static balance position with feet parallel, and have partners gently push each other to throw the other off balance. Then have them balance with one foot in front of the other, to demonstrate how much more effective this position is than when feet are parallel. It is much more difficult to unsettle a partner who is in this position. It is the one that should be used by the attacker in preparation for all slaps, punches and throws, as well as any other time stable balance is required.

MOVES

SLAP

Preparation:

1. Stance – one foot in front of the other, for support
2. Attacker grabs the front of victim's shirt with same-side hand as front foot.
3. Eye contact
4. Attacker's other hand is held high, focusing the audience's attention on the hand, and therefore the hit to come.

Action: Attacker brings hand across (in front of) victim's chest to contact with his own hand, which he claps – fingers to heel of the hand that was holding the shirt.

Cover: Clapped hand immediately drops to his side, out of the way so that audience doesn't realize that it was clapped. Victim grabs "slapped" check with "same-side" hand, and turns face away in appropriate direction, showing pain.

Knap: The attacker clapping his own hand.

Follow Through: Attacker's high "slapping hand" continues swing, over his own shoulder as he twists away from the victim.

- Slap – Back Hand:

Action: Victim looks at attacker after slap and pretends to shield her face from him, raising the "cover" hand away from her face and placing it in front of her, a few inches away from her face. The attacker uses the backside of his follow-through hand to contact victim's palm.

Cover: Victim grabs "slapped" check, and turns face in appropriate direction, showing pain.

Knap: Attacker clapping victim's hand.

Follow Through: Attacker's hand continues swing.

- Slap – head to knee

Preparation: Attacker stands in front of victim. Victim is doubled over – perhaps after a punch to stomach.

Action: Attacker brings up one knee and places his hands on the back of victim's head. Attacker pulls victim's head back slightly, indicating the move is coming. He then guides the victim's head forward, letting go when it gets back to its original position. The victim's head travels towards the attacker's knee, stopping well before hitting it.

Cover: Victim snaps head back, as if bouncing off attacker's knee.

Knap: Attacker slaps knee with both hands, which have slid off of victim's head and traveled towards his own knee.

Follow Through: Depending on the choreography, victim could crumple to floor, or step back for next counter move.

Note: If a script calls for a single slap to the face, without any follow-up moves, it is often best to simply perform a real slap, taking care not to slap too hard. A fake slap may not be worth the set-up, and the preparation may be out of place for the style of the play. A real slap, on its own, always plays better than a faked one.

PUNCH

- Punch – Cross cut

Preparation: See above for slap, except attacker's free hand is level with victim's face, closed in a fist.

Action: Attacker punches towards hand clasped on shirt, which opens to clap. The clap could also be done with a closed fist to the palm.

Cover: Attacker's clapped hand drops quickly to the side of his own body. Victim grabs spot that was hit and shows pain. Head snaps back or to the side, in the appropriate direction.

Knap: The attacker clapping his own hand.

Follow Through: Attacker's hand follows through over victim's shoulder, for clip to the jaw, or curves to the side, if punch was to the check. Hand goes back to being clenched in a fist right after the clap, if it was opened.

- Punch – Upper cut

Preparation: Attacker has one hand on victim's shirt and the other in a fist, low and to the side.

Action: Attacker comes in from below, clapping the hand that was on the shirt with the back of his own fist.

Cover: Victim snaps head back. Victim may grab spot that was hit.

Knap: The attacker clapping his own hand.

Follow Through: The attack hand travels up, past victim's head. The other hand, that was clapped, drops down to the attacker's side.

- Punch – elbow to stomach

Preparation: Attacker stands in front, and to the side of victim. Both face the same direction.

Action: Attacker makes fist with hand closest to the victim and grasps it with her other hand, signifying to the victim that the punch is coming. Attacker thrusts her elbow towards the victim's stomach, stopping just before reaching it. This is the ONLY move that is "pulled"; stopped short before contact.

Cover: Victim grabs area that was "hit."

Knap: Both the attacker and victim make grunts, or cries of pain or anger to cover the fact that nothing is physically making the sound of connection between the elbow and the stomach.

Follow Through: Depending on the move that is to follow, victim could fall to his knees, stagger backwards, or prepare for a counter-move. If victim stays in place, a "head to the knee" hit could follow.

- Punch – blocked

Action: When attacker comes in for a cross cut, victim reaches forward with hand opposite that of attacker's. Victim's wrist contacts attacker's arm and slides down to his wrist, which she grabs by turning over her hand. She then takes his wrist, walks around behind him and, allows him to bend his arm at the elbow, holding his hand behind his back. The final appearance is one of an arm lock, but the attacker is not using any force.

KICK

- Kick – Stomach

Preparation: Victim holds hand out in front of his stomach, palm turned towards attacker, in a protective gesture. Attacker counts out steps necessary to reach victim's hand with a bent knee kick to the palm. Knee is bent to control distance to victim more accurately. A locked knee can only hit the spot at the end of its reach. A bent knee can adjust distance to target as needed.

Action: Attacker gently kicks palm of victim's hand with the top-side of her foot, NOT the toe.

Cover: Victim grabs stomach, doubles over and expresses pain.

Knap: The attacker's foot connecting with the victim's palm.

Follow Through: Attacker steps back, away from victim.

- Kick – Chin – same as above, but with a higher kick, or victim is on knees.

- Kick – Groin – same as above, but the attacker's foot (top of the foot, NOT the toes) connects to victim's inner thigh, well away from the groin. The victim's hand does not reach out to provide the knap. Selling the pain is the most important aspect of the move.

- Kick – Head

Preparation: Victim is lying on his side, head resting on bent arm. He raises his head, sees attacker and raises the free hand as if to protect himself, turning the palm outward, below his chin, away from his face. Attacker stands at the victim's feet and counts out steps to ensure that she will reach the victim's head with her inside leg (the leg nearest the victim). This is important, to ensure that the follow-through step will take her away from the victim, rather than onto the victim's head.

Action: The attacker steps towards victim, walking along beside the victim, towards his head. She brings her foot up and kicks the victim's open hand with the top of her foot. This will generally be done in three steps. The first step is with the inside foot at the victim's feet. The second step is with the outside foot at the level of the victim's waist. The third step is the inside foot making contact with the victim's hand (top of the foot, NOT the toes) and following through in an arcing step to land away from the victim's face.

Cover: The victim rolls onto his back, grabbing the spot that was hit and expressing pain.

Knap: The attacker's foot contacting the victim's hand.

Follow Through: The attacker steps out of the kick, continuing in an arcing direction, which takes her away from the victim's head.

- Kick – Knee to stomach

Preparation: Attacker places hands on victim's shoulders. Eye contact is made.

Action: The attacker brings her knee up towards the victim's stomach. The victim places his hands in front of his stomach, palms facing downwards. The attacker contacts the victim's hands with his knee.

Cover: The victim grabs her stomach and expresses pain.

Knap: The knee connecting with the victim's hands.

Follow Through: The attacker steps back away from the victim.

THROW

■ Throw – Down onto a table

Preparation: Victim stands in front of a table or counter. Attacker stands behind her and off to one side.

Action: The attacker grabs the back of the victim's shirt and gently pulls the victim back into a slight arch. This tells the victim that the throw is coming. The attacker guides the victim forward, towards the table, letting go as soon as the victim reaches vertical. The victim brings up her hands, to protect herself from the impact, throwing herself towards the table. Victim's hands make contact with the table, slapping it as her head snaps backwards, as if it has bounced off the table.

Cover: The victim either collapses onto the table, or turns away from the table, holding nose in pain.

Knap: The victim's hands on the table.

Follow Through: The victim proceeds to a counter move, or stays down, depending on how hard the hit was supposed to have been.

■ Throw – Against a wall

Preparation: Victim and attacker stand about ten feet away from the wall, which is clear of furniture or other objects.

Action: Attacker grabs back of victim's shirt and pulls it back slightly, signifying that the move is about to be executed. He guides the victim towards the wall, in a throwing action, but without force. The victim runs towards the wall, making contact with it in a cage position. For a showier throw, the victim could jump at the wall, making contact with it off the floor.

Cover: Victim's face, or even her whole body, can jerk back off the wall with the impact.

Knap: The victim slaps the wall with open palms.

Follow Through: Victim slides down the wall into a heap, or bounces off of it and continues fighting, depending on how hard the impact was supposed to appear.

- Throw – against the floor

This is done the same way as a throw to a table, except that the victim begins from a kneeling position.

HAIR PULL

- Hair pull – standing

Preparation: Attacker stands beside, behind or in front of victim.

Action: Attacker places her hands on the head of the victim. Victim grabs her wrists with both hands.

Cover: The victim attempts to pull the attacker's hands towards his head. The attacker tries to remove them. Because of the energy needed to achieve this, tension is created. The audience views this as aggressive energy directed at the victim, when, in fact, it is exactly the opposite.

Follow Through: Both parties can stand still, except for the motions of the struggle, or the attacker can "lead" the victim around by his hair. She could end by throwing him to the floor, onto a tabletop or into a wall, depending on the choreography of the fight scene.

- Hair pull – down on the floor.

Preparation: Victim is sitting on the floor. Attacker is above her.

Action: Attacker places one hand on the victim's head. The victim grabs his wrist with both hands.

Cover: The attacker pulls away from the victim, the victim pulls the attacker's hand towards her head.

Follow Through: The attacker can make it appear that he is pulling the victim to her feet, or, by walking backwards while the victim inches her feet backwards, it can appear that the victim is being dragged across the floor by her hair.

FALL

- Fall – Back fall
  - ☐ Step back with one foot. Stop. Front leg is left in place.
  - ☐ Weight is transferred to the back (supporting) leg.
  - ☐ Lower body, keeping butt as close to the supporting leg as possible.
  - ☐ Butt cheek opposite the supporting leg touches floor. Sit on it.
  - ☐ Back rolls down to floor. Head does not touch floor.
  - ☐ Hands slap floor at the sides of the body as head snaps slightly, as if it has bounced off of floor.
  - ☐ Head rests on floor, body goes limp.
- Fall – Back fall to roll

Follow steps 1 through 5 above, then, instead of slapping the floor and snapping the head, place hands on floor and execute a shoulder roll, either ending on feet, ready to keep fighting, or first placing toes on floor and sliding the rest of the body along the floor, end lying on stomach.

- Fall – Front
  - ☐ Step forward with one foot. Stop. Back leg is left in place.
  - ☐ Weight is transferred to the front foot. Deep lunge.
  - ☐ Reach forward to floor with both hands, aiming for spot inside (between feet) and in front of front foot.
  - ☐ Land in cage position.
- Fall – Side
  - ☐ Slowly lower body straight down to the floor, bending knees and controlling descent.
  - ☐ When body reaches a squat position, touch floor beside body with one hand.
  - ☐ Slide hand along floor, away from body.
  - ☐ Sit on floor with one butt cheek (same side as hand on floor), following hand along the floor until arm is extended and body is lying sideways on floor. Head rests on outstretched arm.

HOLD

- Hold – head lock

Preparation: Attacker places one hand on his own hip.

Action: Place victim's head in triangle. Or lock head in bent arm and lower hand to hip.

Cover: The believability is all in the victim's expression of pain.

- Hold – choke hold

Preparation: Attacker faces victim and places her hands on the victim's shoulders, thumbs touching in front.

Action: The victim holds her wrists and pulls her hands towards her body. The attacker tries to pull them away. The tension created makes it appear that the attacker is trying to choke the victim.

Cover: The victim expresses distress.

FIGHT CHOREOGRAPHY

The moves can be taught and practiced in isolation, then strung together in any way that suits the participants and the action required. If the fight is for a serious drama, it will be executed in a realistic, possibly subtle manner, with real anger, fear and pain expressed by the actors. If the fight is to be comedic, the actions and reactions can be very exaggerated. For example, in a serious fight, a punch to the jaw might be followed by a counter punch to the check. In a comedic fight, a punch to the jaw might result in the victim flying backwards, falling back and into a shoulder roll, ending back on his feet, shaking himself off and going in for a counter attack.

Stringing the moves together could be as simple as seeing where one move ends. The ending posture will suggest the starting posture for the next move.

TEACHING A STAGE COMBAT UNIT

Teaching stage combat is a very popular unit in a high school setting. It is a lot of fun for the students to learn these moves. They don't need much encouragement to practice them. They might be warned about using stage combat outside of the theatre, however, as some students get very good at it and can look quite realistic. This can lead to trouble in school hallways.

When teaching a unit of stage combat, it is best to work slowly, mastering one move with many repetitions before moving to another. At every stage, partners can be encouraged to develop a short scene that results in violence and whatever move was learned in that lesson. As the sessions progress, the fights at the ends of the scenes can become longer and more involved, including all of the moves learned up to that point.

Partners: Unlike all other lessons in creative drama and actor training, it may be best to stick with one partner throughout the unit, rather than working with someone new every few minutes. That way, participants can be paired with someone of approximately equal size and strength. It also allows for the development of the communication and understanding between partners that must occur in order to remain safe and execute the moves believably.

Assessment: This could be based on a quiz, testing the knowledge of the terms, safety considerations and the moves themselves. A practical test could also be employed, having students demonstrate the techniques learned. A final project could include a choreographed fight between partners. The criteria could outline the categories of moves needed, as well as the stipulation that the fight must be preceded by some dialogue that establishes a relationship and a reason for the fight to break out.

IMPROVISATION

Improvisations are a great training tool for acting students. Once students have spent many sessions playing warm-up exercises, simultaneous pair improvs and more easily planned small group performance exercises, they will be ready to try improvisations with the rest of the group acting as an audience. All of these introductory exercises can be found in the companion book, **STAGES: Creative Ideas for Teaching Drama.** The following exercises are more challenging. The setups are more complex and the class will view the work. They should not be attempted by beginning students, as they need to feel safe and may not be ready to be watched or to take the risks that these exercises demand of them.

SMALL GROUP IMPROVISATIONS

ADD A SCENE

Two players begin a scene in the center of the circle. A player on the outside calls "freeze" when he sees a physical posture that gives him an idea for a new scene. Instead of replacing one of the players, however, the student who calls freeze starts a new scene based on the tableau of the first two. All three play the new scene. A fourth and fifth person could be added, changing to a new scene with each additional player. The leader could then call freeze and have the fifth person leave. The four players left go back to the scene with four, and so on until only the original two players again continue their scene. In an advanced class, the leader could call out a number and return to the scene that contained that number of players, who would pick up where they left off in their scene. Scenes could be called in random order.

SUBS IN

A small group of players begins a scene after being given a location and relationships. At any point, the leader can call "freeze" and send substitutes in for each of the players, either one at a time, or all of them at once. The new players must pick up the scene where the other players left off, carrying on as the same characters, in the same roles.

Variation #1. The leader could also call specific instructions to one or more of the players.

Sample instructions:

Exit the scene and re-enter as another character

Exit the scene and re-enter with an object relevant to the scene

Recognize a relative in the audience and pull him into the scene

Find a way to end the scene

EVIL DOUBLE

A small group of players begin a scene based on a suggestion of location and situation. One of the players in the scene has an evil double waiting off stage. Once the scene is well established, the evil double enters the scene and taps his character on the shoulder. The player steps out of the scene, as his evil double proceeds to mess things up for the original character by being mean to others, saying the wrong thing or making other mistakes. After 30 seconds, the original player changes places with his evil double and tries to fix what is going on. Once things are running more smoothly again, the evil double takes over once again. The original character has one more chance to make things right and end the scene.

SWITCH ROLES

A group of three players, numbered A, B and C, begin a scene after being given a location and relationships. They are asked to make strong character choices, with distinct voices and physicalizations. Once their characters are well established, the leader calls "Switch," at which point all the players shift roles; A becomes B's character, B becomes C's character and C becomes A's character. The scene continues on as before. Two more switches bring all the players back to their original roles, at which time they find an ending for the scene.

Variation #1. To make it easier, play with only two characters. To make it more challenging, play with four characters.

EXPERT

One player is a talk show host. The other is the guest, who is given a field of expertise on which to be interviewed. Example: The life cycle of the dung beetle. However, both players sit with their hands in their laps, while someone else sits behind each of them, in another chair, with her arms through the sleeves of a jacket, which is draped over the front player. In this way, the front players do the characters' voices, but the back players do the characters' arms. Objects are placed on a table between the front players for the arms to use as props. The front players must incorporate their use into the dialogue.

Variation #1. Players stand at a table. The front players put their hands into shoes and lean their elbows on the table. They do the voices and legs of these very short characters, while the back players do the arms.

OFFSTAGE CONTROL

Pairs are given a location and a relationship, either by the leader, a volunteer suggestion from the audience, or from a deck of cards or out of a hat. They set up and play their scene, but off-stage voices provide the dialogue. They must make their actions match whatever their voices are saying. Each player onstage has his own offstage voice.

SHOULD HAVE SAID

Players A and B are given a location and relationship to each other. Example: Two teens on a date in a movie theatre. Each player has an alter ego standing off to the side, who can say, "Should have said," at any time during the scene. When the offstage voice says it, his player must say something other than his last line of dialogue. It might be simply the opposite of what he just said, but it doesn't have to be. It is just different than the line he just used. The other player responds to this new line and the scene continues, until one of their handlers says, "Should have said," again.

Variation #1. Instead of saying something different than his last line of dialogue, the interrupted character must say something that rhymes with what he just said, and continue the scene with that new reality. Example: "I think I have to go home" – SHOULD HAVE SAID – "Here, I brought your dog a bone. Where is the little rascal? I haven't seen him all night."

HE SAID / SHE SAID

Players A and B are given a location and relationship. Example: A teacher and student meet at a beach. As they play the scene, each has a narrator off to the side, providing the directions that the players must follow. Example: Player A – "Hi." Narrator – "She says as she picks up a handful of sand."

FOREIGNERS

Group decides on, or is given a location and an activity. No preparation time is given, except to decide which country each character comes from. The scene is improvised with each character trying to keep his or her own accent clear and not copy another's.

Sample locations and activities:

International exchange students at an orientation

Judges at an Olympic event

An international food-tasting festival

A train derailment in Europe

An international conference of doctors or scientists

Business partners discuss an international merger

A group of passengers waiting to board a late flight

COUNTING WORDS

Each player in the group is assigned a number between one and ten. The group is then given a location and situation to develop during an improvised scene. Players must speak in sentences containing exactly the number of words corresponding to the numbers they were given. Audience members can be assigned to keep track of counting words for the players, although the players themselves will also need to count as they speak with each other. The scene can be made more interesting if players assigned a low number are asked complex questions and players assigned large numbers are asked questions requiring only a yes or no answer.

Variation #1. As a simpler version of this exercise, it could be set up as a talk show, with an interviewer having no number restrictions on the questions, but the group being interviewed each having a number restrictions. The situation could be that a group that works together is being interviewed together.

Sample groups:

A reality TV family
A team of scientists that have made a discovery
Members of a sports team
A team of archaeologists that have made an important find
A documentary film crew
Any group of professionals offering a service for hire

Rodent extermination
Pet training
Personal counseling
Private detectives

Variation #2. The leader could assign everyone in the group the same number count per sentence. That number could change at any time during the scene.

SIT, STAND, LIE FOR A REASON

In groups of three, the improv begins with one player lying on the floor, another sitting on a chair and the last one standing. The players develop a scenario in which this is logical. The instruction is that one of them must find a reason to change her position once every minute. When that person logically, in the context of the story, changes positions, the other two must also switch, as there can only be one player in each position at any given time.

CHANGE THE CHANNEL

In the small group, one person controls the TV remote and the rest of the group members are individuals on their own specific TV channels. The controller points his "remote" at any one of the individuals, who must come to life as a person in a show on that channel. This switches often. When the controller comes back to a previous channel, the person goes on with the same show. The rule can also be set that it must be a different show each time, but on the same channel. The channels can be themed: the sports channel, news channel, sci-fi, soap operas, infomercial channel, reality TV, etc.

INSTANT SOLILOQUIES

The small group is given a location and a situation that contains a lot of potential for conflict. At any time during the scene, the leader can call "freeze" and point to, or call out one of the players to step forward, and delivery a soliloquy in character, revealing his character's true feelings or intent. This may be quite different from whatever he has been saying to the other characters in the scene. Like a Shakespearean soliloquy, the other characters have supposedly not heard this character, but, of course, they actually have. They may choose to use this information as the scene progresses. By the end of the scene, each of the characters should have had a soliloquy.

MONOLOGUES

A small group is given a location and relationships to the others in the scene. Like Instant Soliloquies, each character voices inner thoughts and feelings, but this scene doesn't have any dialogue, only monologues. Each character in turn presents his perspective on the situation. He can be interrupted at any time by another character presenting her point of view. This goes on until the end of the scene, as the stories intersect and collide, with one character finally ending it in some way.

KIDS' EXCUSES

In trios, one player becomes the parent or teacher, while the other two are young children, caught doing something they ought not to be doing. The adult tries to find out what is going on, while the kids make excuses, fabricating what happened. They use their imaginations to make the scenario wildly improbable.

WAITING FOR GERRY

Two players begin a scene in which they are waiting for a third character to arrive. As they wait for this person named Gerry, they begin to gossip about him/her. They talk about what they like and don't like about him/her, what he/she is like, does for a living, etc. After about three minutes, Gerry arrives, and must become the person who was described by the first two characters.

THIRD ONE IN

A group of three players are given a location and situation. One of the players is sent out of the room, so that she cannot hear the ensuing improv. Once the players are well established in the scene, the leader brings in the absent player to join the scene. She must pay attention to what is happening and fit into the scene as another character.

SAVE THE STARS

Two players begin a scene based on a suggested scenario. The scenario should be boring and mundane. For example, two friends enter a restaurant for lunch. Every time one of them is about to do any physical action, like sit down on a chair, the player calls out "stunt double," whereupon his stunt double enters the scene and performs the physical action for him. It is up to the stunt doubles to make the action look as dangerous as possible. They will usually get badly hurt in the process of performing the stunt, but bravely soldier on to complete it before limping off or otherwise removing themselves from the playing area, so that the scene can continue. Once things get dangerous again, for example, picking up a fork, the stunt double will have to be called in again.

NOUNS AND VERBS

Each group picks a noun from one deck of cards and a verb from another deck. They must create a scene, keeping the noun and the verb central to the plot line. The leader may prepare the cards before the session, or each person writes out one noun and one verb on separate cards, which are then collected for use.

VERBS

Scenes are played using only one word at a time. All words used must be verbs. To begin, each group chooses or picks an activity that they will all be involved in. It is improvised, using one verb at a time. They end the scene by completing the activity.

Sample activities:

Building a house	Flying a kite
Setting up a campsite	Catching a tiger
Training a dog	Sailing a boat
Hunting a bear	Making a meal
Cleaning a room	

ADJECTIVES

A small group is given a location and situation. Before they begin the improv, an adjective is drawn from a hat. All players must play the scene with the adjective in mind, no matter how that may or may not be obviously related to the subject of the improv.

Sample adjectives:

Sad	Happy	Soft
Balletic	Harsh	Angry
Shiny	Flowing	Beautiful
Dark	Vampiric	Horrible

INTERVIEW AS ONE – IN ONE VOICE

Set up as a TV news or talk show, two people are interviewed by a host. The two must answer all questions in one voice. They are given a topic on which they are experts, but not given time to explore what they know about the topic or what they will say. They must intuit the answers and speak together, as if they were both the same person.

PLAY IN A MINUTE

Small groups decide on a fairy tale, movie or other well-known story to re-enact. They decide on the casting, and the stopwatch begins. They have one minute to present the whole play to the audience, complete with action and dialogue.

ANIMALS AT A PARTY

One player is chosen to host a party in her home. She welcomes the other players in her group, one at a time. Each guest takes on the characteristics of a specific animal. Remind the players that they do not BECOME the animal. They remain human, but share some characteristics that we attribute to animals (see Like an Animal, in Creating a Character). For example, a person who is playing a deer might startle easily when the doorbell rings at the arrival of another guest. She would also listen very carefully to the rest of the group, and try to leave at the first sign of danger. A person playing a bear might look for the most comfortable seat in the house and settle in, but be very interested in the food being served and push to the front of the line for a buffet. By the end of the scene, the host (or audience) guesses at the animal portrayals at her party.

ENTER AND EXIT

A small group of players is given a location and situation. The audience (or leader) gives a key word to each of the players. Whenever a player hears her key word said by any other player, she must exit the scene in a way that is logical to the playing of the scenario. She waits offstage and must re-enter the scene when she hears her key word said again. This continues for each player throughout the scene, making for a scene with many unexpected, but explained entrances and exits. Key words are common words that are used often in regular speech. Example: because, yes, no, but, like, maybe, here, etc.

SCENE WITH CONDITIONS

Groups must create a scene that contains a set of three random conditions, which are picked from a deck of cards in the leader's hand. The conditions could also be written by the audience, and tossed into a hat for selection by the small groups.

Sample conditions:

There is a character that only speaks at the end
There is a couple in love

One character walks with a cane – for a reason
One character gets injured

There is a surprise in the middle of the scene
Something sad happens

A character brings bad news
A character wins something

One character can only ask questions
One character is a small child

One character can't use words of a certain letter
The weather turns very bad

One character can't use her left arm (or leg, etc.)
One character can't speak English

The scene contains a natural disaster
The scene contains a wedding

Two characters are twins – one evil, one good
Something breaks during the scene

One character says, "Oh yeah!" after everything else said

PLAY IT AGAIN

A simple scene is played out according to a given location, relationship or situation. Then, the same scene is repeated twice, in two specific genres, as named by the leader.

Sample genres:

Newscast	Thriller	Melodrama
Romance	Documentary	Tragedy
Slapstick comedy	Silent movie	Horror

Crime story	Western	Spy Thriller
Reality TV	Magic Show	Soap Opera
Shakespearean Tragedy		

HOW WAS YOUR DAY?

Small groups share stories about a typical day's events. They choose one on which to base an improv. Very mundane days are best. The group takes on the roles needed and improvises the day's events, making the trivial very important, to humorous effect.

DO IT IN SONG

The group is given a location, relationship or situation. Instead of creating a scene with dialogue, they do it singing. It could be done in a specific genre, in order to make the improv even more challenging.

PAIR IMPROVISATIONS

GET THE HAT

The players are given a relationship. Each player wears a hat. The scene is over when one player removes the hat of the other. This must be done without turning the improv into a scene about stealing hats. The topic of conversation is about anything else but the hat. They try to catch the other player off guard and snatch the hat. Players can try to protect their hats, but not touch, carry or hide them. Hats must be worn on heads.

FEATURES

Player B leaves the room while the group decides what his special feature will be. He returns and player A plays the scene, subtly giving him hints about his feature by the way in which she treats and responds to him.

Sample features:

His nose is three feet long.	He has an extra arm or leg.
He has a short tail.	He has a long beard.
He has no hair at all.	He is very short or very tall.

Variation #1. Instead of a special feature, player B must figure out what his occupation, or physiological problem, attitude or mental state is.

WHAT WILL SANTA BRING ME?

Like Features, player B leaves the room, while the group decides what he wants Santa to bring him for Christmas. When he returns, player A takes on the role of a shopping center Santa, who asks him what he wants for Christmas. Going with the hints that Santa offers, B answers Santa's questions and tries to figure out what he is asking for.

Variation #1. This exercise can be played with many other scenarios involving an object.

Sample situations and objects:

Something brought back to the store for a refund
Something brought to a repair shop
Something used in a TV cooking show
Something demonstrated in an infomercial
Something found in a student's locker

TALK SHOW CELEBRITY INTERVIEW

Player B leaves the room while the group decides what he is famous for. He is welcomed back into the space and onto the set of a TV talk show, with a host who is treating him as a celebrity. He must answer all of the host's questions even though he doesn't know who he is. He tries to figure it out and goes along with it once he does.

Variation #1. Rather than being a known celebrity, it could be played as an interview with someone who is new to fame.

Sample new celebrities:

An artist is being interviewed on her latest success, but must figure out whether she is a singer, actor, dancer, composer, painter, etc.

An inventor is being interviewed and must figure out what she has invented.

An archaeologist is being interviewed about his lasted valuable find, but doesn't know what it is.

JOB INTERVIEW

Player A conducts a job interview as the boss, knowing what the job is. Player B must answer all the questions, but he doesn't know what job he has applied for.

Variation #1. Many other situations can be played in which the person doesn't know what is going on, but the audience and interviewer do. For example, a criminal is interviewed by a cop, but doesn't know what crime he is supposed to have committed. He must play along and try to figure it out. He cannot deny that he did it.

WHAT HAPPENED BEFORE? (OR AFTER?)

Two players create a short scene, based on the suggestion of a situation. Once completed, the leader asks the question, "What happened before?" whereupon the pair plays another scene showing the backstory to the first scene. They could also be asked, "What happened after?" and they would have to add a follow-up scene to the first one.

FIRST LINE

Two players begin a scene based on a line chosen at random from a book. It could be a novel, textbook or any other book of interest to the group. The same book could be passed from person to person in the audience, in order to pick the next line to give to each new pair to play the exercise. The line should be chosen by flipping through the pages and placing a finger on any page, then reading the line found at that spot.

Variation #1. The pair bases an improvisation on the note from a fortune cookie.

PHYSICAL CONTACT

Players cannot speak to each other unless they are touching. Once given a location, they must play a scene and find realistic reasons to touch in order to be able to speak. The rule is that a new contact must be made for each time a player speaks.

UNLIKELY COMBINATIONS

Players create a scene with suggestions received by picking a card from each of three decks. One deck contains occupations, another locations and the last, objects. Both characters become the same occupation. The location and object must be important in the scene. So, for example, they could be asked to play a scene as:

Two nuns in a rowboat with a vacuum cleaner
Two hairdressers in the park with a banana

With a good selection in each deck, the combinations are endless.

Sample occupations	Sample locations	Sample objects
Lawyers	Beach	Spatula
Undertakers	Sailboat	Backpack
Mechanics	Rain forest	Umbrella
Make-up artists	Desert	Tour guidebook
Movie producers	Cruise ship	Baseball bat
Talk show hosts	Car	Felt pen
Teachers	Semi-truck	Fan
Bakers	Small island	Bike
Lumberjacks	Restaurant	Running shoe
Bounty hunters	School bus	Tennis racquet
Police officers	Office tower	Bouquet of flowers
Fire fighters	Notre Dame Cathedral	Dictionary
IT technicians	Eiffel tower	Tent

BEGINNING AND ENDING

Players are given two different tableaux from the leader or a volunteer in the audience; a beginning tableau and an ending tableau. They begin a scene based on the first tableau. The scene is over when the action flows naturally into the ending tableau.

MOVIE

Players are given characters and a location. A "director" stands off to the side and shouts instructions at random that the characters must react to. For example:

slow motion – rewind – fast-forward
freeze frame – pause – play

FOREIGN FLICK

Players play an action scene in gibberish. Each player has a translator off to the side to translate each line into English.

Sample scenarios:

> Alien invades suburb during neighbourhood barbeque
> Tourist offered goods to buy at famous site
> A rodeo rider approaches a bull in a pen
> An exterminator is called to a restaurant kitchen

DUBBING

Players are given a location and situation. They perform a scene in pantomime, moving their lips as their partners off to the sides dub in their lines of dialogue.

LEAVE SOMETHING BEHIND

Players are given characters and a location. Example: a mother and daughter at a shopping mall. One player is assigned the objective to accidentally leave something behind when she exits the scene. They begin the scene. The character with the objective must find a reason to leave and accidentally forget an object in the playing area.

ACCEPTANCE / REJECTION

Two players are given a situation. One player accepts the situation as being a good thing, and the other rejects it and wants it to change. By the end of the scene, they must have switched. This must happen in the context of the scene.

INSTANT REPLAY

Two players are given a situation. They limit the scene to about eight to ten lines of dialogue each. As soon as they finish the scene, another two players are asked to repeat the scene, imitating the action and dialogue exactly.

Variation #1. The original pair could be asked to repeat the scene in gibberish, instead of real language.

Variation #2. The original scene is timed. The same pair is asked to repeat the same scene, but in half the time, and then again in one quarter of the original time.

Variation #3. The scene could be repeated, but with the opposite intentions for each of the players. For example: If someone was trying to hurt the other in the first playing of the scene, this time she would try to help him, but use the same lines of dialogue.

Variation #4. The original two players create a scene in which they are encouraged to make strong physical choices to go with their dialogue. While they play it, two other players watch with their ears plugged, or wearing headsets, so that they can't hear what is being said. As the instant replay, they must redo the scene, but not having heard the dialogue, the actions will be the same, but the storyline different.

POCKET DIALOGUE

The entire group writes out three random lines of dialogue on three small pieces of paper. Two players are given a location and a situation. Before they begin the improv, they each pick three slips of paper from the hat and place them in their pockets. As they play the improv, each takes a paper out of his pocket, at random intervals, and uses it as the next line of dialogue. His partner reacts to it in the context of the scene.

CATEGORY SCENE

Pairs are given a location and situation. Just before they begin the scene, they pick a category out of a hat. During the improv, they try to mention as many things as possible that fit within the chosen category. It may come up as a comparison, or analogy, or be referenced in many other creative ways. The audience keeps track of the points scored by each player for slipping in something from within their category.

Sample categories:

Fruits	Vegetables	Car models
Countries	Names of candy	Types of junk food
Cities	Kinds of birds	Modes of transportation
Kinds of cutlery pieces		

PLAY IT BACKWARDS

Players play an entire scene backwards, beginning with the ending. The first word could be good-bye. The scene ends with a hello. This is difficult to do. The first time, a pair may need to play a simple scene forward, and then play it again backwards.

FIRST AND LAST SENTENCE

The group generates many random lines of dialogue that are written on individual slips of paper and placed in a hat or bucket. Two players each pick one of the slips to use as the first line and the last line of their improv. The players can be assigned as the one to start and the one to finish, or leave it to chance.

SPLIT WORLD

A common situation is given to the two players, but each is given a different environment that must be made real and maintained throughout the scene. For example, two people are discussing a tricky problem with the boss at work, but one player is in a canoe on a lake and the other is washing dishes in a kitchen. They are near each other on stage and can infringe on the other's space, making it necessary for them to incorporate the other's movements and justify them for their own environments. Each player can pretend that the other is in his environment as they speak to each other. The audience should be able to see the two environments in the actions of each of the players.

YIN / YANG

One half of the stage is a positive energy environment, and the other half is a negative. Two (or more) players are given a scene that necessitates a lot of movement all over the stage. Whenever they cross over the dividing line, their responses to the situation being played, and to each other, go from negative to positive, or vice versa. The situation in the scene must continue, even as the intentions of the players change.

Sample situations:

Setting up a campsite: gathering wood for the fire, pitching a tent
Building a house or cottage
Playing in a playground (as small children)
Creating a sculpture from many pieces of recycled material
Surveying a building site for future construction

Variation #1. More states of mind could be set for more areas of the stage.

Example: Down Stage Left = paranoid, Down Stage Right = surprised

Up Stage Right = depressed, Up Stage Left = angry

Variation #2. Different set pieces or objects in the playing area could hold different energies and create different states of mind in the players touching them.

Example: Sofa = sadness, table = excitement, chair = contentment, small prop = fear

SOUND EFFECTS

Two players are given a situation and begin a scene. At any time during the scene, an offstage technician plays a sound effect: a roll of thunder, a phone ringing, a doorbell, a dog barking, etc. Each sound effect must be recognized and justified by the players, who incorporate it into the action of the scene and carry on.

ACTING TECHNIQUES

The baseline goal of an actor is to be believable as a character, but beyond that, actors strive to be riveting and unforgettable. The audience wants to get lost in the world of the play. Stylized, non-realistic theatrical pieces aside, they want to see actors that are not only fully inhabiting their characters, but are alive and engaged, making bold choices and taking risks.

The question is, can that simply happen as a result of an actor's passion, or are there techniques and training that can result in this total embodiment of a role and a brilliant performance? I believe that it is important for directors and educators to understand the basis for different techniques and choose the ones that can appropriately be used with beginning actors in monologue and scene studies. Some techniques will also have specific training exercises that may be effectively used in the classroom. In order for any technique to result in a better performance, it must be used practically, rather than studied as an intellectual pursuit. The younger the actor, the more game orientated the process can be. There may not be a need or desire to use an actual technique or its vocabulary at all, instead allowing the child to move and create a character organically. It is once the child has grown enough to become self-conscience that he or she loses the ability to be natural. At that point it may have to be retaught through a technique. Naturalistic acting can also be made more interesting through the use of techniques.

My favourite story of how acting styles differ is the reported exchange between two brilliant actors, Sir Laurence Olivier and Dustin Hoffman, while shooting the movie *Marathon Man* in the 1970s. Dustin came to the set to shoot a scene in which his character was said to have been awake for three days. Sir Laurence asked him why he looked so bad. Dustin explained that he had been awake for three days. As a Method actor (someone who tries to "live" the role he is playing), this was Dustin's preparation for the scene. Olivier is quoted to have said some version of, "Why don't you try acting it? It's much easier." Hoffman later said the story was taken out of context. He was going through a divorce and had been partying very heavily as a result. He used the explanation as more of a joke than description of his process. Nevertheless, the story has always been used when discussing Method acting versus other techniques. Olivier, for his part, was a very adventurous actor who took risks in portraying his characters, and certainly wasn't only reliant on any specific technique learned in a classroom long ago. However, he is quoted as saying, "All this talk about the Method, the Method! WHAT method? I thought each of us had our OWN method!"

THE EXPERTS

What follows is an overview of the most well-known acting techniques, as well as examples of how some teachers have modified and applied them.

Stanislavski: Any discussion on acting technique must start with Constantin Stanislavski (1863-1938), who pioneered what became known as Method Acting. He never called it that. It was so named by **Lee Strasberg** (1901-1982) in New York, who first taught Stanislavski's Method as the head of the Actors Studio, from 1948 until his death. What Stanislavski said about his own technique was:

My system is the result of lifelong searchings… I have groped after a method of work for actors which will enable them to create the image of a character, breathe into it the life of a human spirit and, by natural means, embody it on stage in a beautiful, artistic form… The foundations for this method were my studies of the nature of an actor.

Before his founding of the Moscow Art Theatre in 1898, no one had devised an actual system for making an actor a great artist. He began with the premise that the actor must treat everything on stage as part of a real world, and put himself into that world truthfully. He called this the Magic If, "based on your own experience in life, … you will see how easy it will be for you sincerely to believe in the possibility of what you are called upon to do on the stage." The actor must ask himself how he would react if this situation were happening to him in real life.

Out of his system have come the modern concepts of beats (units of measure within a play), with each beat having an objective for each character (his desire), which should always be described as a verb, resulting in a playable action. It begins as an action, not an emotion. "The right execution of a physical objective will help to create a right psychological state." Some suggest that the Method as taught in North America missed the "action" part of his system, relying very heavily on the "emotion memory" for becoming the character. He also maintained the character would have a superobjective, the overall desire of the character during the play.

All other systems of acting technique have been an expansion, exploration or reaction to Stanislavski's work. As such, it is useful to study his writings. An accessible place to start is his book, *An Actor's Handbook: an Alphabetical Arrangement of Concise Statements on Aspects of Acting*. It is made up of quotes from his longer works.

Michael Chekhov: Stanislavski considered him to be his greatest student. Michael Chekhov (1891-1955) was the nephew of the famous playwright Anton Chekhov. He taught in Europe after leaving Russia, immigrating to the United States as a result of WWII, where he taught his own version of Stanislavski's technique. He believed that an actor could imaginatively create a real event in the life of the character on the stage.

All you experience in the course of your life, … all you brought with you into this life at birth – your temperament, abilities, inclinations etc., all are part of the region of your so-called subconscious depths. There being forgotten by you, or never known to you ,they undergo the process of being purified of all egotism. They become feelings per se. Thus purged and transformed, they become part of the material from which your Individuality creates the psychology, the illusory "soul" of the character.

He believed that Stanislavski's technique could lead to a style of acting that was simply naturalistic and thus not very interesting. He trained his actors in a more physical and imagination-based system that also used the intellect. He coined the term, "psycho-physical" in reference to his acting technique. His "psychological gesture" is described as a single physical gesture that expresses the thoughts, feelings and will (objective) of a character. Once actors discover that gesture for a particular character, they can perform it (or think it) to immediately again find the full essence of that character. The exercises in Chekhov's technique lead actors into ways of finding that psychological gesture for the characters they play. He first published his technique in *To the Actor* in 1919. Many teachers have explored his technique in other books in modern times. His student and executor of his estate, Mala Powers, provided a recent revised and expanded version, first published in 2002.

Sanford Meisner: As a young man, Sanford Meisner (1905-1997) received a scholarship to study at the Theatre Guild of Acting, where he encountered **Lee Strasberg**. In 1928, he was one of 28 students chosen by Strasberg and two other founding leaders to form the Group Theatre. Meisner and several other students became disenchanted with Strasberg's use of something he called the Affective Memory exercise. The premise of this exercise was that an actor would recall an actual past event in her life in order to recreate a real emotion on stage. In 1934, a fellow member of the Group Theatre, **Stella Adler** (1901-1992), returned from studying with Stanislavski in Paris with the news that he had moved on from relying on past memories to inform a character and now believed that using physical action, imagination and a belief in the given circumstances within the text were more important. After the Group disbanded in 1940, she opened a studio that rivalled Strasberg's in importance. A collection of her lessons was finally published in 2005, under the name *The Art of Acting*. Her revelation marked

Meisner's development of his own theories of acting, which are now known as the Meisner Technique. From 1940 on he taught this at the Neighborhood Playhouse. His book, *Sanford Meisner on Acting*, which he coauthored with Dennis Longwell is a description of sessions he conducted with students, training them in his technique. The book begins with a physical description of his studio, where two of his most important maxims hang on each side of the blackboard, "Be Specific" and "An Ounce of BEHAVIOR is Worth a Pound of WORDS." His definition of acting is that "Acting is behaving truthfully under imaginary circumstances." Rather than playing a straightforward action or emotion, an actor must explore the subtext of a play and use interactions with the other characters on stage to inform a performance. His most famous exercise is called the Repetition exercise, where an actor makes any comment based on his partner. The comment is repeated between them until it spontaneously changes. The intent is to remain truthful and not manipulate the change.

As his book does not lay out his technique in point form, but describes it through a narrative, it might be useful to see how it was clarified and manifested by **Matthew Harrison**, in an acting workshop, which I attended. Matthew studied at the Neighborhood Playhouse School of Theatre in New York, and developed his own way of using the Meisner Technique. He is the founder of the training facility The Actor's Foundry in Vancouver. He suggests that in beginning a scene study, you need to make very specific decisions, identifying the following:

> **COR** of the scene (its story):
> C – circumstance: what's happening in the scene, what's the back-story?
> O – objective: what do you want in the scene? (and/or subconsciously need)
> R – what is/are the relationship(s) to the other(s)? ("She is the one who...")

> **ARC** of the scene (structure):
> A – arc: what changes in the scene? Is it from positive to negative or vice versa?
> R – realization: what's the major realization in the scene? What decision follows it?
> C – cutting into three: how does the scene break down into its own three acts?

APPLICATION by the actor (acting):
A – action: what are your partner-related verbs? What are you trying to DO to your partner on each line?
P – personalization: how do you personally relate to the emotional circumstances?

Another way of looking at it is to create a CHARACTER STATEMENT:

I have to *partner-related verb* to *relationship* because I need *my objective* otherwise *consequence of failing* because deep down I *underlying truth*.

For example, the character of Luke Skywalker, of *Star Wars*, might say: "I have to convince (partner-related verb) my mentor, the one who holds the key to my destiny, (relationship) that I will not fall to the dark side because I need to save my friends (objective) otherwise they will die (consequence) because deep down, they are my new family, and a universe without them isn't worth saving (underlying truth)."

Acting is three things – a process:

1. Scene analysis: COR and ARC
2. Emotional grounding: APPLICATION
3. Focus (moment to moment in the scene): This is what the audience sees. #1 & #2 are preparation. You learn them, then leave them at the door.

Your preparation and performance goes from the general to the specific.

1. Story
2. Character Statement (COR & ARC)
3. Your understanding: What is your personal connection to the circumstances of the character?
4. Specific hook: What specific personal image do you hold from your understanding that brings you to this moment of reality for your character?
5. Physical action: Literally a physical movement or tableau from your hook that brings you to this moment of physical intensity needed by your character.

In addition to teaching and coaching many successful actors, Mathew Harrison has posted many essays on-line for actors and teachers.

Uta Hagen: A German- born actress who originated the role of Martha in *Who's Afraid of Virginia Woolf?* on Broadway in 1963, Uta Hagen (1919-2004) also became a very respected teacher. She wrote two books, *Respect for Acting*, with Haskel Frankel, and *A Challenge for the Actor*. Her technique begins with putting one's self into the role, rather than using external factors. She wrote the books almost twenty years apart, and disassociated herself from the first, when in the second she says that action is more important in defining the character than using one's own emotional memories. Instead of using the term "substitution" for this emotional memory work, she used "transference" in the later book, acknowledging that while an actor uses herself in the character, there is some distance involved. She also provides many exercises for training the actor.

Michael Shurtleff: A long-time Broadway casting director, Michael Shurtleff (1920-2007) put his theory and practice into his book, *Audition: Everything an Actor Needs to Know to Get the Part*. He developed 12 guideposts for analyzing a scene and thus preparing for an audition. They begin with the character's relationships and end (even after discovering everything you can within the scene) with adding a sense of wonder at the unknown in the other character, and within yourself.

David Mamet: Another student of the Neighborhood Playhouse, David Mamet (born 1947) has written many acclaimed plays and screenplays, among them *Glengarry Glen Ross*, for which he was awarded the Pulitzer Prize. He developed his ideas on acting training in his book, *True and False: Heresy and Common Sense for the Actor*. In it, he begins with the premise that, "The actor is onstage to communicate the play to the audience. That is the beginning and the end of his and her job. To do so the actor needs a strong voice, superb diction, a supple, well-proportioned body, and a rudimentary understanding of the play." Therefore, he contends, the idea that the actor "becomes" the character has no meaning. He should simply say the lines in the manner that the author indented. He decries long, involved, self-absorbed acting training.

Although not outlined in his book, he calls his technique Practical Aesthetics, and says it is a natural progression of Stanislavski's work. What he, along with actor W.H. Macy and director Gregory Mosher, have taught their actors resulted in a very clear, succinct book by a group of their students, called *A Practical Handbook for the Actor*. They begin with the Meisner statement that "acting is living truthfully under the imaginary circumstances of a play." They further break it down into action – that which you physically do to meet your objective, and moment – referring to what is happening on stage at any given instant. Essentially, the actor must analyze the scene in order to be prepared to improvise every moment on stage. This handbook offers many ways of doing just that.

Ivana Chubbuck: There are many present-day acting coaches, teachers and authors who have put forward their own methods of achieving greatness on the stage. One such teacher is Ivana Chubbuck, who has an acting school in Los Angeles. She has put her theories into a guidebook called *The Power of the Actor: The Chubbuck Technique. The 12-Step Acting Technique that will take you from Script to a Living, Breathing, Dynamic Character.* She describes the difference between her technique and those that came before her: "I teach actors how to use their emotions not as an end result, but as a way to empower a goal. My technique teaches actors how to win." Her use of "win" refers to a character meeting her goal (objective) in a scene. The book is filled with definitions of the 12 steps, with examples and exercises to explain and experience them. While Ivana works primarily with film actors, her technique is equally applicable to the stage.

Tony Barr: A well-respected acting teacher, Tony Barr (1921-2002) wrote *Acting for the Camera.* While his technique is aimed at film work, it is generally applicable to the stage as well. As he says, "if I were teaching for the stage, I would start in the same place: stop acting, start listening, keep it simple, without loss of passion!" The only difference between them is the "distance of communication." In a theatre, an actor has to work through the other actors to reach an audience that might be quite far away, while the camera brings your audience so close that you are communicating with another actor in real space. His book lays the groundwork for truthful acting in both mediums.

TERMS AND TIPS

With this wealth of material in print for the beginning teacher or actor to read, I need only define some common terms, and to offer a few additional tips on the art of acting, as gleaned from working with many very fine teachers over the years. Also, remember that using the exercises of the Scene Studies chapter are unlikely to hurt anyone, and can make the process of acting fun. Some of the techniques above rely heavily on digging into an actor's past for the moments of greatest pain. This can leave actors feeling raw and emotionally vulnerable. Choose the techniques you use with young actors carefully. The world of the play is still a world of make-believe, and best left there.

Action: Verb – what you do. Actions are 100% repeatable, emotions are not. You don't need to feel the emotion to play the action. The action doesn't happen in isolation, but is the final consequence of your intention. When playing a character, instead of asking, "Why am I doing this?", which would try to analyse the character, ask, "What am I doing this for?" and simply do the character's action, letting the audience do their job, which is explaining "why." Also, "why" takes you into the character's past (not playable), while "what" pushes you forward into the present action (playable).

Adjectives: In analyzing a character, do not use adjectives; they are not helpful in playing the character. Rather than saying someone is charming, tell him to charm the other character.

Beat: A unit of measure in a scene, the moment when something changes.

Body Position: If you hear something from another character that affects you, it may help to subtly change your body position to receive it, let it affect you.

Breathe: Don't forget to breathe. A tense body will not make for a good performance. Physical tension comes from fear of failure (see Focus, Looking Stupid).

Choices: Make strong choices for your character. Take risks. Connect the action you choose to play with something inside you. You feel the emotion, but play the action.

Circumstances: What is happening right now? What time of day is it? Your character may have a plan, but then something interferes. Live the moment-to-moment reality. To do this, keep your surrounding circumstances specific. See your immediate obstacles.

Character Sketch: Not just a description, but full of what the actor wants to DO as the character.

Entrance: To make a great entrance, know what just happened the moment before.

Focus: Your focus is always on the other character, not on yourself. You should be too busy focusing on what is around you to worry about what you are doing. Trust yourself.

Judgement: Never judge your own character's behaviour, but create a relationship to her experiences. Take what your character says at face value. There isn't always sub-text. Discover reasons and justifications for your actions, especially if playing a villain.

Lines: Learn them, then let them take care of themselves. You don't have to play them. If the line is sincere, don't say it sincerely, find something else. Find out what is happening under the lines, it's more interesting (see Subtext).

Listen: Don't wait for your next line; really listen to the other character's and respond.

Logical: Your characters don't have to be logical, no one we know in real life is.

Looking Stupid: Actors afraid of looking stupid always will. Fear of making a mistake is the problem. Remember there is no right or wrong way to create. Keep your eye on the target – what are you trying to win? What is your goal/objective?

Magic: The magic happens when you see the effect your actions are having on the other character, and allow that to influence your own responses.

Moments: Stay in the moment. Don't give your line and step back. Stay present. As in life, you never know what could happen next.

Objects: Things you handle on stage. Create a relationship with them. Put yourself in the physical context of the scene.

Objectives: Sometimes called goals, desires, needs, will or something to be won. What does your character want in this beat? This scene? This play?
- Attitudes can't be played, actions can.
- Look for the active verbs to perform in order to get what your character wants.
- Always form your objectives in positive terms: what you

want, not what you DON'T want, what you WILL do, not what you WON'T do.

- Frame your objectives in such a way that they will impact the other character.

Obstacles: What are the things getting in the way of meeting your objectives?

- Read the play or scene and find out what is blocking your character. Is it circumstances, another character, or your character's own fears or actions?

Overcome: Rather than trying to show your character's problem, show how you are trying to overcome the problem. Always explore the opposite, show the positive side.

Playing characters with "conditions": A character that has to cry or be drunk.

- **Sad:** Of course, some dramas are very sad, but it is the audience who is supposed to cry. Generally, if you do it for them, they don't have to. Find the motivations for the character. Remember, play an action, not an emotion. What does the character want? The more she wants it the harder she tries to get it, so the more the audience will feel for her. Raise the stakes. Besides, sorrow is not energizing, it drains the life out of a scene. Make a more compelling choice. How does the character handle a sad circumstance? With bravery? With bitterness? Keep remembering what she wants, and how she is going to get it.

- **Tears:** The most effective way to play a character that is supposed to cry is to try your best not to cry. Watching a character trying to hold it in is more compelling than a meltdown. This goes for any strong emotion. Don't try to play the emotion, play against it. Try to hold it in and keep going for what you want.

- **Drunk:** The most effective way to play a drunk or high character is to try to act sober. Be very careful with your words, trying very hard not to slur them. Try extra hard to walk upright in a straight line, to not waver or fall down. The harder you try, the drunker you'll look.

Practise: Actors always want to "get it right" every time. Let it go. Don't pianists sometimes play the wrong note? Keep training, keep practising.

Relationship: What is your relationship to the other characters?

- This can be phrased as "She is the one who ____,"
- You, as a person, are always in relationships, responding to them. You change with different people. You are a walking contradiction. So is your character.

Senses: Sometimes you have to release your intellect and let your senses expand and explore. What you see in the scene is what you know. Just deal with what you see.

Secondary Life: What you actually have to physically accomplish during the scene. It gives you a route through the scene.

Spine: The through-line of the scene or play. Noun verb object.

Stakes: What is at stake for your character if the goal is not achieved? Make it strong.

Story: First question to ask is, "What is this scene about?" The answer is always an action that is happening in the relationship between the characters.

Strategies: Sometimes called Actions, Tactics. What are the things your character is doing to meet an objective?

- Sometimes the script will give you clear strategies, actions to play that help your character go for her goal. Other times, you may have to fill them in for yourself, based on your understanding of the play.
- One way of discovering which strategies to play when, is to find all the possible strategies within a scene, and rather than deciding which one you will play on which beat, go through the whole scene with one, then go through it again with another. Once you have tried them all out, one at a time, allow each one to come through on its own. It will keep the scene fresh and in the moment.
- Ask, "Why is my character saying this line right now?" It isn't just to advance the plot. It will be related to her trying to get what she wants.

Substitute: Take a person you know in real life as a model for the other character on stage with you. Use that to inform your character's relationships with him or her.

Subtext: Everything happening under the lines, what your characters thinks. Your brain finds images, ways of relating to the environment, the other characters, everything.

Therapy: Acting may be therapeutic, but it isn't therapy. Don't beat yourself up remembering every bad thing that ever happened to you to bring to the character. If you are working with young people, beware of the emotional recall component to some techniques. Keep them safe.

You: Avoid physical cliches and imitations. Just bring yourself to the role. No one else is you. You have something unique to offer as this character. All you can ask of yourself is to show up and do your best. Stay in the moment and experience it. Work through the text and find meaning for yourself in the words.

Vulnerability: Ask yourself how the other character is affecting you. Let it affect you.

PLAYING A COMEDIC CHARACTER

One thing that is widely agreed upon by creators and especially the performers of comedy is that one cannot TRY to be funny. Nothing can kill a comedic performance faster that the audiences seeing the effort that the actor is making to be comedic. This is something that Stanislavski noted when he began working with his dedicated troupe of actors at the end of the nineteenth century. "The more the actor wishes to amuse his audience, the more the audience will sit back in comfort waiting to be amused" (Reynolds Hapggod, 1965). He used "amused" in the broadest sense, as he was also referring to serious work. Amused could be replaced with "engaged." Nonetheless, the sentiment applies.

So how does one present comedic material, and make it funny without trying to make it funny? By making it real, being so invested in the material, and taking it so seriously, that the audience will find it funny. As is pointed out in *Truth in Comedy*, "... the only way to do a comedy scene is to play it completely straight. The more ridiculous the situation, the more seriously it must be played; the actors must be totally committed to their characters and play them with complete integrity to achieve maximum laughs" (Halpern, Close, 2004). This was said in reference to creating improvisations, but the maxim also holds for successfully acting in a comedic play. Playing a comic character in a scripted work requires, in the words of LA actor and coach Michael D. Cohen, "...precise timing, intense character commitment, and an authentic connection to heighted reality." This is difficult to teach on the page, but does reflect my first point, to make it real.

Basically, if you are playing a funny character, chances are he doesn't know he's funny. He is likely very sincere in his actions and words. He doesn't crack himself up, so he cracks up his audience.

CREATING A CHARACTER

Whether an actor is analyzing a character from a script in order to physicalize him effectively onstage, or creating a new one, there are processes that can be successfully utilized. The following exercises focus on the "how to" of creating a character. They can be used in classroom work, during a rehearsal process for a play, or in creating pieces of devised theatre.

Students can be encouraged to examine many different aspects of a character's personality. People are very complex, with seemingly contradictory traits, just like characters. Using these techniques will make the process of discovering a character fun for beginning students of acting. All of this would precede the work that would then need to be done to determine what is happening in the play or scene (the specific circumstances that the character must deal with – obstacles), what the character wants (needs, desires), and what his actions (strategies, tactics) will be to gain his goals (objectives).

DOMINANT BODY PART

This exercise encourages exploration of a character based on how this person moves and carries him- or herself.

Method: To create a new character

Step 1. As the students walk around the space in "neutral," the leader calls out a specific body part and encourages students to focus on that body part, allowing it to change and control the way in which they walk. They actually "lead" with that part of their bodies to discover how that feels. Example: Nose. How would a walk change if the nose were controlling it? Would the head be held higher as a result, or lower? What else might change as a result of focusing on the nose?

Other body parts to explore: hip, stomach, neck, arm, leg, foot, eyes, back, etc.

Step 2. This exercise can lead to characterizations, by having students imagine there is something specific or special about the dominant body part. Example: Nose; it is too big, too small, running because of allergies, perfect – after having a nose job, etc. Students are encouraged to keep walking and explore what kind of a character would be in possession of such a nose. Would this person be an introvert or an extrovert (low status or high)? What sort of job or profession would this person have? Where would he live? Would he have friends? What would his relationship with his closest relatives be like?

Step 3. After exploring this exercise with various body parts, ask students to pick their favourite character from the ones they have created. Have them find their own spaces in the room and create worlds for their characters. The leader narrates them through the day of this character, beginning with getting up in the morning, fixing breakfast (or grabbing a coffee on the run), going to work and so on. Narrate them through a good day and then a bad day in the life of this character. As the leader narrates, the students pantomime the actions of their characters.

Step 4. Once they have established the daily patterns of their characters, have them repeat the day's activities, but allow other characters in the room to interact with theirs.

Step 5. In partner improvisations, place any two characters in a location and have them interact with each other. They retain the characters they have created, but now use them in various environments.

To explore and analyze an existing character: If this exercise is used in the analysis of an existing character, choose the dominant body part of the character, based on the information that the script provides.

Step 1. Use the Exercises: Going through the steps of this exercise once this decision is made will enhance the actor's portrayal of the character. In the final playing of the role, the audience may not even be aware of the dominant body part, as it may make only the very subtlest of differences to the physicality of the character, but it is a valuable rehearsal tool to use in the early stages of character discovery.

Step 2. Improvisation: Having each character in a play do this exercise independently, simultaneously, will allow the actors to explore how this character will move on stage. Once discovered, the characters could improvise scenes that are outside of the script, perhaps providing backstory to the plot, or exploring alternative responses to the plot points, or doing existing scenes in their own words.

Step 3. Exaggeration: In addition to, or as an alternative to performing improvisations with the characters, actors could go through a scene from the play, exaggerating the effects of their dominant body parts. This may result in making new discoveries for the playing of their roles. Once the exaggeration is removed, the lingering effect may be a subtle physical, or psychological difference for the actor in the role.

CHARACTER RECALL

This exercise invites students to create a character based on observation. It makes students more aware of others in their worlds, as observing and understanding the actions and reactions of others will make them better able to create believable characters on stage. It will also produce more realistic characters in their improvisations and playwriting projects.

Methods:

To create a new character: Students are asked to follow a person in a public place for twenty minutes. They should be very discreet. The idea isn't to get arrested for stalking, but to simply observe a fellow human being. They are asked to make careful mental note not only of what the person is doing, but also of how they are doing it.

At the next class students are given two minutes to perform a pantomime of the people they followed. The group should be able to tell not only where they are and what they are doing, but also a sense of the age, mental state and personality of the character.

Follow-up assignment #1. Student writes a character sketch in which this character is given a complete background, guessing the person's age, occupation, whether she lives alone or has a family and anything else she can create based on what she witnessed.

Follow-up assignment # 2. Students write a monologue in the voices of their characters. They explore what their characters would say to someone else in a particular situation. This can be a written assignment as well as a performance for the class.

Variation #1. Instead of following a stranger, students could recall the actions and characteristics of people they know well. A pantomime, character sketch and monologue could follow. As the person's background is already known, the other analysis exercises can be added to the description: Effort Action, Animal, Colour, etc.

Have them watch these people, or others, in different specific situations. How do these people react to:

- Stressful situations
- Sad situations
- Being in a hurry to finish something or get somewhere
- Being surprised
- Being in charge of a situation
- Having to follow someone else's lead in a situation

To explore and analyze an existing character: A variation of this exercise that may be useful to actors playing specific roles in a play is to ask them to find people in their own lives that remind them of the characters they are playing.

- **Lists:** Have them list characteristics of the person known to them, in an effort to better understand the roles they are playing.

- **Observation:** Watching this person in life may help inform him of underlying motivations for his character, as well as assisting him in physicalizing the character.

- **Substitution:** In order to play a relationship on stage, it may be helpful if an actor thinks of someone that the other character reminds her of. She can use her relationship with this person to help inform her relationship with the character.

FAMOUS CHARACTERS

This exercise uses characteristics of well-known people, both real and from literature, to inform created characters and those that are new to them in scripted work.

Method:

To create a new character: Have the group identify a well-known person and make a list of his or her defining characteristics. Be very specific, translating all descriptions into actions. Example: Someone is described as ruthless. What does it mean to be ruthless? Translate that into playable actions. How does a ruthless person affect others?

- stare people down

- ignore other's ideas
- disregard other's feelings
- use physical force to get what he wants
- defend only his own self-interests

Once a list is complete, go on to another famous person. Find contrasting characters. Then, give lists to players who use them for characters in improvised situations. The name of the person should not be at the top of this list. Rather, give the character a new name or identifier, as this exercise is about playing an actor's own interpretation of these actions, not trying to imitate the well-known person. This would also be helpful in playwriting.

To explore and analyze an existing character: If presented with a character in a script that needs fleshing out, it may be valuable to name a well-known person or character from literature that shares some characteristics with this new character. The actor can add some of his or her traits to what is known about the character to be portrayed.

LIKE AN ANIMAL

Students will create characters based on animal traits. People have personified animals, giving them human characteristics based on what they look like or what they do. This has led to cliché similes: sly as a fox, wise as an owl, hungry as a bear, etc. In this exercise, rather than apply human characteristics to an animal, students use an animal as the basis for a human character.

Method:

To create a new character:

Step 1. Students are asked to move about the space as a jungle animal. They can choose which animal they would like to be, making the sounds and actions of that animal.

Step 2. Students stand and walk upright, but maintain the characteristics of this animal.

Step 3. Students begin to speak and interact with each other, but retain a trace of this animal in their speech and, more importantly, in their physical characteristics and their attitude. They are human characters that are based on their animal's qualities.

Step 4. Repeat the exercise with everyone becoming a barnyard or domestic animal, and then taking those characteristics into a human character.

Step 5. This can be repeated for various animals. Then, students choose their favourite character and create physical environments for them. They may leave their environments to visit other characters in their environments. Remind them that they are playing human characters, not animals. They bring the characteristics of their animals into these people.

Examples: A hibernating bear might become an author who likes to write in his den, with a warm fireplace and comfortable chair. He may become quite irritable if anyone disturbs him. Once his book is finished, he wants to go out for a huge meal, with salmon being his favourite food. His voice is gruff and he isn't fond of company.

A pink flamingo might become an interior decorator who is very flamboyant and loves to use colour. She is gregarious and loves to go to parties, interacting with everyone there. She loves to laugh and makes people feel at ease in her company. She is always well dressed and groomed, following the latest fashions and very confidant. She is also extremely graceful.

Step 6. Students are placed in pairs and improvise a scene involving both of their characters. Switch often to give various characters opportunities to interact. This could be done simultaneously, with the whole group participating, or, with an advanced group, they could watch each other's improvisations.

Variation #1. They repeat a favourite improvisation, editing as they play it. The scene needs a beginning, middle and end, with a conflict to be solved. Characters need goals (objectives). The scene can be scripted and rehearsed, then performed for the group. A discussion could follow on how the actors used their animals while in the scene.

To explore and analyze an existing character: Describing the character as a specific animal may help in physicalizing her. Moving like the animal in an exaggerated fashion in an early rehearsal may aid in the discovery of the character.

LABAN EFFORT ACTIONS

Rudolf Laban was an American modern dancer during the early days of modern dance in the mid-twentieth century. He developed a method of categorizing the way in which the human body can move. He looked at the speed at which a person moved, quickly, or slowly and sustained, and called it time. He studied whether a person was direct in getting to where they were going, or indirect, taking the scenic routes of life, and called it space. Lastly, he observed whether a person performed movements that were very ponderous, strong and heavy, or light and airy, and called it weight. He further discovered that if these three categories were combined in every configuration, there were eight possible combinations. He called them eight Effort Actions. Every human on earth could be put into one of those eight categories, as could every character ever written. Each category has a descriptive name. The Effort Actions can be used to define a character in a script, or as the base in creating a character.

These Effort Actions can define a person's physical movement style and inform personality traits; the way in which a person functions and interacts with others.

EIGHT EFFORT ACTIONS

NAME		TIME	SPACE	WEIGHT
Press	=	Sustained	Direct	Heavy
Punch	=	Quick	Direct	Heavy
Float	=	Sustained	Indirect	Light
Glide	=	Sustained	Direct	Light
Wring	=	Sustained	Indirect	Heavy
Slash	=	Quick	Indirect	Heavy
Flick	=	Quick	Indirect	Light
Dab	=	Quick	Direct	Light

FINDING THE EFFORT ACTIONS

Method: Spread students out in the playing area. Ask them to focus on spots at the other side of the room and go straight there. Once they are there, direct them to go back to their original spots, still in a straight line, but with slow, heavy elephant steps. Then explain to the group that what they have done is a personality type called a "Press," someone who is very direct, doesn't give up easily, but just plods along towards her goal, no matter who or what might stand in her way. Go through each subsequent Effort Action, naming it after they have discovered its qualities. Finally, explain that these are called Effort Actions, and relate their origins.

USING THE EFFORT ACTIONS

Method: Divide the group into pairs and have all of the students work simultaneously. Give each of them an Effort Action to play, and a situation to develop in their improvisations. If this group is experienced in improvisational work, have them view each other's improvs. The specific Effort Action could be chosen by each individual, picked out of a hat, or assigned by the leader. The situation could be replayed after having students switch to a different Effort Action, resulting in quite a different scene.

Variation #1. In addition to using Effort Actions in improvised scenes, students can use them alone, or in conjunction with other methods of creating a character, to write monologues or two-handers (a scene with two characters).

To explore and analyze an existing character: Identifying the specific Effort Action of a character can be helpful in exploring a role. It will inform how the character moves, relates to others and conducts himself. Every situation in a scene can be studied in terms of the characteristics of the specific Action. It will also help identify those moments when a character does something surprising and "out of character."

COLOUR CHARACTERIZATIONS

Another way of looking at someone's character is to describe him or her as a colour.

YELLOW	Bright, sunny, cheerful, extrovert, caring, speaks before thinking
ORANGE	Extrovert, popular, irresponsible, forgetful, disorganized, doesn't follow through with plans, insensitive, lives for the moment
RED	Extrovert, intense, plays emotions to the limit, extreme behaviour
PINK	Very spiritual, kind, in his/her own world, spaced out, introvert or extrovert

PURPLE	Very intelligent, witty, snobby, bossy, may be hurtful and cruel, extrovert
MAUVE	Combination of purple and pink, intelligent and spiritual, witty, kind, introverted
GREEN	Earthy, natural, not afraid of change, brave, helpful, extrovert
BLUE	Very organized, punctual, leader, serious, sensitive, afraid of change, hides emotions, introvert
GRAY	Will take on other people's personalities, like a spy who wants to blend in
BROWN	More extreme than gray, will actually imitate others
BLACK	Evil or mysterious, powerful
WHITE	Very innocent, pure, usually only young children are pure white

A character may be a combination of colours, or have a dominant colour and another that is secondary.

In the same way that it is said that opposites attract, characters that are opposite each other on the colour wheel will play off of each other well in a scene. Example: Red/Green, Yellow/Purple, Blue/Orange, Black/White.

PERSONALITY TYPES

People have used personality tests to define themselves. There are dozens of systems, but most of them draw on the same ancient source, Hippocrates. In ancient Greece he laid out a series of personality traits that, grouped together, could tell people which of the humours of the blood ruled their lives. Each had positive and negative qualities.

HIPPOCRATES' HUMOURS OF THE BLOOD

| SANGUINE | Talkative, expressive, impulsive, emotional, likes to be the center of attention, charming, enthusiastic, forgetful |
| CHOLERIC | Domineering, impatient, strong-willed, born leader, dynamic, organized, confident, goal-orientated |

| MELANCHOLIC | Analytical, artistic, thoughtful, perfectionist, moody, hard to please, suspicious, prone to depression |
| PHLEGMATIC | Easy-going, quiet, dry wit, sympathetic, unmotivated, selfish, shy, fearful, worried, avoids responsibility |

A character might be a combination of humours.

An easy way to understand these character types is to imagine that one of each of them was involved together in a group project. The Sanguine would volunteer to present the material once the project was completed. The Choleric would keep everyone organized and on task. The Melancholic would do the research and the artwork. The Phlegmatic would offer moral support while doing as little of the work as possible.

AN INTERVIEW

A way of spontaneously creating a character, which can then be fleshed out with analysis under all the preceding categories, is to conduct an interview with each student.

Method: One at a time, students are asked to sit on a chair in the middle of the space while the leader conducts an interview, asking for their names and ages, occupations, hopes and dreams. They are instructed to be anyone they would like to be, except themselves. Encourage them to speak positively about their choices in life, and attitudes towards themselves and others. Negativity doesn't play as well on stage (see Playwriting chapter for hints on writing monologues). They can be asked what they remember to be the best days of their lives, or the worst, and about their relationships to other significant people in their lives, but not what colour, humour, animal or Effort Action they resemble.

Follow-up Assignment #1. Students write out character sketches in which they analyze their characters and make decisions about which categories they fit into.

Follow-up Assignment #2. Students write monologues as these characters, choosing situations for them to react to. They can then be performed for the group.

CHARACTER SKETCH

The exercises in this chapter are useful for exploration in a classroom setting. They could include the following information:

1. What is this character's background information: age, family make-up, physical description, occupation, hopes, dreams and desires?
2. What kind of animal would he be and why? Give an example of past behaviour.
3. What is his dominant body part and why? How does that affect him?
4. Which Effort Action is he? Give an example from his life that demonstrates it.
5. Describe this character as a colour. Give an example from past behaviour.
6. Which of Hippocrates' Humours does he most resemble and why?
7. Is this a low or high status character? Is he comfortable with his status?

If writing this character sketch about a character from a play or from real life, the following questions would be important to ask:

1. What does he say about himself?
2. What do others say about him? This may not, however, be true!
3. What does he do? This is the most important, for actions speak louder than words.

Judgement: It is not the actor's job to stand in judgement of a character. It is important for the actor to like the character she is playing and to find justifications for all of her actions. If this is a difficult concept for students, rather than explaining it, have them do a character sketch on the antagonist from a play they are studying. Just have them answer the first question on background: what has he done before the play begins, and what is he doing in the play? What are his hopes and dreams? Now have them participate in a writing exercise, without calling it a character sketch. Ask them a series of questions about themselves, having them write down their answers. For example: What are your goals for the next year? Do your parents try to control your life? What do you really want? What are you willing to do to get it? What is your relationship to money? Now have them compare this writing with the character sketches they wrote. The difference will be the judgement.

Everything the students do will be justified, but they will stand in judgement of the character.

This is why I encourage actors to speak of the roles they are playing in the first person. Use "I," not "she." If they personalize it, they will be less likely to judge.

Usefulness: Character sketches done on characters in a play must be useful to the actor. It should be easier to play the character once those facts are established. Negative judgements lead to generalized cliché portrayals of a character. For example: It isn't helpful for an actor playing a villain to simply say, "I'm evil. I'm a murderer." A better way would be for him to look at his actions and describe what he does for reasons he considers valid: "I killed my neighbour to protect my land." Remember that everyone is doing the best they can under the circumstances they find themselves in. Also, it is more helpful to talk about actions than states of being. Rather than "I am," use "I [verb]."

STATUS

Characters in life and art have differences in status. This could be the result of position, wealth, or force of personality. In a theatrical context, the struggle for status is often the basis for relationships. Plays will have a mixture of high and low status characters and those who want more status. Understanding a character's status will explain a lot about the choices she makes.

INTRODUCTORY EXERCISES

THE PARTY

This exercise is an introduction to the concept of status. It is most easily understood by saying that high status people are generally outgoing and low status people are not: extroverts and introverts. Naturally, there are exceptions, like Howard Hughes, but this works as an introduction.

Method: Students form pairs, with one partner on one side of the room and one on the other. They are all at a party. The students on the right side are very shy and introverted, afraid to meet people. Fortunately, each of them has a friend here to help. The students on the left are very extroverted, outgoing and confident. It is up to them to go and get their introverted friends, introduce them all around and make sure that they have a good time at this party. The exercise is repeated with the roles reversed.

ONE UP

Method: In pairs, students simply take turns trying to outdo each other. They carry on a conversation in which everything they say makes them out to be more adventurous, smarter, richer, and greater in every way than their partners. The conversations get as ridiculous as possible and simply end at the command of the leader. No one can actually win this one.

Variation #1. As a means of demonstrating that status can come from pathos and sympathy as well as brains and power, the exercise can be repeated with each partner trying to get below the status of his partner with an even worse hard luck story. The result may look, at first glance, that the student's status is diminished with every statement, but in fact, while a hard luck story may not give anyone power or influence, the sympathy and attention it can garner is a form of status in itself.

GET HIGHER/LOWER

The objective in this exercise is to show status in a physical way.

Method: Pairs work with each other non-verbally. They size each other up and try to take status from the other person. It will begin with a student pulling himself up to his full height, throwing back his shoulders, attempting to look down on his partner and may escalate to finding something to stand on to gain a physical advantage over his partner.

Variation #1. Repeat the exercise with the reverse objective. Students physically give status to their partners, making themselves lower, physically and figuratively. It will begin with bowing and showing deference, trying to get closer to the floor.

PHYSICALIZING STATUS

A discussion about physicalizing status could follow the playing of these introductory exercises. What are the physical characteristics of high and low status characters?

High Status:
- Good posture
- Makes eye contact easily

- Smiling and outgoing (or frowning and intimidating), extroverted
- Open body postures – strong and confident
- Firm handshake, confident stride when walking

Low Status:
- Slouched posture
- Doesn't make eye contact
- Shy and introverted
- Closed, protective body postures
- Afraid of contact, small steps, tense, not relaxed, body movements

This discussion leads into how to take status or how to give it to another character.

Take Status:
- Order people to do things for you
- Put other people down, treat them in a condescending manner – or – treat them well and gain status by popularity instead of intimidation.
- Use big words, name drop, boast about past deeds
- Pause a lot in speech, to make people wait for your next words
- Follow all physical patterns of a high status character

Give Status:
- Ask for advice
- Give compliments
- Offer to do things for others
- Give up physical comfort for others. For example: offer your chair
- Get physically lower than others
- Put yourself down
- Follow all physical patterns of a low status character

STATUS IMPROVISATIONS

Improvisations involving status are somewhat advanced, as in addition to creating a story, the issue of who has status must be considered. Students must be reminded to stay in the world of the improv, and not taking the struggle for status personally. If the group is new to improvisations, a more accessible place to start is the improvisations in the companion book, **STAGES: Creative Ideas for Teaching Drama**. It is important to only try status improvs with a group accustomed to performing improvisations with an audience of peers, and that should only be done after the group has lots of experience with simultaneous improvs and planned performance improvs.

Method: Warm up for status improvisations with an audience by having students partner up for some simple situational improvisations with the focus being status. Students are given characters that are either high or low status and a situation in which to play a scene. Everyone works simultaneously.

Sample Scenes:

> Co-workers at a fast food restaurant. A is high status – been on the job for two months. B is low status – first day on the job.

> Bank robbers planning their next job. A is high status – pulled lots of jobs before, B is low status – messed up the last job.

> Friends at a beach. A is high status – lots of friends, B is low status – new kid in town.

RANKING

In this improv for an audience, status is completely arbitrary and quite a lot of fun to play with. Students are encouraged to find ways to give people status, and take it away. This is best played with all three students being of the same gender, so that it can't become a two-against-one situation. This exercise is not for beginners.

Method: This exercise is played with three people. They enter the playing area and silently decide on a ranking for everyone, including themselves. They do not share this information with the audience or with each other. Person number one is the most important person in the scene, number two is below him and number three is at the bottom. They place themselves as one, two or three. They are given a location and begin the scene, treating their number ones the best and their number threes the worst. After the scene ends, the audience should be able to guess the rankings chosen.

Variation #1. To make it more challenging, it can be played with four people, two of each gender. Remind them to listen to each other, something more difficult with four players. It will also be more challenging to keep the numbers straight during the scene, and make their own status in the hierarchy clear, both to each other and to the audience.

RANKING WITH CARDS

Method: A group of four or five players create a scene based on a suggested location; one in which status is important. Each player pulls a playing card from a deck, but cannot see it, as it is held to his forehead by an elastic headband. The player does not know his own rank, but does know the other players', and treats them accordingly. As the scene progresses, each discovers his own rank by how others treat him.

Variation #1. Instead of knowing all but his own ranking, he only knows his own. He tries to assert the amount of status he believes he deserves, without first knowing where he falls in the ranking compared to others in the scene. At the end of the scene, ask all players to line up according to their presumed ranking.

Sample locations:

    A royal palace
    A high-end private art gallery
    A corporate office
    A university faculty club
    A police station

PULLING FACES

In this status exercise one player is given status by virtue of her position, but the lower status player can pull status on her. This is where players find out that playing a low status character can be much more fun than playing one with a lot of status.

Method: The scene contains characters with a boss/underling relationship. The boss has all the status. However, it is the objective of the underling to pull silly faces/imitations of the boss whenever possible in the scene without getting caught by the boss. The scene can be played for a specific length of time, perhaps two minutes, with the audience counting how many faces were pulled successfully. The next underling to play the scene tries to beat the previous score.

SWITCHING STATUS

This exercise points out that status is not only the result of one's position in life, it is also a choice to give or take status from another person.

Method: The scene contains two characters, one in a high status position, the other low. Example: boss/employee or beggar/shopkeeper. They start the scene playing their status; however, at any time the leader can call "switch" and the status is reversed, although the roles stay the same. The shopkeeper must find ways of giving the beggar status, who finds ways to take it. That is, until the leader calls for another switch.

FIND A FRIEND

Perhaps the ultimate struggle for status, in this exercise students come to realize that achieving high status is often more effectively done through kindness than through intimidation. This exercise can be hard on the ego and should not be played early in a session, and never by beginners to improv. Students need experience with improvisation before they learn to not take it personally. Play the scene with a gender balance, as it is too difficult to avoid "ganging up" on the one lone member of the opposite gender.

Method: This exercise is played with groups of four or five students. They are given a situation in a specific location. Their only objective is to stay in the scene but have one of the other players leave. It is an exercise in survival. The only way to ensure that you will not be made to leave the scene is to find a friend who wants you to stay. The scene is over when it is clear to the audience that one of the players should leave, whether he has physically done that, or is still fighting an already lost battle.

SCENE STUDIES

For a group that is new to scene studies, it may be helpful to try these three introductory exercises first, allowing students to use their imaginations before learning how to analyze text in a scene. This idea, along with the exercises, INTENTION AND WHAT ARE WE FIGHTING FOR?, came from a workshop with Rosemary Dunsmore, from Toronto.

INTRODUCTORY EXERCISES

NONSENSE RHYMES

Using children's short poems instead of scripted scenes, students enact them for the class.

Method: In pairs, students are given a short children's nonsense poem or rhyme, and find a way of communicating its meaning for their audience. A good place to start is Dennis Lee's book of nursery rhymes, *Alligator Pie*. Here is an example of one poem, called "Thinking in Bed." This first verse is a perfect length for this exercise.

> I'm thinking in bed,
> Cause I can't get out
> Till I learn how to think
> What I'm thinking about;
> What I'm thinking about
> Is a person to be—
> A sort of a person
> Who feels like me.

OPEN DIALOGUE

These short scripts can act as a bridge between the nonsense poetry enactments and scenes from plays.

Method: In pairs, students are given open dialogue scripts. They study them for a few minutes and present them to the class, making the circumstances of the scene clear by how they have answered the following questions in their preparations:

- WHO are you?
- WHERE are you?
- WHAT has just happened? What is happening?
- WHEN is it? What time of day?
- WHY is this happening?

- WHAT do you want from the other character?

Sample Open Dialogue Scenes:

A: Open up. It's me.	A: I didn't expect to see you here.
B: Do you know what time it is?	B: No.
A: I don't know. Late.	A: It's been a long time.
B: What were you thinking?	B: Yes.
A: Well –	A: I never thought –
B: Did you get it?	B: I guess not.
A: Don't worry about it.	A: How have you been?
B: Close the door.	B: Well, you know. Are you –
A: I can't do it.	A: What?
B: That's okay.	B: You know.
	A: Oh, yes (or no)

AMBIGUOUS TEXTS

The next stage is the introduction of scripted scenes that are fairly ambiguous, and open to interpretation. Scenes are taken from plays that are not known to the students.

Method: In pairs, students are given short scripts and asked to go through the dialogue, answering the same Who – What – Where – When – Why questions for each of the characters, then playing it for the group. You may also introduce the idea of having an intention with every line (see Intention exercise, later in this chapter), or leave that for later in the unit.

Sample text:

A: Hey.

B: What are you doing here?

A: I think I have a right to be.

B: She doesn't want to see you.

A: Did she say that?

B: After everything that's happened, I would think that you –

A: We need to talk.

B: You don't feel any remorse at all, do you?

A: Are you going to tell her I'm here?

B: You left.

A: I had to.

B: Why?

A: We both know why.

SCENE STUDY TECHNIQUES

MEMORIZING A SCENE IN A HURRY!

While this exercise may not be for students who are completely new to script-work, it is very interesting for those more experienced. Once you have introduced it as a class exercise, actors can use it on their own with whatever scripts they are learning. This exercise came from a workshop with Peter Skagen, from Calgary.

Method: Hand a script to each partner in the scene. Scenes from movies work well, as they tend to be shorter than stage scenes, with shorter lines for each character. Give them the basic set-up of the scene; only which character each actor will play and where they are. Both actors have a blank piece of paper or bookmark to cover all unread lines of their scripts. They do not even glance at the scripts before the exercise begins.

1. First character reads her first line aloud.
2. Second character guesses aloud what his response might be.
3. Second character checks script for actual response and delivers it.
4. First character guesses her response to that line, moves her bookmark down the script, checks it to find the real line and re-delivers it.
5. Second character does the same and so on, until they reach the end of the scene.
6. They begin again at the top and read the scene, as written, with each other.
7. They begin again WITHOUT SCRIPTS, performing the scene for the class. They will be amazed at how well they know the lines; at times word perfect.

This can also be done in pairs, simultaneously, if time does not allow for each set of partners to do it for the class, but it is a very interesting exercise to watch.

A single actor, learning her lines before an audition or workshop, can use this same technique. The actor simply reads the other characters' lines and covers her own, making a guess at them before revealing them. It must be done as the very first read of a scene, when the actor truly does not know where the scene will go. This is an extremely fast and effective method for getting the lines into an actor's head. It also starts informing the actor's choices for her character, as she will automatically start thinking about why her character responds as she does to what she is given. Whether she has correctly predicted her character's responses, or is surprised when she sees what the real line is, the process helps to start understanding her character, as well as remembering what she actually does say.

SOLO READ

As an alternative to using the exercise, Memorizing a Scene in a Hurry, here is another approach to classroom scene studies.

Method: After performing a physical relaxation exercise, have all actors find their own spaces, and read the script very slowly, out loud for themselves. They read for all of the characters in their scenes. They do not have to try to figure out what is going on in the scene, but just let their imaginations wander as they read, allowing for any images or connections to the lines to surface.

Follow this reading by having them do a journal entry, relating the scene to something from their own lives, or to anything that it reminds them of that they have read of heard about before. Have them record how it makes them feel. Some students may also want to create a visual art response to what they have read.

It is important to take a lot time with the words at the very beginning of a rehearsal process. Actors need to take the words of the playwright and begin to make them their own. There is no need to rush into putting a scene up on its feet.

FIRST PARTNER READ-THROUGH

First read-throughs of scenes are usually done with both actors looking down at their scripts. However, after using the solo exercise above, they are ready for a more involved first read with a partner.

Method: Have partners sit in chairs, facing each other. Ensure that they are sitting in relaxed open positions, with no folded arms or crossed legs. Have them look down at their scripts only when they are not actually speaking their lines to each other. They need to look at their partners both when they speak, and when they listen to their partners speak. Glancing down only to absorb a line or two and then looking and listening to their partners allows them to begin to establish a connection between the characters. Encourage them to keep the line deliveries natural and honest, without pushing them or tying to "perform."

Variation #1. Repeat the exercise, but allow the actors to decide whether to begin sitting or standing. Each actor decides his first position, which doesn't have to be the same for his partner. The scene begins again, with the actors only speaking when they are looking up from their scripts, and not looking down at their scripts when their partners are speaking. If an actor gets an impulse to move, he does so.

After this exercise, encourage them to talk to each other about the discoveries they made.

OBJECTIVES AND STRATEGIES

In every scene each character has an objective or goal, something that she wants from the other character. This is her reason for being on the stage. Each character will use strategies or tactics to get what she wants. In order to understand this concept, it may be helpful to play a simple, straightforward improvisation, in which students are given a single clear objective, and told to come up with three different strategies to use in order to win their objectives. Only one of the three can be purely verbal. The other two must also contain a physical component, something they do to achieve their goals. Instruct them to go on to the next tactic when it is clear that the first one isn't working. Once all three have been attempted, win or lose, the improv is over.

Method: One of the partners is sitting on a chair. The other is told to do whatever it takes to get her partner to stand up and move away from the chair. No actual physical contact is allowed. Each partner has a turn in each role. A discussion follows the exercise: What did they do to get the chairs? Did it work? How quickly did they move on to their next strategies? Some verbal strategies could be to beg, threaten, offer a deal, or present a compelling reason to get up out of the chair. Non-verbal strategies can include crying or fainting, or taking on a physical condition that needs the partner's help. The seated partner is not given a specific objective, but told to get up if a reasonable human being in that situation would do so.

Variation #1. Instead of trying to get the partner to give up the chair, the objective is to get the partner to sit in the chair. Now the partners are no longer quite as passive, as they will need to come up with reasons for not accepting the offers to sit down in the chairs. They need an objective to meet that does not involve sitting down in that chair.

Variation #2. Students are asked to design their own improvisations in which both of them have their own objectives. It should now go beyond simply one partner's wanting something and the other not wanting it. Now both must have their own positive goals that are important to them, but do not mesh with each other. They do not tell each other their objectives before they begin a scene. Tell them that they are not allowed to ask directly for what they want. They must manoeuvre the dialogue and action in such a way that the partners offer them what they want.

Variation: #3. The discussion goes to the actual scene that the pair is working on, to find what each of their goals are, and what they do in the scene in order to reach them. It is unlikely that the objectives will be as concrete as simply wanting an object from the other character. It may be more of a psychological need that must be addressed; perhaps a need to be loved or accepted. The key is finding actions to play to meet their goals.

BEATS

A play is divided into units. The largest units are the acts. Then, each act is divided into scenes. The scenes will change when something shifts; the location, the time or perhaps something subtler that the playwright nevertheless wishes to separate from what precedes it. The smallest unit of measure in a play is its beats. Beats are individual little moments within the dialogue and action of a play. A beat is created when something new occurs, or something changes. It might be the entrance or exit of a character, creating a new dynamic on the stage, or it could be as subtle as a shift in the intention of an individual character within a section of dialogue. Any time that a character has a new objective there will be a new beat, as well as when a character begins to use a new tactic to get what he wants. Student actors need to recognize these shifts.

Method: Pairs read through their scenes together, making note of when a character has a shift, or a change that begins a new beat. Have them talk about what causes each change. Have them mark each beat in their scripts with a forward slash / to separate this new thought, intention, or idea. These beats will influence most of the rest of the exercises they will go through with their scenes. Finding and marking the beats in the script will keep them from running the thoughts together and is the beginning of finding different levels to play within the scene. Beats may change at the beginning of a section of dialogue or in the middle of one character's speech. The biggest gifts in a scene are when a discovery is made, a decision reached or when a character receives news. All of these occurrences will result in a new beat, with a significant shift.

FIND THE WORDS

This exercise is very helpful in studying the text.

Method: Each person makes a list of the one most important word in each beat of dialogue. He does this independently, but while reading aloud with his partner. Each actor reads through to the end of a beat and selects a word. If the scene has a director, she would have a voice in the process and assist in choosing the word that best represents the character's thoughts in that beat. Once they have created their lists, they use them in place of the full sentences, turning the single words into true conversation with each other, as they seek to explore their partner's meanings and reacting to them with their own, but adding no additional words to the single ones chosen.

If this is the first time this exercise is used, consult the fuller explanation under Monologues, later in this chapter, in the Looking for Meaning exercise there. Once the pairs have been led through several "as if" scenarios, they are ready to work on their own. Their own "as if" intonations do not have to be as exaggerated as the ones they were given to explore. Rather, the individual words should start to flow as conversation between them. As each word is said in turn, the dialogue develops.

Variation #1. A single word can be repeated, making the conversation off kilter, as the two may not be at the same stage in the list. One partner may repeat a single word longer than the other, as they take their own journeys through the text.

The partners will begin to develop their characters' relationship and the single words will act as guideposts pointing out the direction of the scene, making memory easier.

LISTENING

The objective of this set of exercises is to explore the intent of the lines and discover the characters' need to communicate.

Method: Partners sit on the floor, leaning on each other's backs. With scripts in hand, they go through a series of readings of the dialogue.

1. Reading through the script, actors listen to their partner's words and respond with their own. Lacking any visual cues will help them tune in to the text.
2. Repeat the scene, with each actor snapping her fingers the moment she is ready to say her own line in response to her partner's, whether he is finished his line or not. They are looking for their impulses to speak, even as they keep listening.
3. Repeat the scene in their own words, keeping the intent of the actual dialogue.
4. Go back to the lines as written, really listening and responding honestly.

SHARE A SECRET

This exercise helps develop a sense of urgency to communicate their characters' thoughts and ideas with each other. It leads to finding the characters' objectives.

Method: Have partners sit facing each other and go through the lines of their script in a whisper. Ask them whether this gave them a sense of urgency, a need to really communicate with their partners. Have them repeat the exercise in full voice, trying to retain that sense of urgency and need to communicate.

Follow this exercise with a discussion on what the stakes are in this scene. Why is a particular character in this place, at this time, having this interaction with the other character? What is it that each character wants from the other? What is each character's objective? What will happen if this objective is not met? What are the stakes? Encourage the actors to make strong choices in deciding the characters' objectives. Make the stakes high. If it isn't important to meet the objective, the scene will lack a sense of urgency, and the energy level will drop.

DISTANCE COMMUNICATION

This exercise is helpful not only in training actors to project into a large auditorium, but also in separating volume and communication. Intimate communication can happen at any volume. Rather than emphasizing the volume of a speech, encourage actors to communicate, with each other and with an audience.

Method: Have all of the scene partners stand around the outside edges of the room and speak the words of their scenes to each other. They must not simple try to out-shout the other pairs, but really try to keep the connection with their partners in spite of the other pairs. Challenge them to do this without shouting. If the group is large, it may be more effective to do this exercise a few pairs at a time, rather than everyone at once.

SUBTEXT / INNER DIALOGUE

A dialogue will work on two levels: what is on the page, and what is left unsaid.

Method: Have students face each other, preferably standing, as our energies are more alive and available to use when we stand. Sitting leads to comfort, which can lead to complacency. Read through the scene together.

The pairs read the scene again, this time speaking quietly any thoughts that come up as their partners speak. They are running an inner dialogue with themselves, discovering the subtext of their words. Sometimes it is what they would like to say instead of what they do say. The subtext is what is really going on in the scene, underneath the lines.

Variation #1. To make this more concrete, actors could each have a friend beside them that they talk to. This friend is the actor's inner voice, and holds a conversation with the actor between and through all the lines of the scene, adding insight and encouragement. If this isn't active enough, add a second friend, and repeat the exercise until the inner voice has been thoroughly explored. Then have the actors play the scene again without the friends, bringing all that information into the scene with them.

INTENTION

Each line that is spoken carries with it an intention. Acting isn't about how to say a line, but in using the line to affect a change in the other character.

Method: Ask the pairs to go through the text of their scenes, and answer the question, "What am I doing with this line?" Every line should have a verb to describe what a character hopes to do to impact the other character.

For example:

> Character A: It's lovely outside. The sun is shining. (entice her to go for a walk)
>
> Character B: This is a very important TV show. (dismiss his idea)
>
> Character A: That new trail has opened in the park. (seduce her to go)
>
> Character B: We can check it out later. (reassure him of your love – or possibly, shut him off, depending on the context of the scene)
>
> Character A: I'll be leaving early tomorrow. (guilt her into it)

Step 1. Go through the scene, first saying the intention, then saying the line.

Step 2. Say only the lines, but play the intention.

Step 3. Add a friend. Beside each scene partner place another person, who gives the actor someone to look at, giving her a thumbs up every time the action of the intention brought her closer to her objective.

Step 4. Play the scene without the friends, but remind actors to watch their scene partners to see if they are winning, getting their points across. Each time they think they have, they say "score." Each time they don't think they have, they say "ouch."

Step 5. Play the scene as written, with intentions.

TOWARDS AND AWAY

These exercises physicalize the relationship between characters in a scene. Actors create a spatial relationship that later translates into emotional and/or physical space.

Method: Pairs work through their scenes with something new to focus on each time.

1. For each line (or complete beat) a character says, the actor finds the impulse to take a step towards her partner; to establish closeness or exert influence or show strength. Or, she will take a step backwards; to gain distance, establish autonomy or retreat. The entire scene is played in this way, either stepping towards the other character, or away from him. Some lines might bring the actor one step closer or further away, and others might require many more steps. Some beats may not result in a change of proximity, but most will.

2. Pairs go through the scene reading the lines on the page silently, to themselves. They position themselves near or far from their partners as they contemplate the lines on the page in turn. The focus is on the relationship between the characters, demonstrated not by the words they say, but in their proximity to each other.

3. Pairs repeat the scene without scripts, creating a "dance" of their relationship. This can be done for active scenes that have a lot of movements, and also for very still, focused scenes with no movement in the final blocking. By expressing themselves physically, the actors will find the moments when they emotionally withdraw or approach the other character in their scene.

4. Pairs play the scene again, speaking the lines. Instruct them to recall when they moved towards or away from their partners previously, and ask them to make the opposite choice now. If they went towards their partners on the first line, instruct them to step away from them instead. In going through the scene in this way, they will discover that there are times when the scene is even better with the opposite action than the one first chosen. For example, at times stepping away can actually intimidate the other character more than stepping towards him. This is about finding levels in the work, rather than playing everything in a predictable manner.

CHECKMATE

Playing a game while speaking the lines is a good exercise to use when the actors are first off book, as it gives them an external focus while further exploring the world of their scene. If the actors don't play chess, use checkers or any other board or card game.

Method: The actors play the game while they speak their lines. The game may act as a simple distraction, but it may also inform the characters' relationship with each other.

PUPPETS

This exercise offers student actors a means of exploring their characters and relationships somewhat externally.

Method: Pairs work through their scenes with puppets, or other objects, such as stuffed animals. Even a simple object, like a pen, could represent a character. Using the lines of dialogue from the script, the object is manipulated by the actor, creating the interaction of her own object with her partner's.

BALL TOSS

This exercise encourages actors to view their lines as offers they make to the other characters in their scenes. It is used once actors are off book.

Method: One actor holds a ball, tossing it to his partner once he is finished his line. This makes what happens in every scene tangible; offers are tossed and caught by the other character. Ask the pairs to move around the rehearsal space as the ball is tossed between them.

As this exercise is repeated, the actors will get into it; catching, holding and returning the ball in ways that speak to the intentions of their characters. The relationship between them will be encouraged to develop further.

WHAT ARE WE FIGHTING FOR?

In a scene with a struggle, and most scenes have one; this exercise allows the actors to explore how to focus their intentions.

Method: Find the one word or phrase that represents the struggle for both of the actors. For example, in a scene about two brothers that want the family business, the shared intent might be expressed as "it's mine." Instead of using the lines of the scene, this single intention is the only line spoken by either of them as they:

- Play Toss the Ball, with this line.
- Play the scene as written, but each actor finds a place to say the words "It's mine."
- Play the scene as written, but instruct each to use the other's real name once, to ensure that he takes it personally.
- Play the scene again, remembering this intention, but only using the lines.

MATCHSTICK

This exercise focuses on how actors must allow what the other character says to affect them, and how they must try to affect their partners with what they say and do.

Method: Pairs go through their scenes while walking about the room with each of them pressing against an end of the matchstick (or toothpick) with only one figure. The actors remain connected to each other by the matchstick, as each tries to guide the other into various positions without allowing it to drop.

SLOW MOTION

Method: Actors go through their scenes in slow motion, drawing out the lines, and fully exploring all of the pauses between the lines.

Variation #1. Before going through their scene, partners can perform a slow motion race (last one over the line wins), physical fight or any other activity that would inform their relationship in the scene.

Hint: Even once a scene is up on its feet, it can still be very useful to go through a scene in slow motion, making sure that both actors are staying present and in the moment-to-moment reality they have created with their scene.

ROLE REVERSAL

Method: The actors literally change characters with their partners, reading each other's dialogue. This may provide insight into their own characters, as they see them through the eyes of the other character.

1. Try it as an imitation of the other actor's interpretation of his character.
2. Try it in the voice inflections, physicalizations and attitudes of their own, original characters, but use the dialogue of the other character.
3. Find their own way of approaching their partners' characters and do a true reversal of the scene.
4. Switch back to their own characters; see if anything has changed.

MAKE A MISTAKE

This exercise throws out all previous choices made for the character in this scene, to free the actor and allow for "happy accidents" to occur.

Method: Students go through their scenes making all the choices they consider "wrong" for the character and scene. Encourage them to react to events and other characters in (seemingly) wildly inappropriate ways.

After going through the scene with these opposite choices, ask them to note how many times what felt like a bad choice turned out to be just perfect for the moment, or how exploring the opposite of what they thought would be the wrong choice brought them much closer to the truth of the moment, or made things more interesting.

This exercise is useful for several reasons.

■ An actor shouldn't be predictable in his choices. He may have been going for the obvious choices in the scene, and this will show him other possibilities.

■ An actor should never play just one note. For example, it isn't interesting to only YELL, if the character is trying to push the other character. Aggression can be expressed in many different ways. It might be smoldering, it might go very quiet, then explode for only a moment, it might even come out as sadness or laughter. Many different verbs should be sought, a different one for each and every beat.

■ Actors need to stay in the moment, and not get stuck playing a situation exactly the same each time. This may shake things up for a fresh approach to a scene.

MONOLOGUES

While there are exercises for scene studies that will also work with monologues, here are some that work especially well for the solo performer.

INTRODUCING THE MONOLOGUE

In a perfect world, all of the monologues your students work on will be from beautifully crafted plays, with richly developed characters. However, the reality is that with so many stand-alone monologue collections available, you are likely to take advantage of them, allowing your students to choose those they find appealing without taking up a lot of valuable class time. That's okay. In the absence of any clues about the character from her past, or interactions with others, a student actor can make up the details, in order to flesh out her character into a living, breathing complicated person.

- **Background:** Using whatever clues are available within the monologue, create a history for the character, including family background, occupation, hopes, fears, wishes, dreams and desires. This exercise may be written, as a character sketch, or verbalized to a partner who has her own monologue to analyze.

- **What happened before:** Create the moment before the character starts to speak. Where did she come from? Is she settled or on her way to another location?

- **The audience:** Most importantly, to WHOM is she speaking? Make this choice very specific. Picture this person or group of people very clearly. This allows the actor to have an objective, something to win from the other character. Use strong active intentions, like: to beg, convince, cajole, threaten, etc. In Shakespearean monologues (soliloquies), the characters are almost always off talking to themselves. In this case, the other character could be viewed as another side of herself. She may be arguing with her "other self" in order to work out a problem.

- **The story:** What is going on in this monologue? What is the character doing and reacting or responding to? What is the story being told, directly and indirectly? Is there subtext, something going on beneath the words? What is the character NOT saying, but really meaning? So, now we are ready for the words.

LOOKING FOR MEANING

Alone, without distractions (but everyone participating in his/
her own space), participants explore their own monologues.

These exercises help the students get to know the words of
their monologues and the ideas behind them. Everything done
in the memorization phase is out loud, helping them to not
only start to learn the lines, but also to connect to the character and find its voice.

1. **Read aloud:** Students read their monologues to themselves,
   out loud, without any particular emphasis or thought. They
   are just introducing themselves to the words.

2. **Find the word:** Participants read the first line of their
   monologues, repeating it aloud several times until one word
   resonates with them. Repeat that word over and over until it
   feels satisfying and complete. Circle, underline or highlight
   that word, or create a list on another paper. Go on to the
   second line and repeat the exercise, finding the one word
   that encapsulates what is going on at that moment.

3. **Create a chant:** Have them string the individual words
   together to form a sort of chant. This helps them explore
   the character and create a flow for the meaning of the
   entire monologue. The words they have chosen will create
   their own storyline.

4. **Find a movement:** Have them repeat the words again, this
   time finding a movement or action that feels right for each
   word. Some may look like a dance, while others will have a
   separate clean action for each word.

5. **Work with a partner:** Students work in pairs, in order to
   bounce the word off of the other person (who doesn't have
   the same word, character or even the same monologue).
   This helps each student to stay focused, and feel they are
   having an impact with their words. They begin saying their
   words to each other, exploring each one fully before going
   on to the next. This creates a sort of dialogue, even though
   the words are not related to each other. Encourage them to
   really explore each word and say it in as many different
   ways, with as many different intentions as possible. You
   could start by leading them through the first few sentences
   very slowly, giving them the intentions you want them
   to use.

Example: Now that you have found and underlined the most important word (or made a list of them), I want you to turn to your partner and tell each other what the word is.... Good, now take turns repeating your word to each other:

- as if you want to find out if your partner is your friend
- as if you don't really want your partner to hear it
- as if your partner has just told you you're beautiful
- as if you want to hurt your partner with it
- as if you want to comfort your partner with it after your partner fell and hurt himself
- as if your partner won't share his chocolate bar with you
- as if your partner just cooked your favourite meal
- as if your partner just cooked something she knows you hate to eat
- as if you are a small child and want your partner to take you to the park
- as if your partner is your best friend, who was out of town for a month
- as if your partner just gave you a thousand dollars

After going through a few of these intentions with a some of the words, you may feel that they can explore the rest of the words on their own, using each word to play an intention that feels right for that moment of the monologue. They may need to list their intentions beside each of the words on their lists.

Once they have gone through this exercise with each single word said only once, they can do it again, moving to the next word only when they feel they have fully explored the first one. They do not have to be at the same stage of the conversation as their partners. One may be moving through the list more quickly than the other. A conversation might look like this, with actors A and B saying one word each:

Choice – Perfect – Choice – Perfect – Don't – Perfect – Don't
Perfect – Don't – Everything – Sense – Nothing – Quickly
Opens – Quickly – Opens

This would have been based on the opening lines of the following two monologues.

Character A: I know that I am facing a choice. But I feel that I don't have any say in the matter, really. Nothing makes any sense. Everything is moving too quickly....

Character B: This date is going to be perfect. I have planned everything out so carefully. Nothing has been left to chance. And now, the door opens and there he(she) stands....

FIND THE VERBS

Repeat the single word exercise, but with a new list of words. Have the participants highlight all of the verbs (action words) in their monologues. Have them read them aloud, in order, simultaneously, but in their own spaces. The objective is to see if they can give them a flow and tell the whole story of their monologues through only the verbs. Repeat the exercise with movements for each verb.

HINT: If the performer has also written the monologue, this exercise can make sure that the verbs chosen are strong action words that carry the weight of the piece.

SIMULTANEOUS MONOLOGUES

This exercise is for memorizing and becoming familiar with the text of a monologue. As a warm-up for a class or workshop dealing with monologues, participants find a space to work in and say their monologues for memory, aloud and simultaneously, five times. Each repetition has a different objective.

1. **Articulation:** Over-articulate every word.
2. **Speed:** Do an "Italian" run – very fast.
3. **Breath control:** Have the actors go as far into the monologue as possible on one breath. Tell them to take a second breath when needed and continue with the next line. See how many breaths they need to complete the whole monologue.
4. **Movement:** Ask the actors to find a physical activity to do while they say their monologues. It could be as easy as everyone walking around the space randomly, or performing repetitive calisthenics.
5. **Sell it:** Ask the actors to say the monologue as if they are selling the idea of it to the rest of the group; as a

salesperson. Or, they decide what it is that they are trying to convince everyone else of, and really try to get their imaginary audiences to believe them. This goes back to imagining the monologue as a two-hander and playing the character's objective.

WITH DISTRACTION

Participants take turns standing in the middle of a small circle of other actors, saying their monologues aloud, with everyone offering distractions; bugging the person with noises, questions or laughter, all at once. This exercise is simply to test the participant's concentration and memory of her text.

FIND THE ARC

Find the arc of the character's story within the monologue. She goes on a journey. Is this journey going from positive to negative, or vice versa? The levels will change once the following aspects are identified.

1. **Objective:** What does the character want in this monologue? What is she hoping to accomplish with her words? What does she need to win?
2. **Stakes:** Keep the stakes high. What is at stake if the character doesn't get what she wants? Students create a statement by filling in the blanks: "I want _____. This is important, because if I don't get it _____."
3. **Actions:** What tactics is the character using to get what she wants? What is she doing to affect the imaginary partner? Find levels in the way that she does it by identifying the specific tactics: chastise him, reject him, entice him, argue with him, flirt with him, etc. This results in the actor playing some things quietly, slowly, aggressively, sullenly, etc. This will create levels in the performance. Rather than talking about finding emotional levels, talk about the actions and their desired effects. This is more playable than trying to find "the right emotion" for a line.

MAKE DISCOVERIES

The joy for the audiences in watching a monologue is to see the journey that the character takes through the arc of the story. The character can't know where the monologue will end, but makes discoveries along the way. The audience wants to see that process of discovery. The partner is now helping the performer create a dialogue of her monologue, acting as an invisible scene partner, asking questions, pushing it further.

Method: In pairs, partners work on one actor's monologue at a time. Before the actor begins her monologue, her partner asks a question that leads the actor/character in the discovery of the first line. This continues for every line, or at least every beat. This is especially useful for Shakespearean monologues (soliloquies) where characters are usually off talking to themselves. The partner keeps asking for clarification and making observations, prompting the character's discovery of her next thought.

FIND THE SECONDARY LIFE

In a monologue, the character needs to find something to do. Sometimes this is no more than sitting still in the middle of the stage. This is still doing something. For some actors, keeping the imaginary partner in mind and delivering the monologue in such a way as to try to affect that partner is enough. However, beginning actors may be well served by exploring a more active secondary life as a way of grounding themselves on stage and in the text.

Having a secondary life assists an actor in several ways:

- It creates a world for the character to play in, making the performance more grounded and real.

- It gives the actor something to focus some energy on, as, in the hands of an inexperienced actor, words alone can sometimes take on more importance than they warrant, making the performance seem forced and contrived. Sometimes, the more important the words, the more likely people are to toss them off, instead of emphasizing them. It is important that they don't "play the words" but rather allow them to occur on the spot, as if each thought is a new one, occurring at this moment for the first time (as they did in the Discoveries exercise). If beginning actors give the words too much importance, their voices take on an artificial cadence.

- Having something to physically do can give the actor something to focus on and help dispel some of the nervousness of performing. It is helpful if the secondary life requires some manipulation of a prop, rather than just being something to hold.

This set of exercises is one method to use in order to discover the character's "secondary life," also called "stage business."

Method: Participants find a meaningful physical activity that their characters might actually be doing while speaking the words of the monologues. Have them choose a physical prop (not mimed) to use in this activity. It may, but certainly does not need to have anything to do with the specific topic of the monologue. Just as in real life, dialogue, even one-sided ones like a monologue, often take place while the speaker is otherwise engaged. For example, a student tells a friend about her weekend while opening her books and finding her homework assignment. A boy explains why he didn't come home last night while eating his dinner.

Alone, without distraction, have participants simultaneously say their monologues while trying out different ideas, with different props. After several run-throughs they can share their favourites with partners, and decide together what seems right for the monologue. It is also possible that the prop will simply act as a grounding tool during the initial rehearsal process, but isn't needed for the performance.

INTRODUCING SHAKESPEARE

Shakespeare is widely considered the greatest playwright who ever lived. As such, there may well come a time when you will want to introduce him to a theatre class, or present one of his works onstage.

What follows is based on the introductory material prepared by the Manitoba Association of Teachers of English (MATE), to be used in the classroom.

A SHAKESPEAREAN GLOSSARY

Here are some expressions that appear frequently in Shakespeare's works that are no longer in use today:

hath – has

hast – have

thee, thou – you

thy – your

thine – yours

dost – do

shalt – shall

wilt – will

would – wish

thus – this

prithee – I pray thee: please

by my troth (rhymes with "oath") – truly: upon my word

I trow (rhymes with "how") – I trust, or I think

coz (rhymes with "buzz") – cousin: relative

marry – really? An expression used in reply to a question, suggesting surprise or indignation

anon – soon, or right away

bootless – useless

fie (rhymes with "pie") – exclamation expressing disgust or outrage

sirrah (accent on the first syllable) – sir: may imply anger or contempt

for the nonce – for the time being

ay – aye: yes

verily – truthfully: really (may be used as an oath or promise)

beseech – beg: entreat

give me leave – allow me

alas – an expression used when something is amiss, or sad. There is no modern equivalent, but "unfortunately" is close.

Elizabethan language also contains many old verb forms that we no longer use.

For example:

thou art (thou'rt) – you are	thou dost – you do
thou know'st – you know	thou see'st – you see

thou did'st – you did	he hath – he has
he doth – he does	he durst – he dares
methinks – I think	

The word "don't" was not used in Elizabethan English. Therefore, some phrases will sound strange to a modern ear, as the word order may be confusing. For example:

leave me not – don't leave me

stayed he not with thee? – didn't he stay with you?

worry thee not – don't worry

The word ending "-eth" was commonly added to a root word that is still in use today. For example:

speaketh – speaks	knoweth – knows
sayeth – says	singeth – sings

Often letters are omitted in words for the sake of the sound of the line of poetry, or to fit the Iambic Pentameter rhythm.

For example:

th' – the	'tis – it is
thou'rt – thou art – you are	ne'er – never
e'er – ever	o'er – over
o' – of	i' – in
't – it	t' – to
ta'en – taken	'twixt – betwixt – between

While Shakespeare often used the second-person pronouns "thee / thou," this was simply the formal salutation, showing respect in Elizabethan England. He also used "you" frequently in his writing, when a character was speaking to another of his own rank or lower in society. Shortly after this time period, the form denoting status fell out of common usage. Shakespeare lived at a time when the English language was changing. Many modern words were coming into use, and Shakespeare also invented some of his own words, which entered common vocabulary.

SHAKESPEAREAN INSULTS

Thanks to a list made by Jerry Maguire for the Manitoba Association of Teachers of English (MATE), you can create your own Shakespearean insults.

Choose a word from column one, another from column two, tack on the noun from column three, preface it with "thou," and thus shalt thou have the perfect insult. Let thyself go – mix and match and create a barb worthy of the Bard!

COLUMN ONE	COLUMN TWO	COLUMN THREE
bawdy	bat-fowling	barnacle
beslubbering	beef-witted	bladder
bootless	beetle-headed	boar-pig
churlish	boil-brained	bugbear
cockered	clapper-clawed	bum-bailey
clouted	clay-brained	canker-blossom
craven	common-kissing	clack-dish
currish	crook-pated	clotpole
dankish	dismal-dreaming	coxcomb
dissembling	dizzy-eyed	codpiece
droning	dog-hearted	death-token
fawning	earth-vexing	flap-dragon
fobbing	elf-skinned	flax-wench
forward	fat-kidneyed	flirt-gill
frothy	fen-sucked	foot-licker
goatish	fly-bitten	giglet
impertinent	fool-born	haggard
infectious	full-gorged	harpy
jarring	guts-griping	hedge-pig
loggerheaded	half-faced	horn-beast
lumpish	hasty-witted	hugger-mugger
mammering	hell-hated	jolthead
mangled	idle-headed	lewdster
mewling	ill-breeding	lout
paunchy	ill-nurtured	maggot-pie

COLUMN ONE	COLUMN TWO	COLUMN THREE
pribbling	knotty-pated	malt-worm
puking	milk-livered	mammet
puny	motley-minded	measle
quailing	onion-eyed	minnow
rank	plume-plucked	miscreant
reeky	pottle-deep	moldwarp
ruttish	reeling-ripe	nut-hook
spleeny	rude-growing	pignut
spongy	rump-fed	puttock
surly	shard-borne	pumpion
tottering	sheep-biting	ratsbane
venomed	swag-bellied	strumpet
villainous	tardy-gaited	varlet
warped	tickle-brained	vassal
wayward	toad-spotted	wagtail

FAMOUS SHAKESPEAREAN QUOTATIONS

Hamlet:

To be or not to be; that is the question.

Something is rotten in the state of Denmark.

This above all: to thine own self be true.

Neither a borrower nor a lender be.

Though this be madness, yet there is method in 't.

There is nothing either good or bad, but thinking makes it so.

The lady doth protest too much, methinks.

A little more than kin, and less than kind.

The play's the thing wherein I'll catch the conscience of the king.

And it must follow, as the night the day, thou canst not then be false to any man.

This is the very ecstasy of love.

Brevity is the soul of wit.

Doubt that the sun doth move, doubt truth to be a liar, but never doubt I love.

Rich gifts wax poor when givers prove unkind.

A Midsummer Night's Dream:

The course of true love never did run smooth.

Love looks not with the eyes, but with the mind, and therefore is winged Cupid painted blind.

That would hang us, every mother's son.

My heart is true as steel.

The true beginning of our end.

Out, dog! out, cur! Thou driv'st me past the bounds of maiden's patience.

As You Like It

All the world's a stage, and all the men and women merely players. They have their exits and their entrances; and one man in his time plays many parts.

Can one desire too much of a good thing?

I like this place and willingly could waste my time in it.

True is it that we have seen better days.

The fool doth think he is wise, but the wise man knows himself to be a fool.

King Richard III

Now is the winter of our discontent.

A horse! a horse! my kingdom for a horse!

So wise so young, they say, do never live long.

Off with his head!

Romeo and Juliet

Romeo, Romeo! wherefore art thou Romeo?

It is the east, and Juliet is the sun.

Good night, good night! Parting is such sweet sorrow, that I shall say good night till it be morrow.

What's in a name? That which we call a rose by any other name would smell as sweet.

The Merchant of Venice

But love is blind, and lovers cannot see.

If you prick us, do we not bleed? if you tickle us, do we not laugh? if you poison us, do we not die? and if you wrong us, shall we not revenge?

The devil can cite Scripture for his purpose.

The Merry Wives of Windsor

Why, then the world's mine oyster.

I cannot tell what the dickens his name is.

As good luck would have it.

Measure for Measure

Some rise by sin, and some by virtue fall.

The miserable have no other medicine but only hope.

King Henry IV, Part I

He will give the devil his due.

The better part of valour is discretion.

King Henry IV, Part II

He hath eaten me out of house and home.

Uneasy lies the head that wears a crown.

A man can die but once.

King Henry the Fifth

Men of few words are the best men.

King Henry the Sixth, Part II

The first thing we do, let's kill all the lawyers.

Small things make base men proud.

True nobility is exempt from fear.

King Henry the Sixth, Part III

Having nothing, nothing can he lose.

Taming of the Shrew

I'll not budge an inch.

Timon of Athens

We have seen better days.

Julius Caesar

Friends, Romans, countrymen, lend me your ears; I come to bury Caesar, not to praise him.

This was the unkindest cut of all.

But, for my own part, it was Greek to me.

A dish fit for the gods.

Cry "Havoc," and let slip the dogs of war.

Et tu, Brute!

Not that I loved Caesar less, but that I loved Rome more.

This was the noblest Roman of them all.

Yond Cassius has a lean and hungry look; He thinks too much: such men are dangerous.

As he was valiant, I honour him; but, as he was ambitious, I slew him.

Cowards die many times before their deaths; The valiant never taste of death but once.

Macbeth

I dare do all that may become a man; Who dares do more is none.

Fair is foul, and foul is fair.

I bear a charmed life.

Yet do I fear thy nature; It is too full o' the milk of human kindness.

Double, double toil and trouble; Fire burn, and cauldron bubble.

Out, damned spot! out, I say!

When shall we three meet again in thunder, lightning, or in rain?

If chance will have me king, why, chance may crown me.

Look like the innocent flower, but be the serpent under't.

Is this a dagger which I see before me, the handle toward my hand?

Out, out, brief candle! Life's but a walking shadow, a poor player that struts and frets his hour upon the stage and then is heard no more: it is a tale told by an idiot, full of sound and fury, signifying nothing.

King Lear

How sharper than a serpent's tooth it is to have a thankless child!

I am a man more sinned against than sinning.

Nothing will come of nothing.

Have more than thou showest, speak less than thou knowest, lend less than thou owest.

Othello

'Tis neither here nor there.

I will wear my heart upon my sleeve for daws to peck at.

Antony and Cleopatra

My salad days, when I was green in judgment.

Cymbeline

The game is up.

I have not slept one wink.

Twelfth Night

Be not afraid of greatness: some are born great, some achieve greatness and some have greatness thrust upon them.

Love sought is good, but giv'n unsought is better.

The Tempest

> We are such stuff as dreams are made on, rounded with a little sleep.

Titus Andronicus

> These words are razors to my wounded heart.

The Winter's Tale

> What's gone and what's past help should be past grief.

> You pay a great deal too dear for what's given freely.

SHAKESPEARE'S CANON

The following chronology was prepared by Sir Edmund Chambers (circa 1930).

1590-1591	Henry VI, Parts 2 & 3	1600-1601	Hamlet Prince of Denmark
1591-1592	Henry VI, Part 1	1600-1601	The Merry Wives of Windsor
1592-1593	Richard III	1601-1602	Troilus and Cressida
1592-1593	The Comedy of Errors	1602-1603	All's Well that Ends Well
1593-1594	Titus Andronicus	1604-1605	Measure for Measure
1593-1594	The Taming of the Shrew	1604-1605	Othello the Moor of Venice
1594-1595	The Two Gentlemen of Verona	1605-1606	King Lear
1594-1595	Love's Labour's Lost	1605-1606	Macbeth
1594-1595	Romeo and Juliet	1606-1607	Antony and Cleopatra
1595-1596	Richard II	1607-1608	Coriolanus
1595-1596	A Midsummer Night's Dream	1607-1608	The Life of Timon of Athens
1596-1597	King John	1608-1609	Pericles Prince of Tyre
1596-1597	The Merchant of Venice	1609-1610	Cymbeline
1597-1598	Henry IV, Parts 1 & 2	1610-1611	The Winter's Tale

1598-1599	Much Ado About Nothing		1611-1612	The Tempest
1598-1599	Henry V		1612-1613	Henry VIII
1599-1600	Julius Caesar		1612-1613	Two Noble Kinsmen
1599-1600	As You Like It			
1599-1600	Twelve Night, or, What You Will			

THE ENGLISH THEATRE

In the Middle Ages, plays were mostly based on Bible stories. As exciting as they often were to watch, their purpose was to acquaint people with the teachings of the Christian Church. By Shakespeare's time, audiences were demanding a different kind of theatre: romance, history, murder, revenge and comedy. Plays began to feature plots and characters closer to real life.

At first actors performed in any available space, traveling through the countryside, making use of the courtyard of an inn or the great hall of a noble's house. They lived precariously, performing for their supper, a bed for the night, or a little money. Their repertoire consisted of roughly constructed adaptations of classical tales, bawdy comedies and stories shaped by religious and political controversies.

FROM 1558 – 1642

Elizabeth I's accession to the throne in 1558 gave rise to theatre so excellent that it is still considered one of the world's greatest achievements. Unlike Italy, England developed a vernacular drama of superior quality performed by professional troupes for both popular and aristocratic audiences. Consequently, there was no such sharp division between the court and public stages in England as in Italy. Furthermore, although the English borrowed much from Italy, they perhaps drew even more heavily on their medieval heritage. Also, Queen Elizabeth wished to silence religious dissension, and banned religious themes, giving rise to secular dramas. In mingling these diverse elements they created a distinctively native theatre and drama. Troupes required a license to perform a play, encouraging the development of professional companies. Soon proper theatres were built. People of all types – rich nobles, clergy, tradespeople and even servants – were attracted to the performances. Playwrights were desperately needed to supply the acting companies with new plays that would appeal to all these people. Into this world stepped William Shakespeare. He graduated from actor to writer and shareholder to become the most successful playwright of them all. By the beginning of the seventeenth century, theatres in London were flourishing. This golden era lasted until the closing of the theatres by Parliament in 1642, as a result of the Puritan faction gaining control of London early in the civil war. They believed that theatrical entertainment was sinful.

SHAKESPEARE

HIS LIFE

William Shakespeare was born April 23, 1564, and died April 23, 1616. He was the son of Mary Arden and John Shakespeare. His father earned a good living as a maker of gloves, and although he probably couldn't read or write, he was also a respected municipal officer in Stratford. He was once fined, nevertheless, for illegally keeping a manure heap in front of his house.

William soon became better educated than his father. He attended the local grammar school where he studied English and Latin intensively. He doesn't seem to have liked school though, perhaps because the day began as early as 6:00 am, and went on until at least 5:00 in the afternoon. William preferred outdoor sports such as swimming, archery and deer hunting. He also loved going to watch plays when troupes of actors came from London to give performances in Stratford.

Shakespeare never went to university, although Oxford and Cambridge were both flourishing then. Perhaps it was because he was married by the time he was eighteen. Anne Hathaway, his bride, was several years older and they soon had three children: Susanna, the eldest, and the twins, Hamnet and Judith. About this time, too, his father fell on hard times financially, and retired from public life.

William, now an ambitious young man, stayed in Stratford for only a few years after his marriage. During that time he may have worked as a teacher's assistant. Rumour has it that he was a bit wild, and might even have been arrested for poaching deer. In any case, the lure of London and the theatres soon proved too strong. He left Anne and his family at home and headed to the big city to become an actor.

Shakespeare did well financially in London. He belonged to the popular theatre company called the Chamberlain's Men and took in a share of the profits from their performances of his plays at the Globe theatre. Towards the end of his life he moved back to Stratford, where he died a well-to-do citizen in 1616.

HIS WORK

He has been called the greatest dramatist of all time. As a playwright, actor and shareholder in acting troupes and theatre buildings, he was directly involved in more aspects of the theatre than any other writer of his day.

Shakespeare is credited with writing 36 plays, and several more in which he was a contributor. It is impossible to do justice to his genius in a short space, for no playwright's work has been more fully studied and praised. Shakespeare borrowed stories from many different sources, from history, mythology, legend, fiction and even from other plays. However, he reworked then until they became distinctively his own.

Typically, situations and characters are clearly established in the opening scenes, and out of this exposition the action develops logically thereafter. A number of plots are usually interwoven, at first proceeding somewhat independently of each other but eventually coming together as the denouement approaches, so that the resolution of one leads to that of the others. In this way, apparent diversity is given unity. The action ranges freely in time and space, normally encompassing months or years and occurring in widely separate places. This broad canvas creates a sense of ongoing life behind the scenes.

Shakespeare's large casts are composed of well-rounded characters who run the gamut from the inept and ridiculous to the commanding and heroic, from the young and innocent to the old and corrupt. Despite the enormous range of his characters, Shakespeare entered into most if them sympathetically and made them appear to be living individuals rather than mere stage figures. His penetrating insights into human behaviour have remained valid for all succeeding generations.

His plays are divided into three genres: tragedies, comedies and histories. Sometimes a play is difficult to categorize, as the lines may blur. However, as a rule, his comedies contain plot twists involving mistaken identities and his tragedies feature a protagonist with a fatal flaw leading to a tragic ending. Shakespeare's history plays were generally set in the Hundred Years War with France. They made social and political statements of his day, and were not necessarily completely historically accurate.

Shakespeare was by far the most comprehensive, sensitive, and dramatically effective dramatist of his day. He attempted almost all of the popular dramatic types and subjects of his time and in each instance gave them their most perfect expression. In his own day, nevertheless, Shakespeare's critical reputation was lower than that of Jonson or Beaumont and Fletcher. His fame began to grow in the late 17th century but did not reach its peak until the 19th century. Like most of his contemporaries, Shakespeare gave little thought to preserving his plays, which in his time were looked upon as momentary diversions (much as television dramas are today). Their survival may be credited in large part to the desire of Shakespeare's fellow actors, especially Henry Condell and John Heminges, to preserve his memory by publishing 36 of the plays. (This original edition, which appeared in 1623, is usually referred to as the First Folio).

LANGUAGE

No playwright uses language as effectively as Shakespeare has done. His poetic and figurative dialogue not only arouses specific emotions, moods, and ideas, it creates a network of complex associations and connotations that links the immediate dramatic situation with all creation.

Shakespeare wrote much of his dialogue in iambic pentameter, a verse rhythm that his contemporary audiences would have been used to hearing. An iamb is a unit of meter containing one unstressed and one stressed syllable, or beat. daDUM. Pentameter is a set of five iambs. There are usually 10 syllables per line.

Each line begins with an unstressed syllable, followed by a stressed syllable. This creates a pattern of five sets of beats per line:

> da DUM /da DUM /da DUM /da DUM/ da DUM
> Some rise / by sin / and some / by vir/tue fall.

Sometimes, Shakespeare varied the rhythm, changed the stress pattern or added an extra syllable, depending on the effect he wanted for the line. For example, in this, perhaps his most famous line, spoken by Hamlet, he added an extra unstressed syllable to the ending:

To be / or not / to be / that is / the ques/tion.
daDUM / daDUM / daDUM / daDUM / daDUM / da

One could also argue that he changed the stress pattern in the line, to read:

To be / or not / to be / that is / the ques/tion.
daDUM / daDUM / daDUM / DUMda / daDUM / da

Generally, characters of a high social standing would speak in iambic pentameter, while those of a lower class would speak in prose.

SHAKESPEARE'S ACTING TROUPE

First called the Chamberlain's Men, his troupe changed its name to the King's Men after James I took the throne in 1603. Members of the troupe gained more lasting fame because Shakespeare was one of their fellow players. The leading performer was Richard Burbage (c. 1567-1619), who created such roles as Richard III, Hamlet, Lear, and Othello, and was generally acknowledged to be the greatest actor of his age. Another member of the company was Nathan Field (1587-1620) – considered by many as second only to Burbage.

THE ACTING STYLE

The acting style of the Elizabethan performer can only be guessed at. Some scholars have labeled it "formal" and others "realistic." Some of the conditions which suggest a "formal" style are the performance of female roles by male actors, the non-realistic style of the scripts, the conventionalized stage background, the large repertory, which would have made detailed characterizations difficult. Arguments for a relatively realistic style include Shakespeare's "advice to the players" in *Hamlet*, contemporary references to the convincing characterizations given by such actors as Burbage, the emphasis upon contemporary life and manners in many comedies, the truthfulness of human psychology portrayed in the serious plays, and the closeness of audience to actors during performances. Judging by contemporary accounts, many actors moved audiences with the power and 'truth' of their playing, but this tells little about their style, for what is considered "truth in acting" varies markedly from one period to another.

THE THEATRE

Most of the plays performed by the King's Men took place in the Globe Theatre, which was built in 1597/98. The theatre they used before that time was simply called The Theatre. The Globe held multiple levels for both the actors and the audience. Theatres had no box office, tickets, or reserved seats. "Gatherers" collected money at the entrance to each of the three principal divisions of the auditorium: pit, public galleries, and private boxes (or lords' rooms). The public theatres catered to all classes, but the pit (or yard), which provided standing room only, was used primarily for the lower classes, while the public galleries, with their bench seats, were patronized especially by the middle classes, and the boxes were considered most appropriate for the aristocracy. By the end of the 16th century, a few spectators were being allowed to sit on the stage itself. As stage stools gained in prestige, the lords' rooms fell increasingly to prostitutes and others.

In the early part of Elizabeth's reign, the days upon which actors were permitted to perform varied considerably from one year to another. Then, in 1574, a royal decree proclaimed the right of companies to perform daily. This ruling remained in force until 1642 except for one modification – James I forbade playing on Sundays. Bet even though it was legally possible for companies to play at almost any time, the actual number of performances given annually was considerably curtailed by forced closures attributed to plague, officially decreed mourning, certain religious observances, and unseasonable weather. It has been estimated that during the early 17th century performances were given on approximately 214 days each year (a total equivalent to about seven months).

Flags were flown from towers high above London's theatres on the days when performances were to be given. A white flag represented a comedy, a black, tragedy, and a red flag was flown for a history play. Announcements of coming attractions were also made from the stage during performances.

As there were no artificial lights, performances were held during the afternoon. Roofless theatres allowed the productions to take advantage of full daylight.

COSTUMES

Because scenery and properties were used sparingly and because the actor was always of primary concern, costume was probably the most important visual element in the Elizabethan theatre. Not only was it an integral part of each individual performer's appearance, it was crucial in such mass scenes as processions, battles, ceremonies, pantomimes and masques.

The conventions that governed costuming between 1558 and 1642 differed little from those in effect during the Middle Ages. Most characters, regardless of the historical era in which they supposedly lived, were clothed in Elizabethan garments. Thus, by far the majority of costumes were contemporary dress such as was worn by persons in real life.

Other kinds of costumes were used sparingly. The deviations from contemporary dress may be divided into five categories.

1. Ancient, or out-of-style clothing, used to indicate unfashionableness, or, occasionally, to suggest another period.
2. Antique, consisting of drapery or greaves added to contemporary garments, used for certain classical figures.
3. Fanciful garments used for ghosts, witches, fairies, gods and allegorical characters.
4. Traditional costumes, associated with a few specific characters such as Robin Hood, Henry V, Tamburlaine, Falstaff and Richard III.
5. National or racial costumes, used to set off Turks, Indians, Jews and Spaniards.

Although some of these costumes were conventionalized versions of garments from past periods, they were not historically accurate. With rare exceptions, even the history plays were costumed in Elizabethan dress.

The troupes bought most of their costumes. Sometimes noblemen gave them garments, and frequently servants who had been willed their master's clothing sold it to the actors. Occasionally the royal family made grants to the troupes to replenish their wardrobes. Since the actors relied heavily upon costumes, the acquisition and maintenance of a sizable wardrobe was important. Each company probably employed a tailor to keep the garments in good repair and to make new ones.

EXERCISES TO INTRODUCE THE BARD

Once a group has been introduced to Shakespeare by way of a little background, it is time to study the language. Shakespeare wrote his plays for the audiences of his time as popular entertainment. As such, they understood what was said. Although he did make up some of his own words, his audiences would have understood their meanings from their context. Much of his humour is very bawdy, something that modern students may miss until they understand the way he uses the language. The goal here is to become comfortable with the language, using it to communicate ideas, rather than as nothing more than incomprehensible "poetry" to memorize verbatim.

GLOSSARY

- Go through the vocabulary and demonstrate the words and phrases in sentences, for the group.
- Invite students to turn to a partner and carry on simple conversations using Elizabethan word usage.

INSULTS

- Invite students to exchange insults with a partner, made up of the words in the columns.
- Divide the students into two groups, with each group standing in a row facing the other. One participant at the end of one row throws an insult to the first participant in the other row, who throws one to the second participant in the first row, and so on, until everyone has had a turn to create a Shakespearean insult.

QUOTATIONS

- Discuss the quotations, finding those that are still in use today, and those that have a modern equivalent derived from Shakespeare's original words.
- Research additional phrases that are still in use today that were first noted in his plays. For example:
  - ☐ To be in a pickle, in trouble, came from *The Tempest.*
  - ☐ The say that someone is a laughing stock comes from *The Merry Wives of Windsor.*

IMPROVISATIONS

With the glossary, quotations and insults in hand, participants use them in the following improvisational exercises.

Translations: In pairs, students are given a situation to develop. Each of the actors has someone off stage to translate the modern language of their improvisation into Elizabethan tongue. In this way, the actors don't have to worry about developing a scene and using the language at the same time.

Language: In pairs, students are given a situation or location, and asked to improvise a simple scene using Elizabethan English.

Quotations: In pairs, students are given a relationship, and improv a scene that ends when someone finds a logical way of using one of the famous Shakespearean quotes. Participants could hold a complete list of quotes, and choose one as the improvisation continues, or the quotations could be copied on slips of paper and placed in a bucket or hat, to be picked by each participant before the improv begins.

Insults: In pairs, students are given a situation, and try to use as many Shakespearean insults as they can logically fit into the action of the scene.

Scenes: Once they have begun working on Shakespeare's plays, have them improvise scenes that are missing between characters, providing background to relationships, or alternate endings to situations, based on other choices made.

COMMERCIALS

- In pairs, students write a short radio commercial, advertising a service, using Elizabethan English.
- In pairs, students write a short TV commercial, selling a product, which they demonstrate. They could make it a modern product, or one that would have been used in early 17th century England. Either way, the language is Elizabethan.

TRANSLATIONS

- Students watch a short scene from a favourite TV series or movie. Keeping the same intent in the dialogue, they translate it into Elizabethan English. This can be done with the whole group, if they are new to Shakespeare, or individually, as a homework assignment, if they are already somewhat familiar with his work.

■ Once they have translated a scene, they can read or perform it for the class. Or, they can give their scripts to other students to read or enact for the group.

■ A discussion could follow on not only the language, but also on the relationships and behaviours of the characters. Shakespeare has often been praised for his understanding of human behaviour long before modern psychological analysis. Parallels may be drawn between the characters from the scenes that the students have brought in and those from his plays.

WORKING WITH THE PLAYS

■ When beginning scene work with students, read through a single scene together, to get a feel for the language, pausing to explain everything that is said, line by line. Use a scene from one of the plays that you and your group is already somewhat familiar with, so they will have an idea of the plotlines.

■ In reading the lines aloud, pay attention to the punctuation for clues on when to pause or stop. Make a slight pause on a comma and full stop on a period, rather than paying attention to the end of each line. Frequently the phrase will continue on into the next line. Many soliloquies and much of the dialogue is written in iambic pentameter, dictating that there will be five beats – ten syllables per line. The phrase, however, is often not completed in that one line. Or, a line may contain more than one phrase. It is also important to remember that even though iambic pentameter has a rhythm of one unstressed syllable followed by a stressed one, the actor should not emphasize this rhythm. Choose words to stress by meaning and desired effect, rather than where they fall in the rhythm. The rhythm will always be there in the background, and can take care of itself, without being pushed by the actor. Iambic pentameter is very close to the natural rhythm of the English language, so it doesn't need to be studied, but just felt when the text is read aloud. Pay attention to irregularities in the rhythm. They will point to something significant being said.

■ Have the students improvise their scenes using their own words, in order to ensure that they understand what is being said.

- Elizabethan society was very verbal, thought based, hence sentences are very long. Main thoughts have subordinate thoughts within them. Actors must stress the main thoughts, or the audience will get lost.

- Once each word of the speech is fully understood, have students repeat their lines aloud, stressing those words which will make the meaning of the line and the character's intention clear. Try to sustain the climax until the end of the line, don't make it anticlimactic by over-stressing words in the middle of the phrase.

- Remember that Shakespeare's plays are all about the language. In the absence of sets to define locations, it was up to the actors to tell the audience where they were and what was going on. It may be helpful to have students draw or paint a picture of the location of their scenes, in order to firmly plant that image in their minds as they play them.

- Because it is all about the language, it is so important to read the scenes aloud. In Shakespeare's day, audiences said that they were going to the theatre to "hear" a play. Now, we say that we are going to "see" a play. Our world is so visual, but in Shakespeare's texts, we need to connect with the words. Let the language work for you. It will carry you, like the songs in a musical.

- Characters can be understood by the words that they speak. Are there a lot of long vowel sounds, creating a languid character, or do they favour clipped consonants and short, tight vowels? It is important to listen to the language not only for meaning, but also for effect, like a fine piece of music. It will offer clues on how to play a character.

- Pay attention to the images that a character uses. The clues to the character will not be so much in discovering the character's background and interior motives, as in a modern play, but in the language they use. There is very little subtext in Shakespeare. Characters usually say what they mean and tell us what they are thinking and feeling.

- Characters are more universally based than in modern plays. A king will always behave like a king. A servant will always be earthy. There is room to play with the character within this, but the actor must first find the universal essence.

- Keeping the period in mind, remind student to move in ways that accommodate the clothes that were worn. Having long rehearsal skirts available may be helpful, as well as headpieces for men and women, and robes, capes and props, especially swords, as befitting the characters. Lengths of wooden dowels can stand in for swords.

- Once they have a grasp of the language they are using, they can go on to other rehearsal techniques to develop their characters and relationships in order to effectively play the scene (see SCENE STUDIES AND MONOLOGUES).

- Some instructors will say it is better to begin with monologues (soliloquies), as they don't have relationships with other characters to worry about, and can work on the piece as a whole, on their own. Others will say that it is better to begin with two-hander scenes, as they will have a partner to share the effort of understanding the scene and making it come alive. Either way, it is good to have young actors and those new to Shakespeare work on both in training sessions. The main goal is to have them not only understand the words they are saying, but to fall in love with the richness of the text, beautifully crafted to display wit, deep emotion and fierce passion, in turn.

ADAPTING SCRIPTS FOR THE GROUP AND AUDIENCE

Generally, when Shakespeare is presented on a modern stage, at least a little bit of license is taken with the length of the play. Modern audiences don't seem to be able to watch an unabridged version of *Hamlet*, clocking in at just over four hours. Most of the comedies are between two and three hours in length.

With young actors, I have found it beneficial to cut scripts down to a manageable 60 to 90 minutes, without intermissions. There are youth adaptations in publication, or you can cut a script yourself. The secret is to keep in the dialogue that is needed to further the plot, establish relationships and the character's main thoughts, with just enough of the poetic language to retain the feel of the piece.

The following example is the balcony scene from Romeo and Juliet, edited for student use in a scene study. I attempted to not break up the rhyming couplets, leaving more poetry than absolutely necessary in some passages, and having to take out more than I wanted to in others. The 190-line scene is now 95 lines long. Overall, the tone of their encounter and longing not to part is retained, but condensed enough to make it manageable for young actors and audiences.

Romeo and Juliet   Act II scene II

ROMEO But soft! What light through yonder window breaks?
It is the East, and Juliet is the sun.
It is my lady; O, it is my love! O that she knew she were!
See how she leans her cheek upon her hand!
O that I were a glove upon that hand,
That I might touch that cheek!

JULIET Ah me!

ROMEO She speaks.
O speak again, bright angel!

JULIET O Romeo, Romeo, wherefore art thou Romeo?
Deny thy father and refuse thy name;
Or, if thou wilt not, be but sworn my love,
And I'll no longer be a Capulet.

ROMEO Shall I hear more, or shall I speak at this?

JULIET Tis but thy name that is my enemy.
Thou art thyself, though not a Montague.
What's in a name? That which we call a rose
By any other name would smell as sweet.
So Romeo would, were he not Romeo called,
Retain that dear perfection which he owes
Without that title. Romeo, doff thy name;
And for thy name, which is no part of thee,
Take all myself.

ROMEO I take thee at thy word.
Call me but love, and I'll be new baptized;
Henceforth I never will be Romeo.

JULIET What man art thou that, thus bescreened in night,
So stumblest on my counsel?

ROMEO By a name
I know not how to tell thee who I am.

My name, dear saint, is hateful to myself,
Because it is an enemy to thee.
Had I it written, I would tear the word.

JULIET   My ears have not yet drunk a hundred words
Of thy tongue's uttering, yet I know the sound.
Art thou not Romeo, and a Montague?

ROMEO   Neither, fair maid, if either thee dislike.

JULIET   How camest thou hither, tell me, and wherefore?
The orchard walls are high and hard to climb,
And the place death, considering who thou art,
If any of my kinsmen find thee here.

ROMEO   With love's light wings did I o'erperch these
walls;
For stony limits cannot hold love out,
And what love can do, that dares love attempt,
Therefore thy kinsmen are no stop to me.

JULIET   If they do see thee, they will murder thee.

ROMEO   Alack, there lies more peril in thine eye
Than twenty of their swords! Look thou but
sweet,
And I am proof against their enmity.

JULIET   By whose direction found'st thou out this place?

ROMEO   By love, that first did prompt me to inquire.
He lent me counsel, and I lent him eyes.

JULIET   Thou knowest the mask of night is on my face;
Else would a maiden blush bepaint my cheek
For that which thou hast heard me speak
to-night.
Dost thou love me? I know thou wilt say 'Ay';
And I will take thy word. Yet if thou sweat'st,
Thou mayst prove false. I am too fond,
And therefore thou mayst think my
'haviour light;
But trust me Gentleman, I'll prove more true
Than those that have more cunning to be
strange.

ROMEO   Lady, by yonder blessed moon I vow,
That tips with silver all these fruit-tree tops –

JULIET	O, swear not by the moon, th' inconstant moon,
	That monthly changes in her circled orb,
	Lest that thy love prove likewise variable.

| ROMEO | What shall I swear by? |

| JULIET | Do not swear at all; |
| | Or if thou wilt, swear by thy gracious self. |

| ROMEO | If my heart's dear love – |

JULIET	Well, do not swear. Although I joy in thee,
	I have no joy of this contract to-night.
	It is too rash, too unadvised, too sudden;
	Good night, good night! As sweet repose
	and rest
	Come to thy heart as that within my breast!

| ROMEO | O, wilt thou leave me so unsatisfied? |

| JULIET | What satisfaction canst thou have to-night? |

| ROMEO | Th' exchange of thy love's faithful vow |
| | for mine. |

JULIET	I gave thee mine before thou didst request it;
	If that thy bent of love be honourable,
	Thy purpose marriage, send me word tomorrow,
	And all my fortunes at thy foot I'll lay
	And follow thee my lord throughout the world.

| ROMEO | So thrive my soul – |

| JULIET | A thousand times good night! |

| ROMEO | A thousand times the worse, to want thy light! |

| JULIET | 'Tis almost morning. I would have thee gone – |
| | And yet no farther than a wanton's bird. |

| ROMEO | I would I were that bird. |

JULIET	Sweet, so would I.
	Yet I should kill thee with much cherishing.
	Good night, good night! Parting is such sweet
	sorrow
	That I should say good night till it be morrow.

| ROMEO | Sleep dwell upon thine eyes, peace in thy breast! |
| | Would I were sleep and peace, so sweet to rest. |

PRESENTING SHAKESPEARE'S PLAYS

Aside from the length of the play, there may also be other license taken with its interpretation.

- **Setting:** Many of Shakespeare's plays can be staged in a new setting. For example, the cultural or political context of a play might lend itself to another period of modern history. While the dialogue will remain the same, the setting may give the words new meaning to contemporary audiences.

- **Casting:** Colour blind and gender blind casting can work well in many of his plays. Some directors have taken a play and reversed all of the gender roles for a new twist on the story. Some plays also lend themselves to casting characters with multiple actors in the same roles. For example, I once directed *Macbeth* with ten witches, who shared the lines written for only three.

- **Technology:** Obviously, Shakespeare's troupe didn't have a lot of technology at their disposal. However, they did make use of what they had. There was said to have been a real cannon that was used in war scenes, as well as actors strung up on wires to "fly" if the script called for it. One can easily imagine that if he were writing today, he would make use of the technology available. It is possible that projections, audio, video and other technical touches might add to productions today. Just use it carefully, and make sure that it supports the action of the play, rather than distracting from it. I once saw a golf cart on stage, with King Richard being driven through a battlefield. It looked a little silly and out of place in the otherwise traditional set. Used well, technology may well enhance a presentation of the Bard.

PART II
PREPARING FOR
A STAGE PRODUCTION

GETTING STARTED

CHOOSING THE RIGHT PLAY

As the director, your first task is to choose a play. There are certain things you need to consider in making your choice.

Know your company: The company may already be formed, and the play will have to be cast from its ranks, or, you may be able to audition the roles. Either way, you must choose a play (or musical) that you know you can cast well from the actors who will be available to you. I was once asked to choreograph a high school's production of *Grease*. However, the perfect actor for the role of Danny got into trouble with the law and didn't return to the school. *Grease* was put on hold, and replaced by the performing arts department creating their own piece of devised theatre/music. This worked so well that the school never looked for scripts again. Their own works were ever more successful, year after year. So, the first question you might ask yourself is whether you have a company that would be better with devising their own work, producing a known play, or commissioning a work specifically for them. There may be a new playwright from a local college or university program that is looking for just such a challenge.

Know your audience: Whether creating your own work, or producing a scripted work, consider the audience that will attend your production. A group of teenagers performing for their peers is different than children's theatre or a public performance. You may decide to challenge your audience and push boundaries, but do understand what you are likely to get as a response and make your choices accordingly.

Know your limitations: Think carefully about what will work within the limitations of your budget, space, preparation time, and anything else that might constrain your vision. Some of my best productions have been done with almost no budget. Your biggest liabilities can become your biggest assets. Jerzy Grotowski, a Polish theatre director, pioneered what he called Poor Theatre in the late 1950s/early 60s. He wasn't actually referring to the lack of a budget, but a technique of theatre production that required nothing but the actors, well trained in physical theatre. With no sets and costumes, all of the focus was on the actors. Consider what you will need in order to realize your dream on the stage. It may be less than you think. You may also decide where to put the limited resources you have. Rather than spreading them thinly over every aspect of the production, you may decide to concentrate them where they will have the most impact. I once directed and produced a large-scale musical on a shoestring budget. I focused on very imaginative costumes, many recycled from materials at hand. The sets were minimal and interchangeable, with boxes and platforms reconfigured for each scene. The actors, singers and dancers, however, looked spectacular, filling the stage with colour and energy. Other shows have relied on lighting to create the mood and atmosphere, allowing the actors to fill the audience's imagination with the world they inhabited. The physical space you will perform in may also dictate the production you chose. A tiny black box theatre may not be able to hold a musical extravaganza, but perhaps there is a public space that can be utilized as a non-traditional performance space. Closely examine the resources at your disposal, and make the most of them for your production.

Know your responsibilities: Just because you have a copy of a printed script doesn't mean you are free to present it on-stage. Check the inside cover of a play published in book form for where to obtain performance rights and how to pay royalties. Amateur rights aren't very expensive but must be paid, including for use in school productions. If no admission is being charged, you may get rights to perform without fees, but that is not guaranteed. If the play hasn't been published, find the playwright and make arrangements for direct payments, or through an agent, as directed by the information you should find on the script. You also have responsibilities to the playwright in terms of how you use the script. Generally, you need permission to change anything that is not in the public domain. In Canada, copyright ends 50 years after the death of the playwright, at the end of the calendar year. For translations, it is 50 years from the death of the translator. Under current USA copyright laws, copyright protection lasts for 70 years after the death of the creator. As laws have changed over the years, don't assume it is in the public domain unless it was first published before 1923.

CASTING YOUR PROJECT

There may be occasions when you will be asked to direct a play that has already been cast. Be aware that not having control of casting the work you direct does have potential pitfalls. Casting actors for the wrong reasons can also result in making your life more difficult than it needs to be. I once caved to political pressure and cast the wrong actor for Dorothy in a production of *The Wiz*. She was talented, and would have made a perfect witch; wicked or good, but wasn't what I envisioned for the role of Dorothy. The decision compromised what I would have liked to do with the production. Check the Audition chapter on ways to effectively cast your project and listen to your own best instincts. If there is someone whose opinion you trust, you can share this responsibility, but share it for that reason, and no other. If the casting doesn't work out quite as well as you'd hoped, do the best you can. You will learn a lot as a director in the process.

PREPPING YOUR SHOW

Aside from knowing the play very well, you will also want to consider the look of your show, and start working with the designers of the costumes and set to make that less of a distraction once rehearsals begin. Get together your team (see PRODUCTION MANAGEMENT TEAM) and have your first meeting: set the roles and responsibilities and share the schedule (see TIMELINE) to ensure that your production is ready by opening night.

AUDITIONS

There is no right or wrong way to conduct auditions, but it is good to think about how you will identify the best actor for each character. You want a process that is going to show you what you need to know and be fair and transparent. All participants should feel that it allowed them to show you the best of what they had to offer as actors.

Where will you conduct the auditions?

- In a small, intimate space, where they will feel as relaxed and at-ease as possible?
- On stage, where they'll show you how well they can project into the auditorium?
- Will you hold the first auditions and the callbacks in the same space?
- Will you need another space for singing or dancing auditions?
- Will you be holding individual, or group auditions? How large is your space?
- Is there an adequate waiting area in addition to the actual audition space?

The space should fit your purpose, allowing you to see what actors can do. Actors will usually feel more secure in a smaller space, rather than on a large open stage. If the stage is all that is available to you, you can make it more intimate by setting up your table right on the stage. If you don't have a front curtain, place yourself upstage, so that the actors are facing you, with their backs to the auditorium.

However, you may have only a short rehearsal time period and are concerned with getting inexperienced actors ready for the stage. You may have a large auditorium to project into, so may want to cast actors who are already comfortable with being on stage. This comes with experience, but there are people who are naturally more comfortable in front of an audience. If that's what you need, run auditions sitting in the auditorium, with the actors showing you how they can fill the house with their presence.

What will they show you?

- A short prepared monologue?
- A scene from the play you will direct?
- A scene in the style of the play you will direct, but not the actual script?

Remember that not all good actors are good at auditions. Some actors are very competent at cold reads, but it doesn't mean that they are great actors. Some good actors are not good readers.

Almost everyone can do well in a monologue that has been worked on for a long while, even weak actors. Knowing this:

- Will a monologue be definitive in your casting decisions?
- Will you see a monologue in the initial auditions and character readings or cold readings from the script on the callbacks?
- Is it practical to make scripts available for several weeks before the auditions? If so, think about having everyone read for lead roles. They will have more lines to work with and they may be the more interesting characters to prepare. Smaller roles can be cast from those that did not get the lager roles that they read for.

INDIVIDUAL VERSUS GROUP AUDITIONS

There are plays that you will be able to cast perfectly well by having the actors bring something to show you in an individual audition. However, there may be times when you will be better served by having a group workshop style of audition. There, you will lead actors through exercises that will show you how they interact with each other, how they take direction and how willing they are to take risks. This may work well when auditioning young actors not previously known to you. You may learn a lot more about them in a shorter time than what you could gain in individual, stress-laden auditions. Group auditions also tend to provide a more relaxed atmosphere, where they will be better able to show you what they can do. As they are in a group situation that is much like a regular creative drama class, they will not feel the pressure to perform, and may well show you more of what you need to see in order to assess not only whether they are right for the parts, but also whether you would like to work with them. The companion book, **STAGES: Creative Ideas for Teaching Drama**, is full of drama games that would be useful in an audition master class.

Another idea is to have a group audition with all of the actors sitting in a circle together and allowing everyone a turn to read for any one of the characters. They may all read for as many characters as time allows. As this process continues, you will start to develop a feel for which actor you would like to see in which part. This could be followed up with specific callbacks, or the play could be cast after only this group audition. This circle reading might effectively be preceded by the workshop style of group audition.

How will you promote the auditions?

- Fliers, posters, bulletins, announcements?
  - ☐ Be very clear on the notices, outlining what you are looking for (a character breakdown stating age range and characteristics).
  - ☐ Describe what actors will need to prepare for the auditions. If there will be movement, include the style and appropriate clothing to wear. If they need to sing, tell them what you will provide, and what you expect to hear.
  - ☐ List the dates for the auditions and for the production, including rehearsal period.
  - ☐ Provide a means of contact for requesting an audition.
- Social media? Word of mouth?

If you are teaching in a high school, and producing a play or musical is an annual event that is eagerly anticipated by the student body, getting the word out for auditions may be as simple as a few notices in the school announcements and in your classes. If you are casting a community theatre production, you may need to go beyond your group of regulars to get the actors who are right for the parts. Taking advantage of community bulletins and newsletters may bring in new people, as will word of mouth by those who have participated in the past.

What can you do if you need something specific for your production and didn't find it in the auditions? I once needed a group of "transformed" young men for the chorus of *Li'l Abner*. I enlisted the assistance of the coach of one of the high school's sports teams. All I needed was for the captain to buy into the project to bring the rest of the team with him. Think creatively to attract the cast you need.

Who will you be casting?

- Can you be colour-blind, and possibly gender-blind in the play?
  - ☐ Be open to casting different races in roles, even in cases where they might be playing family members. In our multicultural society, many families are interracial. It is often possible to cast a female in a part written for a male. Traditionally, more roles are written for males, underutilizing all the female actors looks for roles. Check the playwright's requirements on a royalty play before changing anything, however.

- Are you going for someone who LOOKS the part?
  - ☐ Try to look for the actor with the right energy, or essence for the character. This is more important than someone who looks like your idea of the character (or like the Hollywood actor who played that character in the movie version of your play). Don't get too hung up on how someone looks, as you can usually adjust that if you really need to. Wigs and costumes can dramatically alter appearances. It is more important that they are able to inhabit the characters and make them real people, and that they are actors that you feel you can work with.
- Have you considered double casting, or training understudies?
  - ☐ The upside of double casting is pleasing more actors. This might work well in a school production, but create more headaches than it is worth in a community show. In a double-cast musical, the leads can sing in the chorus on their off-nights. In a play, there may not be enough smaller roles for this to happen. In one double-cast school production, one of my actors playing Dracula dropped out near opening night, so the one actor could play all nights, with both casts, with very little stress for the casts or me.
  - ☐ Understudies could work well in a musical, where again, they could sing in the chorus unless needed. It is more problematic in a play, where they might put in a lot of rehearsal time and never appear on the stage.

Remember that every actor has something unique to bring to a role. Be open to surprises, recognizing when an actor brings in something unexpected, but perfect for a character. Remember that you can set your own stage conventions. Whatever you tell the audience is true, will become truth for them, within the world of your play.

Who will assist you in casting this play?
- A **monitor** in the waiting area can greatly assist in making sure that your auditions run smoothly.
  - ☐ Decide ahead of time how you will communicate with your monitor during auditions. How will the actors be announced or introduced, and brought into the audition room?
  - ☐ Have the forms ready, deciding what information you need for your files. Make sure your monitors (and assistants as needed) understand the forms, the sign-in procedure and any instructions your actors need.

- Be sure that they are well trained and understand how to speak to actors. You don't want actors being unnecessarily stressed because of their waiting room experience. Monitors should take care of the business of the audition, not offer advice or opinions on how to audition. They should respect the actors' need for quiet in order to focus.
- Collect stapler, pens, water, and anything else you'll need on the day.
- Discuss meal breaks, time between auditions and any other timing details before the day begins.
- Arrive thirty minutes before the first audition to get set up, post directions to the space, and give a final briefing to monitors and assistants.

- An **assistant** or two inside the audition space with you is invaluable in your assessment of the actors. This might be an assistant director, trusted colleague, or the musical director, in the case of a musical. It might be the writer, in the case of an original play. If the producer is present, make sure that this person can also be described as a trusted colleague.
  - Being able to discuss each actor with another witness may bring insights you will value. Take two minutes between auditions to do so.
  - Discuss before the day begins how you will communicate with each other during the auditions. No discussions on the merit of the actor should take place in front of the actor. All talk should be respectful and positive, but neutral, not making promises you may have to break.
  - Be respectful of the actors, really listening and watching what they bring in. Don't talk during a monologue or reading, and do take a lot of notes. You will remember less than you think you will. You might also each have checklists to compare at the end of the day.
  - Give every actor equal time.
  - Right after the auditions end pull out the sheets of the actors you want to see in the callbacks. Don't give yourself time to forget anything you saw.
- A **reader** should be available for the actors who come prepared with a scene.
  - The reader doesn't need to be the right gender for the role, and can read for any scenes and the characters in them.

- ☐ This person should be a good actor, known to you, but perhaps someone you already recognize as not right for any of the roles in the current play.
- ☐ The reader is playing the character opposite the actor being auditioned. They may have something to bring to their roles, but should be relatively neutral, and allow for the auditioning actor to bring his or her own interpretation to the role, reacting to what the actor brings in.
- ☐ Sometimes directors think they can best read opposite the actors they are auditioning, as they want to see if they have chemistry and can work with them. It may answer that question, but will not allow them to see the actors objectively. Whether or not an actor personally connects with the director in a scene is not necessarily going to determine how well that actor will be able to play that role. It will also force the director to invest in the opposite role, not allowing her to view the scene objectively.

- An **accompanist** for a musical audition.
  - ☐ Will a piano or keyboard have to be brought into the space? If songs from the musical will be used for the auditions, an accompanist should be there to play them. If other songs, in the style of the musical, are being asked for in the auditions, you may have a piano and accompanist, or a devise for electronic playback.

- A **choreographer** and **dance captain** for dance auditions.
  - ☐ The dance captain (or assistant to the choreographer) could lead all dancers through a warm-up.
  - ☐ The choreographer prepares a short dance sequence (or routine) to teach (or have the assistant teach) to the dancers.
  - ☐ The dance captain leads small groups of dancers through the routine, while the choreographer watches. Or, once the routine is taught, dancers are expected to perform it in small groups without a leader.
  - ☐ The choreographer picks out the people he or she would like to see again. The rest are let go after one run-through. If there are large numbers of dancers that are unknown to the choreographer, the dancers may be given numbers to pin to their clothes.
  - ☐ If there are different dance styles needed for the musical (e.g. jazz and tap), this process may be repeated for each one.

- ☐ The routine will be repeated until all dancers are chosen. In the case of leads that need to dance, decisions will not be final until they have also had their singing (and possibly acting) callbacks.

- ☐ If the musical is heavily dependent on the dancers, or all characters dance, callbacks may be held (e.g. *Cats* or *Chorus Line*). If they dance in the background, and are not speaking characters, all decisions might be made based on that one audition process.

Note: This may not apply to a high school musical with an inclusive philosophy of production, where any and all students can participate if they show an interest in doing so. Those not chosen for lead rules will all either sing in the chorus or dance, as suitability or interest demands. The choreographer and musical director will work with all students who regularly attend rehearsals, preparing them for the best possible performance. While there is no reason to present under-rehearsed productions, this isn't Broadway, and sometimes inclusion is much more important than results.

Will you hold callbacks?

- ■ Can you make your decision after one round of auditions, or do you need to see some of the actors again, in a callback? In professional theatre, there may well be multiple callbacks, but in community and school theatre, you may not need any. If unable to make a clear choice after one audition, one callback should confirm it.

- ■ Are you casting a play that requires people to "match" each other in some way? Do you need to bring in those people together, to see how they will look and work together? Do you need to try different combinations of people together?

Callbacks should help you to accomplish the following objectives:

- ■ To separate the actors you are interested in from those you know you can't use for this project. This will help you focus on what the actors with potential can do.

- ■ If the first auditions were monologues or a group audition, the callbacks could be for the actors you would like to work with, giving them specific roles to read for.

- ■ To spend time working with these actors to test their range and see how well you could work with them. You could give them directions, asking for small changes in the reading, to see how they respond.

- If you have already cast a specific lead, you could have that actor as your reader for the callbacks involving a character that has a significant relationship with that lead, in order to test the chemistry between the actors. If no one has yet been cast, you could bring in pairs of actors for the same purpose, but keep it narrowly focused on only those actors you are seriously considering for each role.

Do consider the time involved, not only your own, but also the time of the actors who are auditioning for you. Probably the worst auditioning experience of my life was before I was a professional actor. As the project was not a paid engagement, the director seemed to assume that the actors' time was his to squander at his leisure. Massive numbers of actors were given a callback, and all told to come to the audition space for the same time. He proceeded to call us into the room in various groups, over and over again. His reason was that he needed to see which actors would look like a match for the family unit the script required. After an hour or two, it was clear which actors were being favoured by how often they were called in to read again. A quick glance over the waiting room told me which actors looked like they might be related. This is something that a look at all the headshots after the initial auditions could have told the director. It was indulgent; a waste of time to have us all there in person for several hours. By the end of the process I had a headache and was happy that I didn't look enough like others he was considering to be cast. This was not a director I wanted to work with.

How will you contact the actors who auditioned for you? **How** will you announce your cast?

- Will everyone hear from you, even those not considered for a callback? If so, a short professional note thanking them for preparing for the audition and encouraging their future endeavours in theatre would be appropriate. As an actor, I can say that these notes are appreciated. As a director, I can say that they take very little time and can create a lot of good will.

- Callbacks might most efficiently be offered by phone, as you will have an immediate opportunity to confirm times and dates. This could also be done by text or email, as long as a request for confirmation is included. The same could be said for making the offer of a role. The more personal, the better. Then, the paperwork required depends on whether there is a paid contract to be offered, or not. In the case of a school production, a posted list may be all that is required.

- The note for those not cast would also be sent after callbacks. Only do this once casting has been confirmed. If someone doesn't accept your offer, you may be going to your second choice for the role.

- Once casting is confirmed, post the list or send out a press release, depending on whether this is a school or community production. I have known drama teachers to post final cast lists at the end of the day on a Friday, to give everyone a chance to absorb the news before seeing the students again on Monday morning. Emotions can run high in the audition process in a closed environment. My best advice is to make the process as transparent as possible, and not to drag it out any longer than necessary. Emotions will build over time, and the results will be more traumatic for those not chosen the longer they have to wait for the outcomes.

Once you have answered these questions for yourself, and know what you are looking to accomplish, you will be ready to go. Design the process that you believe will deliver the results you are looking for. After you have gone through it once, you will know what worked for you, and what you will do a little differently the next time.

THE TIMELINE

The timeline is your calendar from the time you choose your play, until closing night and the final party. It will keep your preparation and rehearsal process on track to ensure the success of your project.

BEGIN AT THE END

When designing your timeline, start at the end of the project and work your way back. In this way, you'll know that you've planned for enough time to get everything ready on time. Opening night is your goal, and that's what you prepare for.

- **The Run:** How many performances will you have? If this is a school production, answering the following questions might help your planning.
  - ☐ Are you double casting, needing an equal number of nights for each cast?
  - ☐ Will you have student matinees, for your own school population and/or for feeder schools in the neighbourhood?

- Do you want weekend shows, or do you want to avoid the weekend?
- Are there holidays to consider in your planning? Will you present right before a school break? Can you sustain quality and interest through a major break in the school year if it falls near your opening night?

- **Dress Rehearsal:** There should be at least one final run, in full costumes, make-up and lighting, done without interruptions. In a musical, or complicated play, there may be another scheduled, in case it is needed. These could be done with, or without an invited audience. In school shows, it might be a matinee on the same day as opening night, or it could be the night before.

- **Tech Rehearsal:** Before the dress rehearsal, you need a final run-through for all the technical requirements to be set.
  - In a school show, that day might look like this:

    9 – 12 pm: The director instructs as to the feel of the lighting in each scene, as the tech director sets the levels of lights on the board. The crew readjusts the hang of the lights, as needed. The lighting board is programmed for all lighting cues. Sound cues are tested. The prompt book is marked for all light and sound cues.

    1 – 6 pm: The cast is brought in to run a "cue to cue," meaning that they begin and end each scene, skipping anything that does not contain a technical cue.

  - In a large complicated show, this might take longer, and be broken into more than one day.
  - This tech day may happen two days before the dress rehearsal, allowing for another full tech rehearsal before the dress. Backing it up one more day would allow for a day off to rest before the dress rehearsal.
  - There might also be a need for a stage crew "cue to cue," where the stage manager takes the stage crew through all of the changes they need to make between scenes. This should happen before the actual tech run.
  - At some point, after the lights are hung, plan for a costume parade, where actors move on the stage in their costumes, under the lights. Leave enough time for adjustments to be made if a costume doesn't work.

□ In a small festival production, there is generally only one rehearsal on stage per performing group. In this time, lasting no more than a few hours, all sound and light cues are set and a 'cue to cue' conducted, with a dress rehearsal only as time permits. There will generally be a set lighting design, with only a little flexibility for changes and specials.

■ **Final Run-Throughs:** The week before the Tech/Dress/Run, will be a build-up of run-throughs.

□ The week will begin with a full rehearsal slot being given to each act of the full-length production.

□ After each act has had its own rehearsal comes the Stumble-Through, where the entire play is run for the first time. The attempt is made to keep going, but stops to fix moments are allowed. Transitions between scenes that have only been run in sequence once before can be problem spots.

□ The Stumble-Through is followed by at least two more complete runs. Time may be scheduled for three days of run throughs, with the third day only used if needed, otherwise becoming a day off before beginning the tech rehearsals.

□ Schedule time at the end of one of the run-throughs to work out and practice the curtain calls.

□ In a perfect world, this whole week is spent in the actual theatre, on the stage, using the full sets and real props. If not, hopefully there is at least one run-through with the set before tech. This means that the time must be scheduled, either before or during this week, outside of rehearsal times, to erect the set, complete the decoration of it, and hang the lights.

■ **Rehearsal Period:** Everything that happens before the last week of run-throughs is preparation leading up to it. Each department will need deadlines as to when their part in the production must be complete (see The Production Team for all the details). The most important point to consider is the overall length of this period. Some directors like to take many months to prepare a production, meeting only once or twice per week until two months from the opening, when they increase it to three times per week, then four times in the three weeks leading up to the final week of run-throughs.

Others prefer a faster, more concentrated time frame, completing the preparation in only two or three months. There are pros and cons to each system. A long rehearsal schedule should be less stressful, with more time to allow everything to sink in between rehearsals. The danger is in sustaining interest and energy throughout the process, and not losing cast members to other commitments. A fast and furious schedule may produce more stress, but will be easier to commit to and energy should remain high.

☐ In terms of the actual rehearsals, an average musical will take about 120 rehearsal hours. This may not include choral rehearsals to learn the music, or dance rehearsals in a show that has a lot of dance in addition to scenes and musical numbers. It is just counting the scene rehearsals leading up to the dress rehearsal.

☐ If there are separate dance and singing choruses, and a choreographer as well as a musical director, they could be rehearsing at the same time.

☐ Allow the leads and the chorus plenty of time to learn the music before scheduling full scene rehearsals. Blocking could begin, however.

☐ A play will require somewhat less time, depending on its length and complexity.

☐ Find the rehearsal times that will work well for the most cast members. Will your school cast be willing to rehearse before morning classes, during their lunch hours, or after school? Will they come in for a full weekend of rehearsals? That might work once or twice during the period, perhaps when learning new choreography, or blocking a large scene, when a longer rehearsal is desirable. It might work once again near the end of the period, for the first complete run-through, for example. Very few students will be willing to give every weekend to rehearsals, however. Noon-hour rehearsals can work, but are best with smaller scenes with only a few cast members. It is too difficult to organize a large group for such a short amount of time. Bring in only the actors that you know you will use for each rehearsal.

■ **Auditions:** How much time should elapse between the final auditions and the first rehearsal? That too, is a personal choice. Some directors like to start immediately, while others might want to give their casts some time with their scripts before beginning formal rehearsals. In some schools, auditions are held just before a school break, with rehearsals beginning as soon as the students return.

By working backwards from opening night to the auditions, you will have worked in enough time for everything that will need to happen in order to produce your show. Always leave enough time to accommodate unexpected problems. Like everything else, once you've gone through the process once, you'll be better able to plan it the second time. Hopefully, it will be a positive experience, and there will be a second time.

PRODUCTION MANAGEMENT TEAM

In professional theatre, the roles and responsibilities of the artistic, management and production staff are clearly defined and will vary only slightly from theatre to theatre. In schools and community theatres, all of the same jobs need to be accomplished in order to mount a successful production, but volunteers handle most, if not all responsibilities. It is good to make up a checklist of what needs to be done, and who will do it. It is important that everyone knows:

WHAT they need to do: what is the job description

WHO they report to: who to ask when questions arise

WHEN they need to get things done: every job has a deadline

The following is a simplified version of a possible production team, suitable for a school or community theatre presentation.

The team consists of four important positions. In a best-case scenario, there will be one person in each position to share the workload, but sometimes, some of these positions will be combined. Each one of these positions will have other people reporting to them.

Director

- Stage Manager
- Assistant Director
- Musical Director (for a musical)
- Choreographer (for a musical)

Producer

- House Manager
- Photography
- Poster – design and printing
- Publicity
- Program
- Ticket Sales

Stage Manager

- Costumes – design, construction, acquisition
- Sets – design, construction, decoration
- Props – design, construction, acquisition
- Hair and Make-up – design, application

Technical Director

- Sound and Lighting Crew Chief
- Maintenance Chief

JOB DESCRIPTIONS

DIRECTOR

- The director has final artistic control of everything concerning the look of the production.
- Liaison with the school administration (in a school production).
- Chair all meetings of the production team.
- Work with the producer on how to spend the money available on the production.
- Choose the script, cast and direct the production.
- Meet with design team to communicate look of the show.
- Communicate with the stage manager, in order to receive what is needed for whatever is seen on stage (costumes, make-up, sets, props).
- Assign duties of the assistant director, if there is one. In a school setting, the stage manager tends to be the only other person in rehearsals, aside from the actors. If there is an assistant director, the job description must be clearly defined, so as to be separate from the job description of the stage manager.

- Accommodate the musical director's need to access the cast for musical rehearsals, and the choreographer's need to access the cast for dance rehearsals. Work in partnership with them on the integration of these aspects into the show.

ASSISTANT DIRECTOR

The job description will vary from one production to another, and from one director to another. This position is meant to be a training ground for a new or emerging director, allowing for the assistant to learn about the director's process, and the theatrical production process as a whole. Remembering this is the best way to not confuse the assistant director with a stage manager. Of utmost importance is that the assistant director ONLY communicates with the director, never the cast or production team members. Any ideas or notes are given to the director, not the actors. Absolute discretion is needed, as the assistant may become privy to the director's thoughts, which should not be common knowledge. Duties might include:

☐ Sit in on all production meetings, as an observer.

☐ Read and study the play, and be ready to offer observations and analysis on it.

☐ Attend all rehearsals, as an observer, but may also include:

- Offer feedback on blocking and directing decisions, when asked.
- Run a rehearsal in the director's absence.
- Take notes for the director during a rehearsal, (especially final rehearsals) his/her own if requested, as well as those dictated by the director. Give to director to communicate to cast.
- Take the cast through a warm-up before a rehearsal.
- Supervise the cast in a line-run or speed-through (Italian).
- Walk through the role of an absent cast member during a rehearsal.

☐ Ensure that the program is complete (liaison between director and producer) and all people and organizations that contributed are mentioned and thanked.

PRODUCER

- The producer is responsible for the following committee heads. He/she must keep in touch with these committee heads to ensure that the jobs are being done by the deadlines set. The producer is the liaison between these heads and the director.
  - ☐ House manager
  - ☐ Photography
  - ☐ Poster
  - ☐ Publicity
  - ☐ Program
  - ☐ Ticket sales
- Liaison between the project and the rest of the staff (in a school production), taking care of the flow of information.
- Bookings: rehearsal space, performance space, meeting space, custodians for the run of the production.
- Order souvenirs (T-shirts, etc.) and save programs and posters for cast and crews.
- Order flowers, thank-you notes or gifts for opening night.
- Organize a production staff party or luncheon.
- Budget: Control the budget and take care of paying bills for production costs, keeping a record of all money coming in and being paid out. Ensure that the stage manager has all budgets for his/her departments.
- Ensure that program coordinator has all information needed for the program.
- Make up list of VIP comps needed, Get them from ticket manager and distribute.
- Liaison with area schools and other groups to book audiences for non-public matinee performances.

  HOUSE MANAGER
  - ☐ Report to the producer
  - ☐ Identify volunteers for all front-of-house positions for all performances:
    - • Generally, a public performance will require:
      - · Two on cash
      - · One to take tickets as patrons enter the theatre

- One to hand out programs
- Several ushers to guide patrons to seats – depending on the size of the theatre

☐ Make sure that all volunteers understand the time commitment involved. For feeder school matinees, you may be the sole usher.

☐ House manager and volunteers should arrive one hour before curtain. Make sure that all are dressed appropriately, as they represent the school or theatre company to the public.

☐ Cash: Arrange for a float and a cashbox. Count money taken at the door every night and keep it in a safe place overnight. Turn it in to the ticket manager the next day. Also keep a record for yourself as back-up.

☐ Programs: Keep in a safe place after each performance. Deliver to the door each evening.

☐ Refreshments for intermission: This could be handed to another school group, such as the Travel Club. They would then manage this job entirely. They keep all the profits, but must make sure that they buy the products and have a group of responsible students and a staff supervisor there each night to handle all jobs related to the refreshments for patrons to purchase. If the profits are to be kept by the theatre club or department, all of the above becomes the responsibility of the house manager, or person assigned by him/her.

☐ Auditorium: Ask student ushers to help straighten up chairs and prepare the house for the patrons' arrival.

PHOTOGRAPHER

☐ Report to the producer.

☐ Cast headshots: arrange appointments as soon as cast is finalized. Make 8x10 copies available to Publicity for front-of-house display.

☐ Rehearsal stills: attend several rehearsals for media photos. Keep copies for school or theatre records. Choose copies for Yearbook committee.

☐ Video each cast's performance during the run.

☐ Cast and crew group photo: take before or after a performance.

POSTERS

- ☐ Report to the producer
- ☐ Arrange for design of poster: will there be a competition for the design? Will a designer be hired?
- ☐ Printing: will printing be done in-house? If not, source a printer to do the job. Decide on the number needed.
- ☐ Identify volunteers to hang posters according to lists obtained from the head of Publicity.

PUBLICITY

- ☐ Report to the producer.
- ☐ Ideas for in-school publicity: catchy announcements, school newsletter, costume parade or flash mob in cafeteria, posters, etc.
- ☐ School sign: book well in advance and put up advertisement for the play.
- ☐ Community:
  - Local newspaper – purchase ad, encourage reporter to attend rehearsal. Write article, submit yourself if no reporter is available.
  - Press release: send to all media outlets.
  - City newspaper: list in free community column.
  - Posters: come up with list of places to hang in the community and other schools – deliver list to Poster Committee head.
- ☐ Media articles: brainstorm for subjects that would be of interest to media; find the hook, what makes this production of this play unique, or of interest to the public?
- ☐ Arrange for the creation of a front-of-house display, with photos of the cast, material on the play, the company and any other information, as directed by the stage manager.

PROGRAM

- ☐ Report to the producer.
- ☐ Printer: book with a printer so you have a deadline. Decide on the type of program – paper or stock card, etc. See if poster visual can be adapted for the program cover or if another graphic is needed.

- [ ] Information for program: personnel lists, cast lists, thank-you list, advertising, scene descriptions, director's message – get everything from the producer as soon as it is available.
- [ ] Decide on number to order.
- [ ] When printed, arrange volunteers for folding. Consult with house manager for delivery instructions. Keep back enough programs for souvenirs for cast and crew. Deliver to producer.

TICKET SALES

- [ ] Report to the producer.
- [ ] Printing: order tickets as soon as dates and prices are set. Consider colour coding for different performances. Order some extra tickets, but sell only available seating.
- [ ] Sales strategy: brainstorm for sales ideas, to have back-up plans if sales are slow. Consider contests, giveaways, etc.
- [ ] Volunteers: arrange for all volunteers needed to sell tickets. Consider table set-up outside of cafeteria at noon hours, etc.
- [ ] Cash: Accurate records must be kept of tickets sold and money collected. Consider numbering tickets, if seating is rush only.
- [ ] Cash sales at the door: The house manager will be responsible for this and give you the money the next day. Add this to your numbers for each day's sales, but keep track of what sold in advance and what was sold at the door. These numbers are important in planning for future shows.
- [ ] Matinee cash sales: the producer will give you the money collected from other schools and groups from the matinee audiences.
- [ ] Comps: The producer will provide you with dates and numbers for VIP comps and request those tickets from you.

STAGE MANAGER
- Report to the director.
- Responsible for the following committee heads:
  - [ ] Sets
  - [ ] Costumes

☐ Props

☐ Hair and Make-up

- As the play is being prepared, keep in touch with these departments to ensure that all is going well and on schedule. You are the liaison between these departments and the director. Ensure that these departments have the funds for the supplies they need and collect receipts as the money is spent. Your liaison for the budget is the producer. Money is received from and receipts returned to the producer.

- Create a prompt book: the "bible" for all rehearsals. (see Prompt Book)

- Attend all production meetings, keep notes and follow up on all issues that arise for sets, costumes, props, hair and make-up.

- Obtain all rehearsal props needed from the props department. Secure them and bring them out as needed. Create a list of all props and their placements at the top of the show. Ensure that the props department has it and uses it during the run. Assign an assistant to check props before each performance.

- Tape out the rehearsal space according to stage dimensions.

- Supervise assistant stage managers: arrange for someone to be at each rehearsal to take director's notes and blocking directions. Ensure the stage is prepared for each rehearsal, with all practice props and costumes available. The stage manager, or one of the assistant stage managers, is the first person to arrive for a rehearsal, ensuring all is ready to go, and the last person to leave.

- Once on the set, spike set pieces for each scene. (Small pieces of tape colour-coded for each scene, marking the placement on the stage for all of the back legs of all furniture and set pieces that will be moved during the play.)

- Give cast the pre-run speech about caring for props, where they will be found, and where to return them if they bring them off-stage during the play.

- Inform cast of any appointments with costume fittings, make-up and hair tests and interviews with the press.

- Ensure Publicity has information needed for the front-of-house display board. Confirm content with the Director.
- Ensure the safety of any consumables needed during the play.
- Inform cast and crews of safety exits and procedures once the production moves into the theatre.
- Run a scene change rehearsal with the set crew that will be working the run of the production.
- Arrange for the final cast party.
- During the run: The stage manager will be on a head-set backstage, trouble shooting, cueing actors, set movements, props, costumes changes, make-up changes. Your headset is connected to the technical director in the control booth, who is calling the show. In some cases, it is the stage manager calling the show, with assistant stage managers in the backstage positions.

COSTUMES
□ Report to the stage manager.
□ Arrange for a sufficient group of volunteers for your crew. Make sure that they have the skills needed to build the costumes and understand the time commitment required.
□ Arrange for the design and creation of all costumes. Consult with the director on the look of the costumes. Keep budget constraints in mind. Rent only when absolutely necessary.
□ Get measurements from actors as soon as casting is final. Arrange for fitting times as needed.
□ Deliver speech to cast concerning the care and respect for the costumes they will wear. Outline your expectations and how your crew will be dealing with the costumes during the run.
□ Arrange and run the "costume parade," when actors will wear their costumes under the lights, for final approval by the director. Leave yourself enough time to make adjustments before the opening.
□ During the run: You and your crew members should be at the theatre by the call time set by the stage manager. Troubleshoot backstage (repairs, etc.). Assign specific crew

members to assist with dressing difficult costume pieces and assisting in quick costume changes between entrances. At the end of each night, ensure all costumes are ready for the next performance. Assign crew members to specific jobs for this.

HINT: A small spray bottle of vodka will neutralize body odour on armpits of costumes between cleanings.

☐ Clean and store all costumes after the run. Return borrowed and rented pieces.

SETS: SET CONSTRUCTION

☐ Report to the stage manager.

☐ Arrange for the design of the set, with instructions from the director on the look of the set. Be clear on how the set needs to function and any details it must include.

☐ Get the materials' budget from the stage manager, and arrange for the purchase of the materials. Keep receipts; give them to the stage manager.

☐ Arrange for sufficient crew volunteers to construct the set. Arrange for a schedule of when this will occur to ensure that deadlines are met.

☐ Set it up in the performance space in order to allow the decoration crew to complete it for performance.

SET: SET DECORATION

☐ Report to the stage manager.

☐ Receive the set design from the designer or stage manager, with instructions on the look of the set. Be clear on any details.

☐ Get the materials' budget from the stage manager, and arrange for the purchase of the materials. Keep receipts; give them to the stage manager.

☐ Arrange for sufficient crew volunteers to decorate the set. Arrange for a schedule of when this will occur to ensure that deadlines are met.

SETS: CREW CHIEF

☐ Report to the stage manager.

☐ Arrange for sufficient crew volunteers to set up and strike sets before, during and after each performance. Make sure that they understand the time commitment.

☐ You and your crew must be available for the last week of rehearsals and the entire run of the show.

☐ Rehearse how set pieces will move during the show. Assign specific crew members to specific set pieces and instruct them on their proper movement and placement.

☐ During the run: You and your crew should be at the theatre by the call time set by the stage manager. At the end of each performance, return set pieces to their place for the top of the next performance.

PROPS

☐ Report to the stage manager.

☐ Arrange for sufficient crew volunteers to build and/or acquire all props needed and to attend several rehearsals and be available for the entire run of the show. Ensure that they understand the time commitment.

☐ Show props: Get this list from the stage manager and start to acquire them. Decide which ones are strong enough to use right through rehearsals and which will need mock-ups, saving the real props for the final rehearsals and run. Use your imagination in all acquisitions, borrowing and making things whenever possible.

☐ Budget: Get available funds from the stage manager. Submit all receipts.

☐ During the run: A props person is needed backstage during the final week of rehearsals, as soon as the real props are being used, and during each run of the show. You and your crew should be at the theatre by the call time set by the stage manager. Ensure props are well cared for and returned to correct location on the marked props table after each show.

HINT: The backstage props table could be covered in brown paper, with the props arranged in a logical order, according to their use in the show. Draw around each prop with a black marker, creating an outline indicating where it should be placed after use. This makes it easy to check for all of the props before each run of the show.

☐ After the run: return all borrowed or rented props. Store the rest safely for future use.

HAIR and MAKE-UP

☐ Report to the stage manager.

☐ Arrange for sufficient crew volunteers. Decide if the show needs a separate crew for hair and make-up, or if one crew can handle both. Will actors be doing any of their own hair and make-up, or is it a period or fantasy piece that will require a lot of assistance?

☐ Ensure that you understand the look of the show and what is required for hair and make-up designs.

☐ Arrange for a workshop to teach actors how to do their own make-up if it is decided that they will do their own. Arrange for crew workshops as needed. Arrange for practice appointments with actors, as needed.

☐ Budget: get allotted funds from the stage manager and submit receipts.

☐ Have all hair and make-up ready for actors' parade under the lights, for final directorial approval.

☐ During the run: You and your crew should be at the theatre by the call time set by the stage manager. Ensure that all make-up and hair stations are set up and ready for use.

☐ Educate crew and actors on proper use and clean up. Ensure that the area is cleaned up and ready for the next performance at the end of each night.

HINT: If using the theatre's supplies, remove all lids and store out of sight to discourage the removable of products by cast and crew.

TECHNICAL DIRECTOR

■ Responsible for the sound and light for the show.

  ☐ Calls the show from the control booth (unless this will be done by the stage manager)

  ☐ Design and create lighting plots

  ☐ Design and create lighting cue sheets

  ☐ Design and create sound cue sheets

■ Responsible for the following crew heads:

  ☐ Sound and Light Crew Chief

  ☐ Maintenance Crew Chief

- Create the show's sound track
  - ☐ Acquire any recorded music needed
  - ☐ Acquire sound effects requested
  - ☐ Set levels at the tech rehearsal
- Set lighting cues at the tech rehearsal
- Co-ordinate the hang and strike of tech equipment

  SOUND AND LIGHTING CREW CHIEF
  - ☐ Report to the technical director.
  - ☐ Arrange for sufficient crew volunteers to run the sound and lights for the show, including the hang and strike. Ensure that they understand the time commitment. Must be available from first hang to the end of the strike, after the last performance.
  - ☐ Train the crews.
  - ☐ Purchase or rent equipment, as authorized by the tech director.
  - ☐ During the run: You and your crew should be at the theatre by the call time set by the stage manager.
  - ☐ Hang and strike the sound and lighting equipment, together with your crew.

  MAINTENANCE CHIEF
  - ☐ Report to the technical director.
  - ☐ Maintain and repair equipment as needed before and during the show.

NOTES ON THE STAGE MANAGER

Stage managers are a very important part of the theatrical process. In professional theatre, they take over the show once it opens. They call the show from the booth, and give actors notes after performances, ensuring that the director's vision for the show is maintained.

This may also happen in a college, university, festival or community theatre, but in high school theatre the stage manager will rarely have that level of responsibility. While having one present at all rehearsals is still very important and she/he may even call the show, generally the director remains very involved with the show throughout the run, and doesn't completely hand it over to a stage manager.

In a high school setting the stage manager might be another teacher, or a senior student, or both, with the teacher acting as a supervisor, but the student taking on most of the responsibilities. A teacher may also act as the mentor for the student stage manager, allowing the student full responsibility, but acting as a support. There may be several assistant student stage managers, dividing up the rehearsals and all the duties.

There are pros and cons to a student assuming the role of the primary stage manager.

Pros:

- It is possible to find students who are very competent and able to do the job. This may be easier to find than a fellow staff member willing to put in the extraordinary time required by the project.

- The student stage manager knows the cast, anticipating the needs of the actors.

- This position will give the student a wonderful opportunity to learn a valuable set of skills that will be applicable to many future careers.

- This position will allow for a high degree of involvement in the theatrical project by a student who is very keen, but does not wish to actually be on-stage.

Cons:

- The student is being asked to assume some authority over the cast. This doesn't have to be a bad thing, but care must be taken to pick the right student, who must be very clear about the role of the stage manager, and not use it as a means to exercise undue authority over fellow students.

QUALITIES OF A GOOD STAGE MANAGER

- Someone who is unfailingly polite, calm and accessible to everyone involved in the project, at all times. Stage managers are never allowed to be in a bad mood, gossip, bad-mouth anyone else on the project, or put down anyone at any time. The stage manager needs to be able to speak to cast members to remind them about rehearsal times, etc. with respect, but authority.

- Someone who will be the first to arrive at all rehearsals, setting up the room as required for that day's scene, and the last to leave and turn off the lights.

- Someone who can efficiently and effectively take notes on everything that the director says in a rehearsal; most importantly, the blocking for each scene, but also possible props, lighting and sound cues, and costume ideas. The stage manager should know the shorthand for stage positions and stage terms and be able to jot everything down clearly, so it can be repeated at a future rehearsal.

NOTES ON THE CHOREOGRAPHER

In a perfect world, there will be a professional choreographer hired to make your musical look great, with trained dancers taking the stage. However, in the real world of school and community theatre, there may be no budget for a choreographer, and willing, but largely untrained dancers to work with. I would make a case for spending money on a good choreographer, even if it means giving up something else in the budget. A young professional, looking for opportunities, may not be too expensive, and the results will be well worth it. There are many ways to help even non-dancers look great in movement sequences, and a good choreographer will be able to do so. However, in the event that your musical requires some dance, and no choreographer will be engaged, the Movement chapter contains some tips to create movement patterns that should help you produce something you can be proud of.

PROMPT BOOK

A prompt book is a script that contains all of the technical markings and stage directions for the show. Made by the stage manager and used throughout the rehearsal period, it (or a copy of it) is also used to "call" the show. Light and sound technicians will follow along with a script marked with their own cues. When calling the show, the stage manager (tech director, or whoever calls the show) will also give a warning for the sound and light cues by saying, "standby for light cue 5." This is done a line or two before the actual cue is called with, "light cue 5 go." The standbys may be included in the prompt book, but don't need to be, depending on the experience level of the stage manager. The prompt book will also be used for calling actors for entrances by giving standby directions to an assistant stage manager to give to the actor. The actor is then expected to be watching backstage for the moment of his entrance.

The prompt book contains:

The script itself

All stage directions (movements) for the actors – entrances, exits, crosses, etc.

All sound and lighting cues

Thumbnail sketches of the set with the position of the actors marked

- The sketches and any detailed instructions will be on the blank backside of the preceding page. Generally, a new sketch will be drawn for every change in the stage picture. Some stage managers prefer to put the dialogue on the left-hand side of the page, instead of the right. They put the sketches and notes on the right, as that is what is of primary interest to them.

- The technical directions (sound and light cues) will be in the margin of the script itself, lighting on the left-hand side, sound on the right – highlighted (and colour coded). They should be represented with the abbreviations SQ 1 and LQ 1, etc. The lighting cues are numbered separately from the sound cues. Music cues are part of the sound cues, as well as any sound that is technically created (not produced by actors).

- What a certain sound cue actually sounds like (i.e. SQ 1 – music, CD #2, track #3) is in a list of all the cues, on a separate page. Lighting cues are described in a separate chart, which will include the actual ID number of the lights used, and their level (brightness). Some info will be given in the script itself (i.e. LQ 6 – Blackout. SQ. 3 – Music fades out). Keep the description brief, out of the way of the SQ, or LQ itself.

- Directions for the actors will be within the script itself – highlighted.

- If the actual set doesn't change for many pages, the stage manager may want to draw it once and photocopy it onto blank pages, with the script copied on the backside of each page, in order to not keep drawing the same set for each page. For an uncomplicated set with little movement or few characters, it may just be drawn once for the beginning of each scene. For a large involved show, it might appear two or even three times on each page, in order to keep track of all the blocking for each character. Characters can be colour coded and their movements diagrammed on the set design sketches.

DIRECTING ACTORS

Directing young people, or any actors with little or no acting experience, can make your life very interesting. They may well bring a freshness and excitement to the process that will feed you and encourage you to work very hard on their behalf, creating the best, most brilliant production your community or school has ever seen. Or, without really considering what you are undertaking, or what will be required of you, it could turn into an exercise in frustration. In taking on the challenge of directing inexperienced actors, especially if your own experience is limited, it is a good idea to think about how you will do this before beginning the process.

DIRECTING STYLES

Is it important to identify your directing style? Maybe all you need to do is pick a play, cast it, show up for the first rehearsal, and see how things go. That might work, but trial and error can be costly. There is no single best way of directing a play, and ultimately, you must design the style that is best for you. With broad strokes, here are several common directorial styles, and how they might work in practice.

THE BOSS

This director leaves nothing to chance. He knows the play well and has a vision for it. Everything that happens on stage will be this director's idea. The Boss takes full responsibility for the play's success or lack thereof. Blocking is precisely planned for every minute of stage time. Years ago, in my theatre undergrad work at university, I was told that for every minute on stage I should spend one hour in preparation. I was to pre-plan everything that the audience would see in the final performance, including every move made by the actors. I was instructed to precisely communicate these instructions to my actors, who would (hopefully) breathe life into my vision for the play.

When to be the Boss
- When studying the play before rehearsals begin. Creating the vision for the play is your job: knowing what you want to

communicate to your audience and coordinating the look and feel of the project are all up to you. All aspects of the play should support the vision. The overall impression left by the piece should be focused and concise. Multiple people rarely achieve this successfully. You may have a small "directorial team" to coordinate this, but if random suggestions on the big picture issues are incorporated throughout the process, the end result is likely to come across as muddled and unfocused.

- When the blocking is set, and you need to get through a run. Experimenting has passed, and time is tight. The rehearsals must keep running smoothly.

- You are in the best position to know how a moment on stage is reading to the audience. This outside perspective is important and something actors can't have.

- When there is more than one choice that will work for a moment in the play. You can encourage experimentation, but finally you will make the choice.

- When one character's choice doesn't work for something else that is going on in the play, and it can only be played in a certain way to make that future scene work. This may be beyond the understanding of the actor in the first scene.

- When you are directing a musical with a chorus of thousands, or a crowd scene in a large cast play. The more you have thought about your stage pictures and where everyone should be, the easier that first blocking rehearsal will be for everyone. Once you have set up your stage pictures the actors can play with their reactions and small movements. Not having the blocking worked out for large crowd scenes before the rehearsal can be chaotic, and frustrating for everyone. With experience, like a great choreographer, you may well be able to set up your stage pictures spontaneously, with all the bodies in front of you, but before you reach that level of comfort, it is best to pre-plan. These ideas may change when you see what the actors have to bring to the process, but you will have a good place to start.

When NOT to be the Boss

- When first exploring the blocking for a scene, in that scene's first rehearsal. Giving the actors a chance to explore where to move or how to play it may open things up in interesting directions that you hadn't considered. At the very least, it will give your actors a feeling of ownership of their characters, and the project as a whole. This can be an exciting time in the rehearsal process, and it is worth building exploration time into your schedule. You know the play so well by the first rehearsal that you will have lots of ideas on how it can be blocked, but you are still willing to allow the actors to explore ideas as well.

Note: This does not mean that you allow for exploration and then, in the next rehearsal, tell all the actors what to do as if their ideas were never considered. Don't ask for input if you are unwilling to even consider some of the ideas you get.

- Ideally, allowing for exploration will result in a collaborative effort between the actors and their director. Ultimately, the Boss makes the final blocking decisions, but with plenty of input from the actors.

- When actors are first exploring their reactions to what other characters are saying, or exploring how their characters will say their lines. Resist giving an actor a 'line read', and asking for an imitation. You really don't want all the characters on the stage to be imitations of you. Each actor has something unique to bring to a character. Allow that to come out. If there is something specific you are after, you can ask your actors questions about their intentions at that moment, as that should be what affects how a line is said, but asking for imitations of lines or movements is a little death for the actor each time it is done.

THE COLLABORATOR

This director really wants the project to be a team effort. He does not want to stand apart from the actors, but truly collaborate with them. I've worked with directors like this, but have yet to find one that remained a collaborator from the very first rehearsal to the end of the process. Eventually, usually, this director makes decisions that at least coordinate the final look of the piece.

When to be a Collaborator:

- When blocking a scene for the first time, discussing characters and their relationships and in creating the backstory for the play.

- When making decisions that affect the whole group, but not the look of the play.

- When giving the students ownership of a project, but not control. You might give actors two choices on how to play something when both will work equally well.

- When rehearsing a project with a very small group of independent, experienced actors with a shared vision in an improvised work.

When NOT to be a Collaborator:

- When you have a play for a public performance. The play needs a vision, cohesion and focus, and someone (who is an outside eye, not immersed in the action on the stage) will need to make the decisions necessary to ensure that this vision is clear and engaging to an audience.

- In a non-scripted work with a larger group of actors, after the group has decided on a theme and vision. Decisions need to be made that support the group's vision.

- When the experimental phase of a project has ended and an end result is expected. The director can keep the rehearsals running productively and effectively. It's frustrating for the cast to feel that the project isn't progressing because the director is unwilling to make decisions.

THE RANTER

It is unlikely that there are any directors who would self identify as a Ranter; that person who yells and screams, thinking that is the best way to get a great performance out of student actors. Some directors fall into this category, unwittingly, at least some of the time, simply by allowing frustration with the actors' lack of focus and commitment to the project to come out as anger. The best way to guard against becoming the Ranter is to follow the preparation suggestions offered here, and then try to relax and stay calm. Inexperienced actors may not put as much energy into a rehearsal as the director might desire. It may result in the director believing that the actors don't remember what to do. It may look like they don't remember their lines. It results in directors loudly saying things like:

- It's not me that is going to look stupid up there on opening night!

- You expect your parents to pay good money to see this mess?

- I've had it! Why am I wasting my time when you refuse to take this seriously?

- Do you want me to cancel the whole production? Because that's just what I feel like doing right now!

- You were supposed to be off-book last week! You've been doing nothing but goofing off this whole rehearsal.

You get the idea. But, experience has taught me that young actors who don't always put a lot of visible effort into rehearsals can still pull off very good performances. Repeat after me: "I will never underestimate the power of teenage adrenalin to propel the performance once the curtain opens." They are likely much more prepared than they appear. As opening night approaches, everyone gets tired. It may be that your rehearsal schedule was actually a wee bit longer than it needed to be, and your actors are getting bored with doing the same thing over and over again. They may not be experienced enough to keep making little discoveries in every run-though to keep it fresh, and so their performances in those critical last rehearsals actually look like they are going downhill from where you thought you had gotten them. There are ways to keep it fresh (see PROBLEM SHOOTING DURING REHEARSALS). For your next show you can also fine-tune the amount of rehearsal time you need (see TIMELINES).

When to be a Ranter:

- I tell pre-service teacher/directors that they are allowed one meltdown during the rehearsal process. It must be saved for when you really, really need to wake up your cast. It cannot be too early in the game, because it will look like it came out of nowhere. The stakes aren't yet high enough. It will turn students off and not have a single positive effect on them. It must be close to opening night, once you have already struggled through several run-throughs and things are not going smoothly. Most importantly, it cannot be directed at individuals, as you do not want it to be taken personally by any one actor. It should focus on how YOU are feeling and stress your concerns about being unprepared to open the show. It cannot include any swearing or name-calling or anything else that will come back to bite you. I know, once you clean up a rant it is hardly worth delivering. Well, perhaps it isn't worth it. But, if one just happens to come out, don't beat yourself up for it. Remember the guidelines and keep it brief. One short, heartfelt, well-placed rant can produce the desired effect of the whole cast stepping it up a notch and focusing on the job at hand. But one, only ever one!

When NOT to be a Ranter:

- With only one rant per show, the time not to be a Ranter is the other 99.9 % of your contact hours with your actors. There are more effective ways of getting what you need from your cast than yelling, ranting or raving. Constant ranting results in actors either tuning out the director, or dropping out of the project.

THE MANIPULATOR

With the best of intentions, the Manipulator pushes buttons and challenges actors to use the pain of their own pasts to draw out the emotions of the characters. While this may indeed result in the actor giving an incredibly real and visceral reaction to the imaginary situation in the scene, it may come at a tremendous cost to the emotional stability of the young actor, who has just bared his or her soul. The Manipulator likely does not have the therapeutic skills to deal with the fallout. One must also consider whether the young actor has the skill needed to bring this out in every performance throughout the run, not to mention sustaining an emotionally stable state of being on and off the stage for the duration. Meisner said, "Acting is behaving truthfully under imaginary circumstances." Using his full technique can lead to solid performances, but all too often, emotional recall is the one emphasized. I have seen first-time actors in workshops give incredible, real and powerful performances by using this emotional recall technique. However, I doubt the neophyte's ability to use it safely or effectively when not assisted every step along the way, which brings into question its usefulness, and indeed, its ethical application with young actors in stage work. Manipulation is not to be confused with encouraging young actors to move beyond their comfort zones, to extend themselves in visualizing the imaginary world of their characters, and putting themselves in their places. The key word here is "imaginary."

When to be a Manipulator:

- There will be times to push an actor to reach deeper for a stronger choice in a scene, but again, this isn't so much manipulative as it is challenging the actor to raise the stakes for a character in a situation. The more important the outcome for the character, the stronger the reaction to a problem becomes.

- There may be times to encourage an actor to remember how something in his or her own life produced the same reaction as the character is now experiencing, but this must be used carefully and gently, and not taken to extremes.

When NOT to be a Manipulator:

- When exploring a character's response to a situation with young, vulnerable actors, encourage them to bring themselves to the role, but stay in the imaginary world of the play. It can be a fine line. Err on the side of caution.

THE FIGHTER

A close relative of the Manipulator and the Ranter, the Fighter wants to pick a fight with an actor whenever a character needs a strong or aggressive reaction to a situation. This often escalates into the director aggressively questioning everything the actor does. It might be that the Fighter is trying to bring about a desired effect in an actor's performance, or it might be that the Fighter simply thrives on confrontation and finds an adversarial atmosphere in the rehearsal hall to be exhilarating.

When to be a Fighter:

- When a strong aggressive reaction is needed and the actor is not investing in the situation. Like the soft-sell manipulation, the Fighter also needs to use very soft punching gloves and keep the actor in character.

- When the director can effectively play "devil's advocate" in a discussion over a character's response or a specific beat in the scene. This goes on only as long as it takes for the actor to make the necessary discovery.

When NOT to be a Fighter:

- When working through a situation in a scene, questions usually work effectively to encourage actors to explore where a character is going. If more is needed, there is likely a game or exercise that could aid in the discovery. It is only on rare occasions, if ever, that the Fighter needs to come out to play. If it becomes the standard operating procedure for the director, it will become personal, and the adversarial relationship created will poison the entire project.

TIPS: BRING OUT THE BEST IN ANY DIRECTOR

Know the play: As the director, you need to know the play better than anyone else in the production team. Read it over and over again, with a goal in mind for each reading. Remember that your very first read will be your closest experience to what your audience will have, as they see it for the first time. See it through their eyes as you read. Jot down those first reactions and any questions that the play raises for you, especially if there are things that are confusing to you. Consult this list as you move through the rehearsal process, to see if you have answered your own questions satisfactorily. For another read, focus on the plot, really understanding what happens, and in what order. Read it backwards, to see what preceded an important event and made it happen. Then read for each character in turn, to find their arc, objectives, strategies and stakes. (see Acting Technique and Scene Studies). Knowing your characters well will enable you to help your actors discover them. Read to find the things that are essential to the understanding of the play, and what aspects you may be able to add your own creativity to in the staging of the piece. Go through it to find all of the beats; the moments where something changes. Some directors will actually memorize the entire play. You may not go that far, but you do know it and understand it thoroughly.

Research: In addition to knowing the play well, do your research on the style of the play and the time period it is set in. There may be times you will switch the time period, but not before researching your chosen era to make sure that it will work with the script. Each period is its own world, with rules and societal norms that will dictate how people behave and the choices they make. It will ring false to the audience if they see characters move or act in ways that don't fit the world you have decided to inhabit.

Have a vision: What is this play going to communicate to the audience? What is it you want them to take away from this production? What will your personal take on the material be? How will you communicate this vision to your cast and crew? How will your audience understand and appreciate the vision you bring to the project?

Let your actors breathe: Theatre is a living, breathing art form. Unlike an artist creating a painting, theatre cannot be static. No two performances of the same play, done by the same actors, should ever be absolutely identical. You are here to train your actors to live in the moment-to-moment reality of the world of the play: to listen to each other, respond to what they are given, not to become robots. The performance of each individual will remain fluid within the set blocking of the piece.

Be generous with praise: Don't hesitate to tell your actors what you love in what they are doing in addition to the things you want to keep working on. If you don't tell them what you love, it may disappear in the next rehearsal, while the actors focus on what you wanted them to fix.

It's okay to have fun: Remember that this is a process and is not just about the fabulous production at the end. How you reach opening night should also be memorable; not for how miserable everyone was, but for how much fun it was to work and make discoveries together. Sometimes, especially after working through a very serious scene, the actors need to fool around a little and take a break. Rather than giving actors actual breaks, where they leave the theatre and take forever to get back and regain focus, I tell them to bring water and use the bathroom whenever they need to. If the rehearsal is only about two hours long, our breaks are the moments when we stop to laugh or play a game that demonstrates a point to be made in the story.

Keep your focus: How the rehearsals run is up to you. Keep your focus and know what you need to accomplish. Your tone of respect will be picked up in everyone's dealings with each other. Only call in the actors you know you will use. Students brought in and not used may well be disruptive to those trying to work.

HINT: Never call rehearsals for "leads" only in a school production. Use the character names from the play when posting your rehearsal schedules. The idea is to foster an ensemble feel, where everyone feels valued. Avoid using the word "lead," and certainly never use the word "star."

Don't be afraid to tell the truth – mostly: Communicate honestly with your actors as much as possible. They are counting on you to bring out their best performance. They need to make honest and specific choices and need you to call them out when they could be stronger. The "mostly" part is in reference to not hurting people's feelings; don't make it personal. It's no one's fault if something isn't working; just try something else.

Safety: Put safety first, always, no exceptions. Don't ask anyone to do something that might result in harm; physical, psychological or emotional. You need them to take risks on stage, but that refers to character choices, not daredevil moves. The cast needs a supportive and comfortable environment in order to put themselves out there.

Develop a relationship with your actors: Make eye contact; rather than standing over them, get down to their level. Really listen to their concerns and their ideas. If anyone is critical of you, it usually comes from an unmet need. If you sense tension, or receive a complaint, talk to the person, and find out what it is he or she needs. Reduce their fear of failing by telling them that this is a shared experience. You are all in it together.

GOOD BEGINNINGS: THE FIRST REHEARSAL

- Welcome the actors and remind them that they are all part of something wonderful. Everyone's part in this play is important to the whole. This is something that all of you will create together, as a team.

- Share your vision of the play, and the production.

  □ What is the story of the play? Describe the spine, or through-line of the story of the play. Keep it fairly short and engaging.

  □ Try to bring in some images that will communicate your vision to your cast. Are there paintings or photographs of the period you are going for, or the look you want to capture? Are there movie clips that will help? Is there some music you can play that will inform the tone of the play, or is there music that will set the period of the play?

  □ How will this story be brought to life? What style are you going for? Will it be very natural? Mannered? Abstract? Movement based, etc.?

  □ How do you want the audience to react to this production of this story? Do you want to evoke laughter, tears, thought, etc.?

  □ Will it be different in any way from what the audience might be expecting? Is it a classic play that is always performed in the same manner? Is that what you will follow, or do you have another idea of how it will be presented? How will it be different?

- What will you be expecting from them, your cast? What are the ground rules? What part does safety play in this production? What about courtesy and respect? It is important that actors are encouraged to keep their personal baggage out of the rehearsal hall. When they enter this space, it is about the play and the process of bringing this play to life. Any personal dramas they may have with other members of the cast have no place in this room.

- Do you want to develop a contract for them? Are there certain things that you want them to agree to
  - ☐ rehearsal times and dates
  - ☐ rules of conduct
  - ☐ late policy for rehearsals
  - ☐ policy concerning missing rehearsals

Do you need them to sign it; do you need their parents to sign it?

- Team spirit – you talked about it in your first point. What are you going to do to make it happen? Starting this and every rehearsal with a warm-up exercise is a good way to develop that group cohesiveness. As rehearsals progress, there may be specific exercises you will do to explore the world of the play, but in the beginning, you just want the actors working together, getting to know and trust each other. Lots of theatre games will work well. If they don't know each other, start with name games.

- That might be the end of your first meeting, or, you may go on to do a table read of the play, or discussion about its story. Having the whole cast sit down together and read through the play may or may not be a great idea. Some young people are not comfortable reading aloud if the material is new. Have they had their scripts long enough to be comfortable with their lines? Is it Shakespeare, or another classical play with difficult language? Will the actors feel embarrassed at how they are reading in front of other cast members? More importantly, reading through the whole play with all of the actors present may not set the right tone for the rehearsal process. If the play has a few leads, and many tiny parts, a table read will only help reinforce what, in the minds of the actors with tiny parts, is the star system of this play. That will not aid the team spirit that you worked so hard to build. It might be better to leave the reading of each scene to the first rehearsal for that scene, which will naturally only include the actors involved in it.

DIRECTING THE ACTORS

BLOCKING

There is no right or wrong way to begin the blocking of scenes, but here is a process to try.

- Read through the scene together.
- Talk about what is happening in this scene. Talk about why the characters are here at this time, and what they want from each other. Some directors like to limit talk and perform improvisations instead. In going through the scene in their own words, you are able to see what they understand of the scene.
- Talk about what happened to these characters in the moments before this scene begins. This may not be the actual previous scene in the play. It may not even be in the play, but occur to the characters "offstage." It is important to know this in order to understand the characters' states of mind and motivations when they first begin this scene. This could also be done through improvisation instead of talking.
- Have the actors walk through the scene, following their own impulses to move.
- Talk about what worked, and what motivated their movements. Every move that an actor makes should be motivated by his need to pursue his objective. More simply put, he should only move if he has a reason to move. Sometimes, you need an actor to move to accommodate some other stage business that is about to occur in another area. In that case, help the actor to justify the movement for himself.
- You may want to use some exercises to clarify the characters' relationships, or discover the beats and changes in the scene. The actions and intentions are very important, but will not all be discovered in this first blocking rehearsal.
- Go through it many more times, stopping to try new movements or clarify moments until you feel you have achieved what you need for the blocking of the scene. Again, this may well take more than just one rehearsal.
- At some point in the rehearsal process have the characters walk through the set and touch everything in it. Help them to find their relationship with the set and the objects on it. Is

the character in his own home, in a stranger's office, at a new lover's apartment? How is the character relating to everything in this environment? How much of it should he touch in the course of the scene? How comfortable is he with what he touches? In the first rehearsal the set may be almost bare. As rehearsals progress, make decisions about what needs to be there, not only for the look of the stage, but for the actors to relate to as their characters.

- Have the stage manager record the blocking that has resulted from the first rehearsal in the prompt book, as well as any props that may be needed.

- In subsequent rehearsals, you and the actors should remain open to changes being made, but there will be a framework in place to build on.

BLOCKING TIPS

- Establish relationships with different levels. Generally, a seated person will have less prominence (or status) than one standing, unless the seated person is surrounded by standing people, in which case he will pop in contrast to them.

- Pay special attention to the stage pictures you create at very important turning points in the play. Consider that picture as an artist would consider a painting. Find those moments and make them memorable.

- Establish certain spots on the stage that have an emotional resonance for certain characters, a place where that character goes to ponder life, for example.

- First-time actors may need to learn the basic rules of the stage, including not blocking other actors, remaining open to the audience (one foot is always pointing to the audience), and turning towards downstage at the end of a cross, to maintain openness to the audience. All rules can be broken, but only with a reason.

STAGE DIRECTIONS

What to do with the script's stage directions! There are varying opinions about how to handle the directions occurring in a script. It is clear that Meisner paid them no mind, as the sample scripts in his book show them to all be crossed out. There have been directors and teachers who black them out of scripts before giving them to students. They believe that it is up to the director and actors to interpret a play for themselves, finding new ways to move and react. Some people believe that all stage directions are merely the staging ideas of the first director from the first production of a play, and don't come from the playwright at all. That is an urban myth that is hopefully no longer believed. Just look at all the plays that are published before a first production to dispel that idea. Most playwrights would be irate at the suggestion that they aren't important. They are most certainly part of the script, put there by the playwright. You will not find them in classical plays because the playwrights generally were present at rehearsals and could verbalize them to their casts. Also, they would not have had any expectation of publication, and therefore didn't see the need to write them in. You may assume that all the stage directions you find in a script are part of the playwright's effort to tell the story of the play. Try playing Pinter after blacking out all of the directions to "pause," or moments of "silence." What would the end of Beckett's *Waiting for Godot* be without the final stage direction? One character says, "Shall we go?" The other replies, "Yes." The stage direction says, "they do not move." The end.

There are two types of stage directions:

- Production Information: setting the stage, character descriptions, the relationship between characters, entrances and exits, scene and act divisions, and so forth.
- Actor Direction: telling an individual actor where to go, what to do, how to react.

The directions are there to further your understanding of the story and its characters. Directors need to follow the spirit of the directions, interpreting and implementing them in ways that convey the playwright's story. It may not always be practical or possible to follow them to the letter. A play must work on your stage, for example, and you may not be able to set it up exactly as the playwright envisions it, but it should have the intended feel. Actor's directions will give the actor the playwright's intentions for that character, but the actor will bring herself to the character in her interpretation of these directions. As a playwright, I certainly do include stage directions, but I try to keep them to a minimum, describing only what is absolutely necessary for the understanding of the story. I do see play production as a collaboration, and want any future director to have some degree of freedom in creating the stage picture of my ideas.

PROBLEM SHOOTING DURING REHEARSALS

There are many tips in the ACTING TECHNIQUE and SCENE STUDY chapters on how to help actors approach a scene. Here are some additional tips that may act as a springboard to solving problems in a scene.

Something Doesn't "Feel" Right for the Actor, or the Director

- **Ask questions:** Find out what doesn't feel right to the actor. Is it the blocking that you have asked the actor to use? Is it something she is getting from another character that she doesn't understand? Identify the nature of the problem.

- **Talk about the moment before:** What is her character responding to in the action of the play? Where did this uncomfortable moment originate?

- **Objectives:** What does she (her character) want in this scene? What is she doing to get it? Is what she is doing working? Maybe she isn't going for it strongly enough. Help find a more important reason for her to want it.

- **Play it "wrong":** When something doesn't feel right for the actor, it may be related to the choices that were made. Have her play the scene making opposite choices. This can help clarify just what is right for that moment. Perhaps a different stage action is needed. If she moved towards another character on a certain line, have her move away instead. Play with the moment, keeping the character's intention (what does she want?) first and foremost in importance.

- **Play a game:** Sometimes, when things just aren't going well, but it's hard to define the problem, playing a game can clarify what is going on for the characters. For example, a scene that is supposed to have tension between the characters might benefit from a short game of one-on-one basketball (could be mimed or real). Perhaps an improvisation with other characters (or animals) would help define the relationship between these characters. Take the actors out of their heads and into their imaginations, in order to look at it a new way.

- **Breathe:** It sounds obvious, but sometimes actors need to be reminded to breathe. It is difficult to focus, concentrate and respond effectively if an actor is tense and holding his breath. Another problem is the huge exhale to show frustration or some other intention. A heavy sigh can take all of the energy out of a scene. Find another way of channelling that intention into another, more productive action and using it to drive the scene, give it energy.

- **Body:** Is the actor's entire body involved in the scene, or is he acting only from the neck up? A need to relax may be part of it, or there may be some nervous extraneous twitching, pacing or shifting of weight that the actor is unaware of, but is very distracting. Find a playable action that has a purpose and becomes something the actor needs to do to meet an objective.

An Actor Isn't Believable

You cast with care, to get the actors that you thought could be natural and interesting on stage, but now, well into the rehearsal process, you don't believe the performance.

- **Listen:** Ensure that the actor is really listening to the other characters, rather than simply waiting for his next line. Ask the other actor to be unpredictable and give him something different a few times, to wake him up and force a new reaction to honestly occur. Talk about what that looked and felt like, encourage it to remain.

- **Focus:** Sometimes actors are not believable because they are focused on themselves, and whether or not they are doing a good job. The more they focus on themselves and try to "act" better, the worse they become. The answer is to keep encouraging them to focus on the other actors, to really look at them and try to gauge whether what they themselves are doing is having an impact on the others. This is the most important aspect of going for an objective. It isn't merely one's own stage action that is important, but whether that action is hitting home and changing the other character. When that becomes their focus, they will lose their own self-conscience performances and become real in the scene.

- **Surprise him:** If an important action has become robotic and routine, find a way of surprising the actor. For example: the character comes on stage and must find and pick up a gun, and point it at another character. This action is essential to the playing of the scene, but the actor doesn't seem to really be into it, or is unbelievable in his search for the gun. Have the actor take a short break, and hide the gun a short distance from where he expects to find it. Now, he really will have to look for it. Repeat the exercise if necessary, until he is able to retain that sense of urgency and truth in looking for it, even after he knows where it will be.

- **Brain engagement:** Give the actor a mathematical problem to solve while the scene is running. Do not allow him to pause to figure out the answer before speaking his lines. Ask for the answer when the scene ends. This will result in brain activity being visible. It is so much more interesting to see an engaged character than an actor who has turned off his brain to play the character. This same engagement must be there every moment of every performance, even when there is no longer a math problem to solve. An actor needs to be present.

- **Raise the stakes:** Talk about why he needs to meet his objective. If that choice leaves the character feeling fine if he doesn't meet it, the choice isn't strong enough. Make it life or death. He must really need to make it happen.

- **Energy:** If the performance lacks energy, have him jump up and down or run on the spot before entering for the scene. Get his heart racing with the excitement his character needs to experience in the scene.

An Actor Is Having Difficulty Finding the Character

- **Talk about it:** Have a discussion on who this character is. Are there people in real life that are like this character? I would suggest that actors speak about their characters in the first person, becoming their characters in discussions. Instead of saying, "I think she wants to hurt him, because...", encourage the actor to say, "I want to get him out of here, because...". The reason for this is simple. When speaking about characters in the third person, it is easy to judge them. Actors must LIKE the characters they play, even the nasty ones. They have to find acceptable reasons for their nastiness and not judge their actions or motives. Judging a character negatively makes it very difficult to play him truthfully.

- **Character sketch:** Have actors write character sketches to explore who they are (see CREATING A CHARACTER). They may work with a Dominant Body Part, an Effort Action, or find the character's colour or animal, all providing something physical for the actor to work with. Then look for what the character wants to accomplish.

- **Improvisations:** It may be helpful to improvise situations that could have happened before the action of the play begins. This will provide an actor with the character's backstory, explaining why she thinks and behaves as she does in the play. You could also improvise scenes that are not part of the play, but help to fill in some details that assist with understanding the character. This will be particularly helpful in working out relationships between characters.

- **Journals and letters:** An actor can keep a journal, as the character, to explore her thoughts and feelings. Actors can also write letters to other characters in order to explore relationships.

- **Relationships:** Sometimes one can define oneself in reference to another character. "He is the one that ___". Maybe this actor is in her own head too much, and needs to focus on the other character on stage, and the effect she wants to have on him.

- **Objects:** What is on the stage that the character relates to? Are there objects that this character would enjoy interacting with that can be brought to the set? The character needs a relationship to the objects she uses, as well as the people she interacts with. The right prop may help ground her in the character.

- **Actions:** Ultimately, it is what she DOES that is important in the scene, and will define her. Help her find her actions (motivated by her desires) and she will find herself.

The Scene Is Flat

Sometimes, even though characters are motivating their movements and everything looks correct, it isn't very interesting.

- **Surprises:** Find a way to surprise the audience. Switch up something that they expect to happen in the stage action. This might be something very small, and will not change the lines or blocking, but will be an unexpected moment. Perhaps the robber tips his hat to his victim before exiting the stage, or a mistress unexpectedly turns and starts to leave before changing her mind and running into her lover's arms. Try not to be predictable in every moment of the stage action. Just ensure that your surprise works within the world you have created.

- **Characters' individual qualities:** As the director, have you paid attention to the differences between your characters? Is everyone playing their roles with more or less the same energy levels, movement styles and gestures, voice inflections, and so on? Go back to the chapter on Character and find everyone's Effort Action, as a start to finding the differences between the characters. Each character should be an individual. Also, watch out for actors who are chameleons, taking on the voice inflections and mannerisms of their scene partners.

- **Find the levels:** Make sure that the scene isn't being played on only one note. Find the levels. What is the arc of the scene? Where are the changes?

- **Find the humour:** This isn't about telling jokes, but subtly allowing humour to colour something. Even a very serious scene will have some humour under the obvious surface of the lines. Finding it can bring more truth to the scene.

- **Find the sex:** It has been said that every scene is about the sex. Once you've identified where the sexual energies lie, you'll have the scene. That is an oversimplification, of course, and not every scene is about sex. What this really means is that it is important to discover the chemistry between the characters. If the scene is flat, is it possible that this is the missing ingredient? Are there sparks of aversion or attraction that have not been explored? How could they be subtly translated into actions?

Directing the Audience's Gaze:

You want the audience to notice something specifically on stage, but it doesn't seem to be working. Unlike film, where a cut to a close-up will do the trick, how do you make the audience notice what is important?

- Use strong stage positions: Where you place important action, or important characters on stage is extremely important. Having the important bits happen closer to the audience is obvious, but it is more than just moving things downstage. Some directors see the downstage right position as the most important one on stage, as we read from left to right. I disagree that this is the case. While beginning a cross from stage left might be the stronger choice, I believe that centre stage is the strongest static position. The audience's eye is naturally drawn to what is happening in the middle, not the periphery. Something placed in the middle can be framed, or flanked in such a way as to draw attention to it. If the important character is alone, or in a small group, downstage will be strongest. If there are more characters, slightly upstage is better, as the other actors can "give focus" (see next point), to the important one. Raising a character can also make her more important. There is a reason that a throne is placed on a dais above the common folk, at the end of a symmetrically decorated room. The same principle can work on stage.

■ Give focus: Whatever characters on stage are looking at will draw the audience's gaze as well. It is the same principle as looking up to the sky because people on the street corner are doing so. If something important is about to happen in a scene, have characters on stage look at the spot.

■ Lighting: If using stage lights, it is easier to make something stand out by putting a light on it, making it brighter than the surrounding area.

The Scene Is Dragging:

Pacing is so important to every play. Almost no scenes are better played entirely slowly. It may be as simple as picking up the pace, but how do you do that effectively and repeatedly? And is it that simple?

■ **Rhythm:** Like a fine piece of classical music, a play needs rhythm. In a well-written play, this may naturally emerge and be easy to find, but often, you need to really look for the play's rhythm, or impose one. It cannot be a single pace from start to finish. There must be sections that are slow (very small ones) and others that speed up. No play will be well served by being played at the exact same tempo throughout. Find the levels.

■ **Timing:** Especially in comedy, the timing of lines is important. Some actors have a sense about when to pause for a millisecond, and when to rush through to the next line, but many must be led through it. Experiment with what makes a line delivery funny. Generally, a tiny pause before a laugh line will help set it up, but each play is different. If something isn't funny that should be, look at the timing.

■ **Pace:** A quick pace is needed if there is to be a sense of energy to a piece. This is not to be confused with running words together and making the actors difficult to understand. It generally refers to the picking up of cues. Also, you will sometimes need to suggest that your actors think ON their lines, rather than pausing to do so. Not every pregnant pause that feels good reads well to the audience. Sometimes, it just slows down the action.

■ **Cues:** Further to picking up the cues; this can sometimes mean that you suggest the actors try to cut each other off. If told to start their lines right before the last actor finishes his, they will likely give you the pace you are looking for. They will not actually cut each other off, but will get rid of the pauses between cues. This wouldn't be something that the entire play is likely to need, but rather saved for those short sections that really need to move.

- **Laughs:** Actors do need to learn how to handle laughs given to them by the audience. In some plays, laughs will be unexpected, or come at different times on different performances of the same play. The actors can't ignore the laugh and plough on through to the next line, but they also can't stop and wait for absolute silence, as that would destroy the rhythm and energy of the piece. The trick is to start talking at the crest of the laugh, just as it is beginning to subside.

- **"Italians":** These are run-throughs done at unnaturally fast speeds. Sometimes casts are reminded of their lines by sitting down and doing an Italian run of the lines, minus the action. However, it can also be extremely useful to do an Italian up on its feet, running through a scene, or even the entire play at breakneck speed. Often this results in some sections remaining much quicker than previously rehearsed, and can help to find unnecessary pauses. At the very least, it will pick up the energy, which might be all that is missing from a scene.

The Scene Is Crowded with Characters and Seems Muddled.

A large cast play will become very much about the blocking, while a two-hander will be more about the relationship between the two characters. The blocking in a large cast play may become about how to create relationships between all of the individual characters, as well as creating interesting stage pictures that tell the story clearly.

- **Bring out the important people in a larger scene:** Are there times when most of the cast on stage should be in the background, while a two-character part of the scene is going on? Choreograph the action so that this can happen naturally, rather than leaving the stage picture static throughout. Be careful to let this flow, using various parts of the stage, rather than always going to a specific downstage spot for all of those breakout moments. Sometimes they could be upstage, with other characters framing the actors and giving them focus.

- **Stage pictures are tableaux:** At any moment you could call for the actors to freeze, giving you an opportunity to examine the current stage picture to make sure that the tableau is reading correctly (see DESIGN PRINCIPLES, TABLEAUX). It may also be a simple matter of balance. There may be moments where you want the literal balance of the stage picture to be off kilter, and other moments when you need the stage to be balanced. All stage action is a huge series of tableaux. Each one should have a purpose and lead the audience in a direction that is consistent with the theme of the play and the director's vision of it.

- **Pantomime:** If there is a lot of stage movement by a large cast, it may be helpful to do a run-through without words, to ensure that everyone knows where they are supposed to be at all times in relationship to everyone else. This will naturally move much more quickly than when lines are spoken, and be much more challenging, but might prove to be useful in directing the action and improving the traffic flow. It will help the actors to be more aware of where they are in relation to everyone else.

- **Ball toss game:** Go through the scene with a ball or beanbag. Each character tosses the object to the next person to speak at the end of his or her line. It will clarify the relationships and proximity of the characters for you. Are the characters where you need them to be to show their relationships within the scene?

It Is Close to Opening Night, and Energies Are Starting to Flag.

Sometimes the play is ready for an audience a little earlier than expected, or even though it isn't ready, the energy and focus of the cast leaves something to be desired. Perhaps, rather than a speech to pep them up, there are exercises that will naturally do this.

- **Novelty runs:** Novel ways of running the play will energize the cast. They can also act as a catalyst to find new ways of playing a scene. They can work so well, you may want to leave room in your rehearsal schedule to use some of them. For example:
  - □ **Pantomime:** It isn't only good to work out traffic jams in the blocking. Running the whole play in pantomime is hugely challenging and a lot of fun. The goal could be to run the entire full-length play in less than 15 minutes. This may energize the cast before a real run-through of the play.

- **Italian:** Like the pantomime, an Italian run can serve a double purpose, tightening the pace and energizing the cast that has become complacent.

- **Switch roles:** Just for fun, run a favourite scene with everyone switching roles. They may not get through the whole thing, but it will be good for a laugh and an energy boost.

- **Music:** Find suitable music for a favourite scene and run it like a dance, but with dialogue. This might also work well for a difficult scene, earlier in the rehearsal process.

- **Sing the lines:** This isn't relevant for a musical, but for a play, singing through a favourite scene, with the actors making up the tunes, would be fun. A style may be agreed upon, or it could be left to the individual to decide if his character is a country singer, an opera singer or a rock star. This may also help in finding the mood or tone for a problematic scene.

- **Gibberish:** Instead of using the lines, a favourite or difficult scene is played with all actors using gibberish, their own made-up language. They will really need to concentrate to keep the through-line of the scene.

- **Style:** A scene, or the whole play could be played in a new style or genre. It could be played like a scene from an action movie, or Shakespearean drama, or soap opera, or any other style that is familiar to the cast.

- **Games:** Play a favourite energizing game at the beginning of the rehearsal. **STAGES: Creative Ideas for Teaching Drama** is loaded with suitable warm-ups, or cast members might suggest their favourites.

- **Celebration:** Have a short celebration before a run. The celebration should be suited to the world of the play, like Christmas morning, or a character's birthday party. Cast members might exchange short notes or small gifts, or have theme-related songs or food. Actors stay in character throughout the exercise.

An Actor Can't Be Heard!

Everything seemed fine in the rehearsal hall, but now that you are on the real stage, some of the actors cannot be heard when you sit in the back row, and that's without a live audience absorbing the sound! Don't panic. There are things you can do.

- **Know the house:** Don't let the performance space and what it needs acoustically come as a surprise to you. Visit it early or see another performance in it if possible before you begin rehearsals. Study it and know what it needs. A small black box theatre allows for intimate performances that require only slightly elevated voice levels. This is vastly different from a large auditorium with lots of hard smooth surfaces and a high ceiling. Unless you are in a building that was designed to be a theatre, there are likely to be challenges, and even in a theatre, projection may be an issue.

- **Voice exercises:** If you have access to your actors for a long enough period of time, use voice exercises to train them (see VOICE). Basically, the voice should be pushed from the diaphragm, not the throat. If an actor tries to raise his volume by straining from the throat alone, the quality of his voice will suffer, as will his throat. He may not last through the run.

- **Share, don't yell:** Talk about projecting as sharing with the audience, communicating with them, rather than simply increasing the volume. If rehearsing in a small space, be aware of this issue early in the process, and sometimes run scenes with the actors standing at opposite ends of the room, rather than close together on stage. Have them try for the same intimate level of communication that they experienced when they were close together, but make sure that their words reach each other. Once you are close to opening, bring that same volume back to the rehearsal, even if the director is only inches from the action, and there is no auditorium to project into at the moment.

- **Slow down, pronounce words clearly:** This is important to recognize early in the rehearsal process. If a character is mumbling his words from the beginning, or running them together, you know that this will be a problem on stage. Fix it early.

- **On stage:** If it is too late for any of the advice above, and dress rehearsal left you wondering how an audience will hear certain actors, work with those actors who need to improve outside of the rehearsal time, on their own. Stand near the back of the auditorium and offer them feedback as they go through their lines. Encourage diaphragm support and ask them to communicate with you as you say their scene partners' lines from the back of the house. Offer lots of praise as they improve to ensure that their confidence in their performances aren't shattered before opening night.

FINAL TIPS

During Rehearsals:

- **Use the actors you call:** I've already mentioned to only call those actors to rehearsals that you know you will use. If it is becoming obvious that you will not use an actor again before the scheduled end of the rehearsal, do send that actor home early. If you have notes for her, save them for the next rehearsal.

- **Playing favourites:** It is important that all the actors feel special, and don't perceive that you are favouring certain cast members over others. This is especially important if an actor was a friend of yours before being cast.

- **Corrections:** Discourage actors from correcting each other. It is possible that one sharp actor will remember a note you previously gave better than another, or has a great idea for how another actor could play a scene. Encourage them early to bring any great ideas for another actor, or issues with them, to you privately. Make sure that the only directorial voice the actors hear is yours. This also applies to assistant directors or stage managers. No one corrects an actor but you. Professionals know this, but sometimes amateurs need reminding.

- **Use the right technique at the right time:** Be aware of which techniques to use throughout the rehearsal process. For example, calling in all the actors one at a time, for a chat about their characters, may work well in the beginning stages of the rehearsal process, but may not be appropriate in a later rehearsal, when the rest of the cast is waiting to do a run-through.

- **Self-indulgence:** Before trying something out in a rehearsal, simply ask yourself if it is something that would just be fun for you, or make you look like a great director, or if it would really help the actors and make the play better. Sometimes lengthy pre- or post-run speeches fall into that category. Be sure that they are focused and to the point.

- **Notes:** Directors need to know when to let a scene run and give notes at the end and when to try new things out on the spot. The most effective technique is to stop the actors as often as needed in the early stages, to allow them to experiment with new ideas as they occur to you, or to them.

Save the giving of notes until actual run-throughs of at least a full act. If you let a single scene run right through, then give notes of things to watch for and try to do differently, only do so if you have time to run the scene again in the same rehearsal. Don't give notes for things to try in the next rehearsal, if that rehearsal is days away. It can be brought up at the next rehearsal and tried out. Once you are into run-throughs, you will be interested in seeing how the scenes flow together, so taking notes and giving them to the actors at the end of the process makes sense, rather than stopping them frequently. Always be brief and to the point in your notes. No cast wants to sit through endless notes at the end of a long rehearsal. Most directors will point out that if something doesn't come up in the notes, it means that there isn't a problem with it. Nonetheless, it is good to also hand out praise for something that worked especially well, in addition to the things that need looking at.

In rehearsal run-throughs, it is fine to give notes to the entire cast, collectively. Once the play has opened, notes are for mistakes that were made, and should only be given to the individuals involved.

On Stage:

- **Blackouts:** Be very careful in your use of blackouts between scenes. I would almost say to never use them, but there may be a few exceptions when they are absolutely necessary, for a big surprise reveal, for example. Generally, ANYTHING, including stagehands moving furniture, is more interesting for the audience than sitting there in the dark. The same principle applies to closing the curtains. Every time you close the curtains or turn off the lights, you lose the audience for a moment and the world of your play disappears. When the lights come on and the action resumes, you have to earn their attention all over again. A fabulous production will do that, but most will struggle at least a little every time.

- **Scene changes:** Speaking of moving the furniture, think about creative ways of accomplishing that. Is a separate stage crew, dressed in black, the best way to go for a particular production? Can actors themselves reset the stage as one scene flows into the other? Every production will have its own solution, but do put some thought and planning into how to do it best.

- **Sightlines:** Be aware of the sightlines for your auditorium while you are blocking the stage action, and be sure to check it once you get to the stage. You don't want important action to be staged where a portion of the audience will miss it.

- **Technology:** Using video, interesting lighting, music and anything else not done by live actors can be wonderful, but must serve the play as a whole. Rather than overshadow the actors, it should enhance them and the production.

- **Pre-show:** What the audience sees and hears as they enter the auditorium is important to capture their attention and set the mood for your play. Do you want to make them feel sombre and serious or happy and bubbly? Which will put them into the right mood to best appreciate the production? Will the audience see a curtain? If so, the music you choose is even more important. If they will see the stage, what will be on it and how will it be lit to achieve the desired effect?

- **Vision:** Stay true to your vision. You thought it through and planned it well. Don't get side-tracked and put something into the play that doesn't belong there. Make specific choices. Don't wander away from the style that you chose. Find many levels, rather than playing the entire piece on one note, but stay within your style. Be especially careful of things that are very clever just for the sake of cleverness. It is your job to tell the story, as clearly and truthfully as you can.

- **Mistakes happen:** No matter how prepared everyone is, actors and crew are human, and mistakes can happen. Warn your actors about this, and set the rule that no matter what happens, they will not break character. Actors can forget a line, even in scenes where that line was never forgotten in a rehearsal. If the pause is long enough for another actor to notice, that actor should think about how she can help. Is there a question she can ask that will bring out his forgotten line? Can the action move on without that line? Somehow, that moment must be gotten through. If all actors are staying in the moment-to-moment reality of the play, mistakes will be corrected, and most times the audience will never notice that a misstep was made. The actor needs to put it behind him immediately and focus on the rest of the scene. It goes without saying that having someone prompt from the wings is not an option. The audience is immediately taken out of the world of the play, and actors may become lazy and rely on the prompter. Once the play opens, they are on their own on stage. It is up to them to make the magic happen.

LEARNING THE LINES

There is so much more to a great performance than just learning the lines, but, as they must be learned, here are a few techniques to help make that happen. They can be used in the classroom, for scene studies, or adapted to the rehearsal hall for a production.

Memorization Tips:

Depending on the learning style of the individual, the following techniques could be helpful:

- Write out the lines, longhand, on the computer, or both – more than once. Writing longhand uses a different part of the brain than typing the words. Many of us type so well that we really don't have to think about what we are typing, making this exercise more effective if we do it with a pen on paper.

- Make an audio recording of the whole scene, with both characters' lines. Leave a short gap between the lines, so you can start to anticipate what your next line will be. Or, make a recording of only the other characters' lines, with a gap in which to say your own.

- Use a bookmark to cover your next line. Read the other character's line, then try to say your own before uncovering it.

- Speeding through. In this technique, the premise is that if you learn to say the lines right through as fast as possible, you are creating a memory loop that goes directly to the muscles of your mouth, using the part of your brain called the cerebellum. You bypass the cerebral cortex, where thought takes place, and make the lines come out automatically. This is especially useful for monologues, implanting the words as a motor memory. Once mastered, you can slow them down and look at them for intent in a rehearsal process.

- Listen. The MOST important tip for memorizing lines is to really LISTEN to the other actors on stage with you. Remember that your character is in relationship with the other characters. By really listening to what the other characters' lines are, you will start to understand why your character says what she does.

- Make connections between a word or phrase said by the other character and the response given by yours. If the other character asks a question it is easier, as you respond with an answer, but if it is a statement, you can still find something to relate to, that can remind you of what your next line is. Maybe it's a colour or something that reminds you of something personal, or anything else that can act as a trigger. Once the line is no longer a problem spot, the trigger will be forgotten, and should not interfere with the action of the play, or the intent of the line. For example:

  Character A: Ever since I was a kid, I've dreamed of doing this.

  Character B: I've lived a long time and seen a lot of players come and go. I think you've got what it takes, if you can just stick to it.

  Character B is reminded to start with "living a long time" as soon as he hears character A say "kid" – the opposite of age and longevity. He may also be making a connection with both dialogues beginning with "I've" – the character talking about himself, his own thoughts. The reference doesn't have to be very clear or direct, or even shared aloud, as long as it makes sense to the actor playing character B.

  This is not to be confused with finding meaning in the words or relationships. It is only a means to help remember specific lines as opening night approaches and some sections just don't want to stick.

- Find hints in the words. In order to get your lines word perfect, find figures of speech, like alliterations, within the line. For example:

  "Wait a minute. So what you are saying is that you wouldn't be here now if you didn't think that it was a wonderful idea?"

  "That is, I suppose, the most sensible idea so far."

  Or, if what you are saying can form a list, memorize it like a list. For example:

"Once I get out of this place, I'm going to live like a king, eat anything that I want to eat, fly to all the places I've never seen and pretend that I don't have a care in the world."

List: live eat fly pretend

Or, for longer passages and monologues, group the ideas into like categories, and create a list of the categories, or create an acronym from the first letter of each new idea. These techniques are great for areas of the script that are routinely forgotten, or lines that get mixed up in their placement in relation to other lines.

- Relate the lines to the actions of the blocking. Once the lines are attached to a specific action – a movement on stage, or location on the set, as well as what the actor is getting from the other characters on stage – it will be easier to remember them. This is why most actors will only start to truly memorize a scene once the blocking has been set. While this is true for stage acting, it isn't practical when acting on-camera, as there may be no more than one or two rehearsals of the scene before shooting it.

- Say the words out loud as you work on them. Hearing yourself say them, and forming the words, is so much more effective than reading them silently to yourself. Just make sure that you either say them neutrally, or in a large variety of ways, stressing different words in the sentences each time and changing intentions, so as not to get stuck thinking about each line in only one way.

Additional Hints

- Along with whatever technique is used to memorize lines, suggest that your actors read them over again just before falling asleep at night. This is when the brain is most relaxed and can absorb the ideas, and, as they fall asleep, the lines have a chance to sink in and stay there, as no other activities will take their place. While they sleep, their brains do some reorganizing of the information they have put in there. In the morning, ask them to go through the script once more, when nothing else has crowded in to take the place of the lines.

- Lines must be learned over a period of time. An actor may be able to keep even a relatively long set of lines in his short-term memory and use them successfully in a film shoot, but stage work requires that they stay there, in sequence, until the end of the run. That's more than short-term memory can manage.

■ You may want to consider suggesting that your students learn their lines without emotion, as you don't want them to develop rhythms and intonations out of context. In fact, you don't want them to develop rhythms at all. The intent behind the lines comes from exploring them in the context of the scene. A performance is a living, breathing entity, and line delivery should reflect the nuances of what an actor picks up from the other characters on stage. Even by closing night, new discoveries can still be made which will affect a performance subtly, if the actors are playing the moment-to-moment reality of the play.

■ If they get into habits when learning lines alone, they may not actually LISTEN to their scene partners or what they are being given. This is a good reason to use some exercises to explore their scenes early in the process (see SCENE STUDIES). Many of these exercises can be done with scripts in hand, and should be done before actors go home to learn their lines in isolation.

■ Even after rehearsals are well under way and actors are off book, it is a good idea for them to occasionally go back to the text, to make sure that they haven't substituted some words here or there of their own, or left out something so often that it has been forgotten. This may not be much of a concern in a full-scale production with a stage manager at hand to remind them, but may pose a problem in smaller productions and class scene work, when actors are sometimes working on their own.

■ Make sure that the actors understand what they are saying. There may be words or references that are unfamiliar to them. This may be a problem in a period piece, and most especially in Shakespearean drama. If the actor doesn't understand the words, there is no way of making the intent of the line clear to the audience.

■ Understand the transitions from one beat to another. This is where actors can get stuck in their memorization of the text, as they are bringing in new thoughts or introducing new actions that aren't referenced in the previous text.

PRE-SHOW WARM-UPS

In my first book, **STAGES: Creative Ideas for Teaching Drama,** the warm-up section, ENERGIZING EXERCISES, is huge, covering all sorts of activities to get participants moving and engaged. Most are in the form of a game, with rules and a structure. All are great for having a group get to know and trust each other, and I would encourage their use at all levels of training when new groups form and must create a community.

I also encourage the use of **STAGES'** energizing circle exercises in all rehearsal and pre-show situations. Each group will likely have their favourites, remembered from classroom training. The warm-ups that follow are supplementary to those in **STAGES.** They help centre actors and share group and individual energies. They are meant for those last few minutes, when the group needs to connect one last time, before going off to focus themselves for the call of "places" before a public performance.

PRE-SHOW WARM-UPS

Any of the exercises from the voice chapter may be done to prepare voices right before a performance. Of course, a musical will demand a more extensive vocal warm-up. Actors may also be encouraged to do their own vocal warm-ups after a group exercise. For a quick vocal warm-up before a play, where voices will be used, but no singing takes place, the group may enjoy singing a round song, which will warm up voices and share energy. **STAGES** has a lovely pagan chant called "The River," or a favourite childhood song could be used.

PASS THE ENERGY: SPHERE OF LIGHT

There are several fast-paced energy passing exercises in **STAGES.** This one is a bit more focused on the individual, as well as being shared throughout the group.

Method: In a circle, one person allows an imaginary spinning orb or sphere of white light to flow feely through her body, before it exits through a finger, knee, hip or other body part. She tosses it with that exit point to another person. The catcher allows the orb to enter his body and exit again to be passed to another person. This continues until everyone has caught it. There could be vocalized sounds with the movements. To build energy, the sphere should move quickly between actors.

GROUP CLAP

This allows the group to build concentration before a performance.

Method: Standing in a circle, one person claps with the person on her right or left. That person can either clap again with the original person or turn to the person on his other side and clap with her. She has the same choice. Two people will always be clapping together as it goes back and forth around the circle. The rhythm should be continuous.

SUN SALUTATIONS

Yoga has so much to offer in terms of body awareness and energy work. This familiar sequence warms up the entire body and centers each person's energy. However, unlike true yoga practice, the individual's focus here is on the group, and sharing its energy with each other.

Method: Begin standing with feet together, palms together in front of the chest, in the "Mountain" posture. The group stays together, sensing each other's readiness to move into the next posture, but without anyone leading or initiating the movements. Breath is taken in and released through the nose, with every change in posture beginning a new breathing cycle. Each upward movement is on an inhale, and each downward movement is on an exhale.

- Reach upwards, resulting in an upper back arch away from the center, palms separate as arms reach upwards – inhale
- Reach forward and down until hands touch the floor, or at least the ankles, bend knees if needed – exhale
- Stretch right leg backwards in a deep lunge; keep the front knee directly over the ankle and the back leg firm, knee on floor. Both hands remain on the floor throughout, raise head (optional: reach arms overhead, palms together) – inhale
- Keep (or place) hands on floor and bring left leg back to join the other. "Plank" posture; arms straight, shoulders over wrists, body straight, feet flexed, toes on floor – exhale
- Bend knees to touch the floor, chest, chin touching the floor, elbows close to rib cage (or simply lower body straight down to floor)
- "Cobra" posture; arms straighten, elbows remain by sides, arch up and back, keeping chest open and shoulders down, legs and feet extended – inhale

- Lift tailbone up to "Downward Dog" posture, straight legs, align head with straight arms – exhale
- Bring right leg forward into standing lunge position, hands on floor on each side of front foot, lift head – inhale
- Bring leg foot forward, hanging down from the waist, hands on floor or legs, head on knees, if possible – exhale
- Roll up through spine, extending arms up above head into upper back arch – inhale
- Return to starting "Mountain" posture – exhale

Variation #1. Just before a show, with participants in costumes that may have limited mobility, this modified version may be preferable. It also has the advantage of keeping participants connected throughout the movements.

Method: Participants stand in a circle, holding hands with their neighbours throughout the exercise.

- Arms reach up and backs arch back – inhale
- Fold downwards into a deep bow – exhale
- Straighten body, reach arms up, step back with right foot, bend front knee – inhale
- Bring feet together, lower body to deep bow – exhale
- Straighten body, reach arms up, step back with left foot, bend front knee – inhale
- Return to starting position, and repeat, or finish in the "Mountain" posture, palms together in front of chest – exhale

FINGERS

Likely the last thing the group does before breaking apart.

Method: After another exercise is complete, the group reaches all hands into the center of the circle, walking towards the center until everyone's hands touch and intermingle. The group may develop their own sound effects to verbalize as the hands brush each other in a final sign of togetherness and encouragement.

ROOTS

This is an individual grounding exercise. Participants could be led through the experience, staying together and sharing energy, or they could learn it and do it on their own, if they find if helpful. It comes from a more complex exercise involving chakras, which are easy to research and reference if the group is interested, but this exercise can be performed without considering that aspect.

Method: Standing comfortably with feet shoulder width apart, participants close their eyes and inhale deeply. On the exhale, ask them to imagine that they are sending any nervousness or negative energy downwards, through roots that are traveling down their spines, through their feet and down into the earth. If you are on an upper floor of a building, imagine the root growing to extend through any number of layers until they reach the earth. On each inhale, ask them to imagine that the earth's energy is traveling up through the roots they have created, like liquid through a straw. Each exhale sends negative energy down, with the inhale bringing up positive energy. Finally, the roots extend to the fiery core of the earth. That energy is brought up through the roots, all the way back to fill every part of their bodies. Now each exhale is reaching down to gather up more of this energy. Once it has filled up their bodies completely, they allow it to burst out of the tops of their heads, and imagine it showering down all around them, like a fountain of sparkles and light. The participants reach out their hands to catch the sparkles, and bounce them out to share them with each other. If standing alone backstage, ready to enter for their scenes, they can imagine catching them and tossing them onto the stage and out to the audience, sending their energy out before they themselves enter.

Once this exercise has been done several times, it can be repeated very quickly, in a matter of a few breaths. This can help to both calm and energize an actor before performing. It can also be used very effectively before an interview or audition.

PART III
DEVISED THEATRE:
CREATING ORIGINAL
THEATRICAL WORKS

Devised Theatre is the name given to any project that is scripted through a group process. Several different projects will be explored here:

The Village
Ancient Rituals
Readers Theatre
Story Theatre
Collage Collectives
Playwriting

Generally, the final result of a devised theatrical piece is non-naturalistic in nature. Of the five processes presented here, three, The Village, Readers Theatre and Collage Collectives, will not tell a story. There will be no through-line or plot development. They will be based on themes, with recurring motifs and other elements that give the pieces cohesion and structure. Theses themes could be anything that the group decides they would like to explore, with an end result that is comedic, dramatic, or any combination thereof.

Story Theatre and Ancient Rituals may have a storyline, with a beginning, middle and end. Although not emphasized here, Readers Theatre could also be used to present a story or scripted play.

The final unit in this chapter is on playwriting. It is included here, as writing techniques could be used to strengthen the scenes and monologues written for inclusion in pieces of devised theatre. There may also be groups that will want to use the techniques to write a play.

ADVANTAGES OF CREATING A DEVISED THEATRE PIECE

Adaptability: Everyone in the group can play a role of equal size and importance. With a large group of actors, it can be almost impossible to find a script that suits the needs and make-up of the group. These projects are made for and by the group.

Process schedule: The rehearsal process may be shorter than mounting a scripted work, as the total length of the piece and staging requirements are completely flexible.

Ownership: Each group member can contribute creatively to the material, thereby establishing a sense of ownership for the project.

Talents: It creates an opportunity for individual talents to be utilized. Singing, dancing, mime, puppetry, writing, or any other talent an actor brings to the group can be included in the final project.

Group building: Group members develop a sense of community as they contribute to the project.

Technical requirements: Whatever is available to the group is what the piece will use, rather than trying to find what a script suggests or demands. Generally, a devised piece will have no set at all, focusing instead on what the actors alone bring to the stage.

DEVISED THEATRE CONVENTIONS

Conventions are acting and staging techniques. Different forms of theatre will have different conventions. For example, traditional theatre has a convention of a fourth wall, that imaginary wall that separates the life on the stage from the people in the audience. Actors respect the fourth wall when they do not look at or speak directly to individuals in the audience, but stay in the world of the play.

In devised theatre, the group is free to break all traditional conventions, and create new ones of their own. Here are some suggestions for creating an original piece.

- Actors can play multiple roles in the same piece
- Scenes can be played out of sequence, with no natural time or plot lines

- Actors can become props and set pieces on a bare stage, fully utilizing all of the conventions of physical theatre
- Casting choices can be unexpected, colour/gender-blind
- Lights and other technical equipment can be visible to the audience
- Voice-overs, soundscapes and music may be incorporated and used as background or to tell a story
- Repetitive movement patterns may take the place of traditional blocking
- Tableaux may be used to convey relationships and meaning, as well as to tell a story
- Split scenes (two scenes taking place together, or taking turns) may be used
- Movement pieces may take the place of scripted dialogue scenes
- Projections, videos and other technical communication modes may be incorporated
- Choral speaking (more than one person speaking at a time) may be used
- Signs and other means of showing the written word can be added
- Voices need not be realistic – monotones, different pitches, volumes, etc.
- Masks, puppets and other non-realistic characters may be incorporated with realistic human actors, or all actors may play non-realistic roles
- Stylized props may stand in for many different objects
- Costumes may be absent, or highly symbolic or stylized
- Movements and gestures may be symbolic or stylized, rather than realistic
- Silence, pauses, freezes, slow motion and fast-forward sequences might be used in place of a naturalistic pace
- Fourth wall may be broken, with actors speaking directly to the audience
- Actors might narrate events, recite stage directions or use other non-tradition dialogues
- Physical involvement between characters might be absent or exaggerated, or not follow expected patterns during dialogue

- Pieces could be absent of dialogue between characters
- Poetry, songs, dances, pantomimes, shadow play, puppetry and other non-naturalistic elements could be included
- Scenes could be entirely absent, or, if included, be episodic and not related to each other, except by a common theme or thread

USING DEVISED THEATRE FOR SOCIAL CHANGE

Theatre can be an effective instrument for social change. Although devised theatre projects can be created with any theme whatsoever, it can be very worthwhile to engage the participants with something that is meaningful to them. As an educator, part of my work with pre-service teachers and adolescents is to encourage a focus on becoming involved in social justice issues, using drama as a medium. Creating devised theatrical pieces lends itself to exploring issues that affect the students themselves or educating them about the social justice issues that affect others in the world. Theatrical work based on social justice issues can be an instrument of positive change in society.

BACKGROUND: AUGUSTO BOAL

Drama as a vehicle for social change is a concept that was pioneered and developed by Augusto Boal in Brazil in the 1960s. In 1964, a military dictatorship took over the government of Brazil. In 1971, Boal was exiled, as his ideas were considered controversial, and a threat to the government. It was in Argentina that he wrote his seminal work, *Theatre of the Oppressed*. (Boal, 1974) His idea centered on taking theatre to the masses, to people who would not be familiar with theatre at all. He believed that only the oppressed could free the oppressed. He used theatrical presentations as a way of educating people about their rights and exploring what they could do to free themselves. In some cases, spectators might not even know that they were watching actors, as they would present in busy marketplaces and other locations where crowds would gather. Audience members would be encouraged to interrupt the action to give their input as to how a situation could be resolved. In one of his theatrical forms, Forum Theatre, audience members, whom he called "spect-actors" would take the place of the actors to continue the action, looking for a solution to the problem that had been presented.

Although inspired by the work of Boal, my practices in devised theatre have taken another direction. The pieces that are created in the projects introduced here are not designed for audience participation, but are primarily tools for creating presentations. The exercises themselves, however, can also be the entire point of the project. If led through the exercises of the Collage Collective in a workshop situation, participants go on a journey of self-discovery concerning an issue, with the goal of becoming empowered to seek resolutions or courses of further action. In this way, these devised theatre projects can be used not only with theatre students and acting companies, but also with groups of citizens that want to explore social justice issues. No background in theatrical training is necessary to benefit from this process. It is also possible for an inexperienced group to use some of these projects, such as Readers Theatre, to create an effective piece of theatre that can affect an audience.

USING DEVISED THEATRE TO EXPLORE ENVIRONMENTAL ISSUES

Along with using devised theatre to explore issues of concern to humanity is the close relationship that it shares with environmental concerns. Creating a piece on animals, their habitats, and our natural world can also be extremely powerful. Climate change and the industries and individual habits that affect our world climate is another area that is accessible in terms of research and can have a huge impact on participants and the audience, if it goes on to a performance. There are many programs worldwide that encourage youth involvement and may act as a springboard for a theatrical response, as youth use their involvement in a project as a theme for a piece created to educate and include their peers. Jane Goodall's *Roots and Shoots* might be an interesting place to start your search for worthwhile projects.

While exploring relevant social and environmental issues works extremely well in devised theatre pieces, the end result could also be derived from subject matter that is completely devoid of social content, or of anything at all of a serious nature. I have guided groups through pieces on zombies, favourite holidays, superheroes and any other great number of fun projects meant only to amuse and entertain the participants and their audiences. The most important theme for a devised theatre piece is the one that excites the people creating it.

TIPS FOR SUCCESS

Outside eye: It can be very difficult for the participants, immersed in the process, to recognize what an audience will get from the result. If the presentation will have a public performance, it is good to have a director, and possibly also a dramaturge work with the participant creators. At the very least, it is important to have an outside eye. This person, or several people, will see the product before an audience does, to ensure that it is cohesive, engaging and comprehensible, with a clear message and appropriate tone.

Audience: Devised theatre pieces can appear to be self-indulgent if not kept clean and concise. If the process itself is the point, with the workshop designed to benefit only the participants, than this is not an issue. Pieces going on to public performance, however, must consider the audience. It must speak to them, as well as feel right to the performers.

Length: Edit, edit and then edit again. Less is more. Carefully reconsider any piece that extends past an hour. What seems absolutely brilliant at 55 minutes may feel like too much of a good thing at 90 minutes. It isn't that a piece can't be long, but the longer it is, the more brilliant it must be. Every moment must earn its right to be included. Recurring images, words or other elements may help to give the longer piece a feeling of cohesion and unity. Instead of keeping the piece entirely episodic and only related by theme, a longer piece might benefit from recurring characters and a story arc, interspersed with more esoteric explorations of the theme.

Accidents: During the creation process, accidents are the biggest gift a group can receive. When something takes an unexpected turn, or goes in another direction when it is replayed, the accident should be explored, not stifled or seen as merely a mistake. It might turn out to be a better idea than the one first tried. It is almost always worth a second look.

Rhythm: Like a well-written symphony, rhythm is very important to the final creation. Having sections of frantic activity balanced with moments of stillness, and solo voices in juxtaposition with full group sounds, will create a rich and varied texture to the piece. If many of the individual parts have a slow steady rhythm, find ways of breaking them up and interspersing or over-layering contrasting elements.

Pacing: Like overall rhythm, pacing is important for the flow of the material. Generally, the pacing should be brisk enough to maintain momentum and energy. Slow, thoughtful moments must be carefully considered and placed within the whole. They may be used to provide contrast and relief from building tension, or create a denouement at the end of a section. Even moving, thoughtful themes can benefit from a pace that maintains the energy of the ideas.

Arc: Even though in most cases this process will not result in a play there should still be a dramatic arc, action rising to a dramatic pitch and providing closure at the end.

Flow: Like rhythm and pacing, the overall flow of the piece is important. How does one piece flow into another? Transitions from one piece to another are as important as the pieces themselves. Make them interesting and meaningful to the theme. There may be times to repeat a certain transition to create a common thread for the piece, and other times when a transition could be used to surprise the audience, to wake them up.

Tone: What message is the total piece meant to convey? How is the audience supposed to feel at the end of it? Is it meant to be controversial and provoke dialogue, or be educational and inform an audience of an issue? Or, is it meant to be a little of both? What is its purpose? What tone is being set and how is it supported throughout the piece?

Technology: If the group has access to technology and the space is conducive to using it, consider the part that video projections, live action camera work, audio recordings, lighting effects and other technology can play in the finished piece.

Theme: Because the pieces are created around a theme, it is important to assess everything created to ensure that the theme is supported. Some parts can be very subtle, as segments do not have to be blatantly stating the theme, but there should be cohesion among the parts.

Humour: Every piece, no matter how bleak the theme, can benefit from a little humour. People in dire circumstances often look for a little laughter to alleviate the pain. Remember that the audience, too, needs a moment of relief now and then. Your message may get lost if the tone is one of unrelenting horror.

Message: If this piece has a message for the audience, remember that the stronger the message, the lighter the words.

Audiences do not enjoy being preached at. Instead, think of it as sharing information, experiences and images. Use characters that the audience will relate to in the narrative sections. Present the information in imaginative ways and allow your message to speak for itself. Allow audience members to come to their own conclusions.

THE VILLAGE

Creating a "Village" can be an effective bridge from creative writing to performing. Unlike a more involved piece, such as a Collage Collective, the Village is solely monologues, with each participant creating one to add to the whole. Groups could choose to base the Village on a fanciful environment, or to explore a social justice issue that is close to them. The hints and exercises in the Playwriting chapter at the end of this unit could act as a guide for the writing of the monologues themselves.

This exercise is inspired by the *Spoon River Anthology*, by Edgar Lee Masters, published in 1915. It is a collection of over 200 short free-form poems, which together form a portrait of life in a small village at the turn of the century. The first poem, "The Hill," acts as an introduction, before each citizen of the village speaks from beyond the grave.

> **The Hill**
> Where are Elmer, Herman, Bert, Tom and Charley,
> The weak of will, the strong of arm, the clown, the boozer, the fighter?
> All, all are sleeping on the hill.
> One passed in a fever,
> One was burned in a mine,
> One was killed in a brawl,
> One died in a jail,
> One fell from a bridge toiling for children and wife—
> All, all are sleeping, sleeping, sleeping on the hill.
> Where are Ella, Kate, Mag, Lizzie and Edith,
> The tender heart, the simple soul, the loud, the proud, the happy one?—
> All, all are sleeping on the hill.
> One died in shameful childbirth,
> One of a thwarted love,
> One at the hands of a brute in a brothel,

One of a broken pride, in the search for heart's desire;
One after life in far-away London and Paris
Was brought to her little space by Ella and Kate and
Mag—
All, all are sleeping, sleeping, sleeping on the hill.
Where are Uncle Isaac and Aunt Emily,
And old Towny Kincaid and Sevigne Houghton,
And Major Walker who had talked
With venerable men of the revolution?—
All, all are sleeping on the hill.
They brought them dead sons from the war,
And daughters whom life had crushed,
And their children fatherless, crying—
All, all are sleeping, sleeping, sleeping on the hill.
Where is Old Fiddler Jones
Who played with life all his ninety years,
Braving the sleet with bared breast,
Drinking, rioting, thinking neither of wife nor kin,
Nor gold, nor love, nor heaven?
Lo! he babbles of the fish-frys of long ago,
Of the horse-races of long ago at Clary's Grove,
Of what Abe Lincoln said
One time at Springfield.

Method: The first piece in The Village sets the stage for the location, which the collection of monologues will fit into. Then, one at a time, each participant adds a personal story to fit the theme set by the first speaker. The theme could speak to any situation that would have a large collection of different people. The monologues can be left as individual stand-alone pieces, performed one after the other, with imaginative staging, or some of them could be combined, using the suggested process in the Playwriting chapter to form dialogues.

Sample themes:

Workers in a factory or specific company
Members of a traveling circus, or old-fashioned "freak show"
Students in a classroom
Refugees in a camp
Members of a family
Models backstage at a fashion show
New immigrants at a Friendship Centre

Crew on a movie set
Tourists on a group tour
Members of a club or society at a convention
Players on a specific sports team
People involved in a disaster; a flood, earthquake, fire, etc.

Sample monologues:

Individuals could write a piece describing:

His/her relationship with another member of the group
His/her reaction to a major event in the group's experience
His/her importance within the group
His/her reasons for leaving the group
His/her introduction to the group
His/her longing to belong to the group

As an exercise, The Village can be a gentle introduction to devised theatre for groups who are new to it. The results could also become a small portion of a larger piece of Devised Theatre, such as Readers Theatre or a Collage Collective.

ANCIENT RITUALS

Exploring the concept of rituals and ultimately creating and performing an original ritual is a good way to end a unit on voice and movement work. It combines elements of choral speech, repetitive movement and musical pantomime (see LITANY FOR THE MOON in the Voice chapter to use as a lead-in).

Method:

1. The group is introduced to the concept of rituals. Modern rituals can be explored, such as weddings, funerals, church services, etc. Research can be done to uncover ancient rituals, such as ceremonies of coronations, burials, sacrifice, worship, rain dances, etc.

2. In groups of six to eight participants, improvisations can be performed using modern, then ancient rituals as their base. As a warm-up to creating their own ritual, LITANY FOR THE MOON or another chant can be distributed, with groups preparing a presentation of it. Creativity in its presentation is encouraged, in terms of voice use: choral speaking and solo voice, staging, rhythms and instrumentation.

3. The requirements for the assignment are handed out and discussed.

4. Each group chooses a ritual to enact. This may be based on an actual ancient ritual, or may be invented by the group.

5. Rehearsal time is given.

6. Each group performs their ritual for the group, or a wider audience. For example, in a high school, the ancient rituals could be presented as a noon-hour performance. Donations or admittance charges could be donated to a charity.

EXPLORING THE STRUCTURE OF A RITUAL

According to Victor Turner, in *From Ritual to Theatre*, anthropologists that have studied the rituals of ancient societies suggest that most rituals had some sort of **passage** as a theme, marking the transition from one stage of life to another. Some of these passages, like the changing seasons of the year and harvest rituals, could be repeated, but many others would have been something a person would only experience once, such as birth, becoming an adult or a funeral rite at death. The passage ritual would typically have three phases:

- Separation
- Transition
- Incorporation

Separation might be physical separation of the initiate, such as a youth who had to be alone in the forest for a period of time as the first step in a coming-of-age ritual. It could also be a spiritual separation, such as coming into a holy place set apart from daily living spaces.

Transition would leave the initiate in a sort of limbo, a time between his pre-ritual state and a new, post-ritual state. This stage would have a ceremony or action that was performed on or by the initiate.

Incorporation is the reintroducing of the initiate into the larger society, but in a new, usually elevated role.

In each stage, there could be symbolic gestures or actions taken by those performing the ritual and those going through the passage as initiates. These actions and symbolic gestures could be seen as "play" on the part of the participants, but they would be imitating the "work" of the community. For example, play-acting the stages of the harvest, while manipulating symbolic objects, might be done to ensure a bountiful crop.

There were many occasions that called for rituals:

- To promote and increase fertility of people, animals for hunting and domestic use, crops and foods that were gathered
- To prevent or cure illness in individuals or the tribe as a whole during times of plagues
- To obtain success in raiding parties or wars
- To welcome boys into manhood, girls into womanhood
- To ensure rainfall, sunshine and the succession of the seasons
- To crown chiefs or leaders
- To anoint priests and priestesses, shamans and shamanins
- To welcome warriors home from battle and reintegrate them into the life of the village
- To celebrate the birth or naming of a child
- To celebrate the passage of a living being into the spirit world

Sample assignment for Ancient Rituals

Requirements:

- The ritual must be between five and ten minutes in length.
- It must have a purpose, with a beginning, middle and end.
- The characters involved must all have a role, or function in the ritual.
- The ritual may be set to music (instrumental only).
- There must be some sections of repetitive movement.
- There must be some sections with sounds, both vocal and created with objects or instruments (tambourines, drums, sticks, etc.). Words or chants could also be used.
- Costumes pieces and props can be added.

Evaluation could be based on the originality of the piece, the fulfillment of requirements and the focus of the group in their use of rehearsal time.

READERS THEATRE

This traditional form of theatre is still widely used as a way of presenting material, both scripted and original. It is great for classrooms and other workshop or performance situations where a lengthy rehearsal process is not desirable. Readers Theatre acts as a bridge between choral speaking and formal theatre. Oral interpreters vocally bring the material to life. If the material is a play or story, the readers voice the dialogue, with a narrator speaking the stage directions or prose, while relying on the audience members to use their imaginations to fill in the action.

Readers Theatre has traditionally worked with very specific stage conventions. Once an audience was introduced to a presentation's conventions, they accepted what they saw without having the stylized mode of presentation interfere with the reality created by the readers. Readers Theatre traditionally used plays or stories as source material.

CONVENTIONS OF TRADITIONAL READERS THEATRE

- Readers sat on stools. They turned their backs on the audience if they weren't in a particular scene. Or, they stood to read and it would be understood that they were not in a scene if they were sitting. Instead of using stools, all readers might stand in a row. They might step forward to read.
- Readers could play multiple characters.
- Off-stage focus was used. The readers looked at each other as if looking at the other character's reflection in an imaginary mirror placed at the back of the auditorium, rather than looking directly at each other.
- Scripts were placed in folders, either held by the readers or placed on music stands in front of their stools. Although dialogue was almost memorized, the material was read during a performance.
- Costumes were not typically used. Readers wore neutral clothing, usually all black. A single piece of costuming, such as a hat, or a single prop, such as a cane, might be used to define a character, especially if a reader was playing more than one character.
- A narrator stood at a podium a short distance from the readers, who played the characters. The narrator spoke directly to the audience, reading the stage directions in a play,

or the prose between the dialogues in a story. In the case of a long story, much of the prose would be cut to accommodate the length of the performance.

Now, traditional conventions may still be used, or the presentation can move closer to formal theatre. Actors might use on-stage focus during dialogue and costume pieces could be added. Instead of sitting on stools, mime boxes or platforms could be used as set pieces or for permanent reader placement, if movement was not being used. Perhaps the only convention retained from traditional Readers Theatre is that actors are holding their scripts. In all other aspects, it might be a fully realized stage production.

The process for developing a piece of Readers Theatre depends on whether an already scripted piece is being used, or if the group is writing their own script.

PROCESS FOR A SCRIPTED PIECE:

1. Choose a play or story.
2. Cast roles. In the case of a story, the narration may be divided between several readers.
   Some of the narration may be turned into dialogue, to allow for more changes of voices.
3. Decide on conventions to be used.
4. Rehearse.
5. Present.

PROCESS FOR A THEMATIC SELF-CREATED PIECE:

1. Choose a theme
2. Gather appropriate material related to theme
   stories, poems, song lyrics, comics, jokes, quotes, news articles, etc.
3. Review and select material to be included. It isn't necessary to use the whole of any one source.
4. Find a logical order for the material. A line or two from a poem can be followed by a few lyrics from a song, which may or may not come back at a later point in the final script. The aim is to present a collection of thoughts on a theme, not to try to force a storyline from the material. Actually cutting out the lines used, from a photocopy of the source material, allows participants to physically move the

pieces around on a tabletop until a satisfactory order is achieved. Create bridges and transitions from one item to the next. It might be that there is a word or phrase that could recur between other pieces, or perhaps there is a line in one source that seems to lead into a line from another source.

5. Read through and edit. Once satisfied, paste or tape the pieces to blank sheets of paper and make a photocopy of the script for each participant.

6. Decide on conventions to be used and assign lines to all participants. Decide how each segment or line might be read. Which sections will be in unison? Which will have a solo voice, or a duet or trio? Is there a section that could be done as a repetitive chant under another section, or be done in canon (overlapping repeats)? Be as creative as possible with how the piece is vocalized.

7. Decide on conventions to be used.

8. Rehearse.

9. Present.

SAMPLE READERS THEATRE ASSIGNMENT: THEMATIC APPROACH

Requirements:

1. Piece should be between four and seven minutes in length

2. A minimum of five different sources should be used, from a minimum of three difference genres.

> For example – 2 poems, 2 jokes, 1 story, or, 1 song lyric, 2 quotes, 2 news articles.

> In a group or five to seven participants, it is likely that they will far exceed this minimum. If every group member brings in just two pieces, there will be ten to fourteen pieces to choose bits of for the final script.

3. All readers should have an equal amount of material to read.

Evaluation could be based on the quality of the material, use of rehearsal time, as well as the final presentation. The presentation grade could be based on the clarity and audibility of the readers, the flow of the material and the characterizations and variety of the voices, as well as fulfilling the source requirements.

This is a project that, in my many years of using it in the class-room, has always met with success. I have never seen a poor result. The material, if chosen with the theme in mind, tends to take on a flow and life of its own. Whether the end results are silly and amusing, or serious and thought provoking, they are unfailingly engaging.

SAMPLE SCRIPT – excerpt of a Readers Theatre script created by a student group

Hallowe'en

Reader A:	Shadows of a thousand years rise again unseen,
Reader A, E:	Voices whisper in the trees, Tonight is Hallowe'en
All: *(in whispered echo, overlapping)*	Tonight is Hallowe'en, Hallowe'en, Hallowe'en
Reader B:	Rapping, rapping at my chamber door Tapping at my chamber door –
Reader C:	Are you scared?
Reader D:	Are you scared?
All: *(in overlapping echo)*	Scared, scared, scared, scared.
Reader B:	On Hallowe'en night, the Great Pumpkin rises from his pumpkin patch and flies through the air to deliver toys to all the children.
Reader A:	And his eyes have all the seeming of a demon's that is dreaming,
Reader D:	And the lamp-light o'er him stream-ing throws his shadow on the floor.
Reader C:	And my soul from out that shadow that lies floating on the floor –
Reader B:	(interrupts) I am the shadow on the moon at night Filling your dreams to the brim with fright.
Reader E:	I am the one hiding under your bed Teeth ground sharp and eyes glow-ing red
All except E:	But we weren't afraid –

And so it continued, interweaving a children's poem about trick or treating, a little Edgar Allan Poe and Shakespeare's witches, and several horror movie quotes. A delightful piece, enjoyed by all!

STORY THEATRE

This process will take a group from a story to the stage, resulting in a piece of theatre. It is a way of taking any story and turning it into a script, which can be performed for an audience.

Method: Divide the group into smaller groups of five to eight participants each. Decide if everyone will be working on the same story, under your direction, or if they are ready to choose and work on stories of their choice.

HINT: With teens and adults, you may wish to go through the steps together with a short nursery rhyme, in groups of three or four. Once they understand the process, divide them into the groups that will each choose and work on their own stories independently. Guide the process just enough to ensure that all of the steps are being followed.

---

1. **Pick a story.** It can work with any story at all. For young children, it may be a nursery rhyme. For school-aged children, it may be a fairy tale or any other beloved children's book. It can also be a story written by the participants, or a novel. Any story can be turned into a staged piece of theatre. Make sure that the whole group knows the story fairly well. This may simply involve reminding each other of the facts of the storyline, or taking turns reading it to each other. Talk about whether you will use the original story, or change some of the details. Will you change the ending? Update the time period? Change the setting? Add in extra characters of your own invention, or from another story? These decisions don't have to be made now, but you might decide whether you will be open to them or not as you set up the story through the following steps.

2. **Decide on the five to eight most exciting moments of the story.** Pick the points where something significant happens, or when something changes. Maybe a new character arrives on the scene, or someone leaves. The number of tableaux will depend on the length of the story.

3. **Tableaux.** Create tableaux representing these important moments. Make sure that everyone in the group is in every

single tableau. If there aren't enough characters, people can become inanimate objects or flora and fauna. It is much more fun to become a tree or a bird than wait backstage for an entrance as a character that isn't in the first scene. It is also more fun to have a person or two form a chair than to use a real one. Having one or two people form a door that can open and close is a lot more interesting than miming a door that no one can see. Create visually interesting pictures, remembering all the rules of design as they apply to tableaux. (See Design Concepts Through Tableaux)

4. **Pantomime**. String the tableaux together with pantomime. Pantomime is "story without words." Not every moment of the story will have been captured in the tableaux, so now is the time to fill in the pieces of the story that happen between the tableaux. If a person began as a tree and changed into a new character, now is the time to explore how that change will happen. Will the audience see this morphing taking place? That might be more fun than trying to pretend it never happened.

5. **Self-narration.** Repeat the pantomime, with each person self-narrating the entire experiences for him/herself. Start at the first tableau, then run through the pantomime from start to finish, with everyone talking at once. No one pauses to listen to the others. Everyone talks through his/her character's experience in this story. Everyone voices the hopes, fears, wishes, dreams and desires held by the character being played. The characters also voice what they say to another character, or what they wish they could say. If a person changes from one character or object to another, he just keeps going in the new character's voice. Even the morphing period from one character into another could have a voice or sounds.

6. **Improvisation.** Repeat Step #5, but take lots of time now, listening to what other people are saying, so they can answer if they are spoken to. Characters keep in all the narration of their thoughts and feelings, just like the last time. Allow for the story to take a lot longer to reach its conclusion, as all listen and respond to each other, as well as voicing all of the asides that express what their characters see and think about the action that is unfolding.

7. **Sharing time**. All share what they had to say and what they discovered in the self-narration process. How did things

change through the improvisation phase? What worked best for everyone? What clever bits did they find themselves saying, or hear each other say? Decide together what lines to keep; which bits of dialogue and narration will best tell the story. Recognize that the audience can only hear one person at a time, so decide who will say what, and when. Keep equal parts of narration and dialogue. None of the original lines from the storybook need to be used, although it is fine to keep iconic bits, such as the little pigs' chant to the big bad wolf, and the wolf's response to huff and puff their houses down. Most of the lines will come out of what people discovered in the self-narration steps. Make sure that everyone in the group has approximately the same amount of material to say.

8. **Write it down.** (optional) If you want the play to stay the same each time you present it, create a script for it. Write down what everyone says and where people go when they move on stage. This is called the dialogue and stage directions. See the samples in the chapter on playwriting for how to set this up on the page. If this is a class project that will only be seen once, it may be left unscripted, with some improvisation remaining.

9. **Rehearse.** Run through the story, repeating the actions of the pantomime with the chosen dialogue and narration. Groups may choose to keep in a tableau or two, at the beginning or ending, or at a moment of high excitement in the storyline. Make sure that the stage pictures and movements are open to the audience, rather than facing each other or the back of the stage area. Are there times when someone is standing in front of another character that is important to the story at that moment? Are there parts where the audience will not be able to see what is going on? Fix up everything to make it audience friendly.

10. **Present.** Perform the finished product for an audience.

Notes: Going through these steps gives the theatrical piece a form and structure. By focusing only on what a particular step is asking for, participants develop a final project that is much richer than something they would devise by simply reading the story and improvising it as a stage play, or discussing it and writing a script. The end result will be a stronger presentation. Each step has something unique to offer. The main elements of **Tableaux**, **Pantomime**, **Self-narration** and **Improvisation** are integral to the success of the final product.

Tableaux: Setting up the tableaux ensures that at least five times during the presentation there will be something worth seeing on stage. There will be a stage picture that has been carefully crafted to tell the audience something important in the story. The tableaux also ensure that every participant is involved in the story at every moment. No one leaves the stage, and everyone is important in the telling of the tale. Every participant is of equal value and all will take ownership of the piece. Using human bodies as the inanimate objects needed in the story also fosters the participants' creativity and innovation.

Pantomime: This step is important as it establishes the action of the piece. Without this step, participants may begin to tell the story verbally, with very little for the audience to watch. A "talking head" scene may result, which means that actors stand around talking, letting their words do all the work, when words and actions together are much more interesting to watch, and fun to participate in. This step also reminds participants where the story is going, and what they need to physically do to tell it. This step is done before adding words, to ensure that there will be a lot of action in the finished piece.

Self-narration: This element is so important, as it ensures that everyone in the group has a say in the dialogue and narration that tells the story. Without this step, it is very common to see one student taking on the role of the playwright and director, instructing other group members in what they should say next. Leaving out this step also will generally result in a play with very little, or at least rather boring narration; perhaps with only one participant simply stating what is going to happen next. The self-narration also frees each participant to speak and discover what is going on for his/her own character. It is spontaneous, which is almost always more interesting than planning what could be said. With everyone speaking simultaneously, no one feels judged, allowing for more interesting discoveries.

Improvisation: Repeating the self-narration step, but starting to listen to each other, is also important. More of each individual's contributions tend to be kept for the final version of the play, because someone else has heard how great they are. As they start to hear what others are saying, they will support each other when they hear something interesting and respond to it. It is important to allow each participant to express what worked for him/herself in that process, before the final script is set.

OPTIONAL WRITTEN SCRIPT

If this project is done as a creative drama classroom activity, the final presentation might be best left as a "planned improvisation." Each step has been gone through by the individual groups, either independently or guided by the leader, depending on the age and abilities of the participants. Then, after several rehearsals, each group presents for the others, and the exercise is complete.

However, if the final presentation is for a wider audience, it is likely that the script needs to be set a little more firmly, so that the group doesn't rely on individuals to simply remember what happens next. It is likely advantageous to create an actual script that can then be memorized and rehearsed more thoroughly.

Someone in the group would write down what is said and where participants moved on stage. This would happen after several improvised run-throughs, once everyone was happy with what had developed. It might be taped and transcribed. Even after the script is written and copied for everyone to use, it might change a little. With every subsequent rehearsal more discoveries are made by individuals and collectively by the group. Rewrites can be done as time allows. At some point, it should be set, allowing the participants to become confident in their roles and lines well in advance of the performance date.

See the Playwriting chapter at the end of this unit on two different ways to set up a script.

FOLLOW-UP PROJECTS AND ACTIVITIES

Once this process of creating a presentation has been followed, there are various ways that it can be used, as either a follow-up activity, if it was a class project, or as a way to further develop it for presentation, or to use it in another format.

- **Genre or style:** The same story could be told in another genre or style. It could be done as a musical, a Shakespearean tragedy or comedy, as film noir, or any number of other styles.
- **Radio play:** It could be audio recorded as a radio play. How would it subtly change if there were no visuals? How would it be enhanced by sound effects instead? (See Radio Plays in Voice)
- **Improvisation:** The group could use the theme of the story to improvise spin-offs from one of the characters' perspective,

to learn about point-of-view. They could also improvise alternate endings, deleted scenes, or "what-if" situations involving the characters. What would it look like if another character, perhaps from another story, was introduced to this cast of characters?

- **Combined stories:** If this project was done in a classroom setting, with several groups each creating their own Story Theatre projects, what would happen if two groups were combined, and given the task of merging their stories into one?

- **Readers Theatre:** The staged version could be rewritten to become a piece of Readers Theatre. Instead of action, it would be done vocally, with choral speaking and individual voices telling the story and creating the characters.

- **Non-linear devised theatre:** The piece could be deconstructed and told in a non-linear style. Perhaps the scenes are now out of order, or some of them are told as a musical pantomime instead of using dialogue. Repetitive movement patterns, soundscapes or any other devised theatre convention could be added to the non-linear storyline.

COLLAGE COLLECTIVES

A Collage Collective is a theatrical piece created by a group who has collected or created material and formed it into a cohesive whole. A Collage Collective can use many different forms of theatrical presentation, including Readers Theatre, dance, tableaux, movement, puppet theatre, singing, and any other talents individuals in the group bring to the process.

In a Collage Collective, all material may come from published sources, like a Readers Theatre project, but frequently the group will develop some or all of the material.

In addition to Augusto Boal, there have been others that have contributed to what I use in my work. In my early teaching of devised theatre, my pieces relied heavily on improvisation and transitional pieces of movement, as well as featuring the special talents of the individuals within the groups, such as singing, dancing or puppetering. A workshop with Chris Gerrard-Pinker, from Winnipeg, in the mid-nineties added elements of individual tableaux and repetitive movement patterns. Another influence is the work of Anne Bogart and her *Viewpoints of Time, and of Space*.

In creating a Collage Collective, a group may work collectively, without a director. This can be a worthwhile endeavour for small groups of student actors, allowing them to grow and develop as they work through the process together. If the project is to be presented publicly, however, the group could benefit from having a director who makes the final decisions, to ensure that the audience will be viewing a cohesive presentation. What follows are instructions for both ways to work, as well as a blend of the two.

PROCESS FOR A SMALL GROUP COLLECTIVE – NO LEADER

1. Choose theme
2. Collect suitable material: poems, scripts, songs, etc.
3. Brainstorm possible scenarios for improvs related to the theme
4. Improv scenarios, possibly video recording them for future scripting
5. Choose material, balancing found material with improved scenes
6. Choose mode of presentation for each piece – song, dance, Readers Theatre, mime, music, puppets, tableaux, circus acts, video projection, etc.
7. Place all material in a logical order
8. Decide which actors will present the various pieces of the material
9. Create transitions from one piece to the next
10. Run through piece several times, editing along the way
11. Set final stage movements and use of set pieces and props
12. Rehearse and present

SOME CAUTIONARY NOTES

It's not a play: Encourage groups to avoid improving so much material with the same characters that they try to turn it into a play. A play takes plot and character development that is usually well beyond the time allotment for a project of this nature. It is better to have several small scenes based on the theme interspersed with other source material.

Audience: Consider the audience for this piece. It will have different tones if set for an audience of peers, young children or the general public. The language content and level, and subject matter should be appropriate for the target audience.

Stage: The performance space will determine the amount of movement and technical aspects the piece will contain. Typically, since the piece is a thematic collage, rather than a play, lighting, sets, and props can be kept to a bare minimum.

SAMPLE ASSIGNMENT FOR SMALL GROUP COLLECTIVE

Requirements:

1. Piece should be between seven and ten minutes in length.
2. Material should come from a minimum of six different sources, from a minimum of four different genres. One of these genres must be improvisation. In this way, the material will be a combination of original and found materials. For example:

    1 story done as Readers Theatre, 1 musical pantomime, 3 improvs, 1 poem.

    or 2 songs, 2 improvs, 1 play excerpt, 1 dance.

    or 1 quote, 2 songs, 2 improvs, 1 excerpt from a scripted puppet show.

Evaluation for this group assignment might focus on teamwork throughout the process as well as the final product. A grade could be given for fulfilling the source requirements, creativity and originality, focus and flow of materials and overall execution.

PROCESS FOR LARGE GROUP COLLECTIVE – WITH DIRECTOR OR LEADER

1. Choose theme
2. Do a variety of exercises to create original material (suggestions to follow)
3. Director oversees writing of the script from material generated by the group
4. Director casts roles
5. Run-throughs, with editing as needed
6. Rehearse and present

COMBINATION OF THE TWO METHODS

The class may be divided into small groups. Each group works cooperatively, without a director. However, the leader takes the class through the exercises to generate material collectively, with each group working simultaneously to develop their own material. If a longer, large group presentation is desired the groups all work with the same theme, and reconvene after working out their own 20 minutes worth of material to add to the whole, as formed by the director. Some found material may be used, but most will be original. Non-original sources may be used to inspire creative responses. Each group could stay with their own shorter presentations, especially if the final performances will remain in the classroom setting.

THEMES

Absolutely anything can be used as a theme in this creative process. For example, you may use a holiday or season that is coming soon, or a theme from any other parts of the curriculum. Encourage students to work with issues that are meaningful to them. Groups working alone can choose any theme they wish, but if the leader will be conducting the various exercises, with each group working on its own project, simultaneously, it may be easier to have all groups working on related themes, so the leader can use common language.

For example, creating a Collage Collective piece based on the theme of social justice allows students to explore the issues that affect them and others in the world around them. Each group of five or six students chooses a specific social justice theme: bullying, poverty, homelessness, mental health, prison systems, racial or other discrimination, etc. The leader guides them through the exercises that will create material based on their specific theme.

EXERCISES TO INTRODUCE AND EXPLORE THE THEME

Visual art response: Before beginning the exercises that will create the material for the final presentation, the theme may be explored using visual art. A large roll of paper is laid out on the floor, providing each group member with a drawing station of approximately one foot in length. Participants sit around the paper at their own stations. Each group member has his own colour to work with: a crayon, felt marker or pencil crayon. On the command to begin, each member begins to draw a picture of what the theme means to him. After one minute, the leader calls for the actors to move, and each person continues the drawing of the actor to his right. This continues until all actors are back at their original stations. A discussion on the results follows, often providing insight into how everyone interprets the theme.

The discussion can be recorded, or individuals can write a reflection on what became of their original drawings, or of the discussion as a whole.

Objects: Group members could be asked to bring in small objects that are related to the theme and are of some significance to them. The object could be the focus of an improvisation, or used symbolically in a more subtle way. Once an object is used in one improvisation, it can be subtly transformed and used in others throughout the piece, becoming whatever prop is needed at the moment. A mid-sized object could be placed downstage, to remind the audience of its significance to the theme. It may be used in a variety of ways throughout the piece, and simply remain in view when not being used. Alternatively, many small objects could be incorporated, or one larger object could be decided on and reappear throughout the piece.

For example, I once used a large round parachute, the kind found in children's playground programs, and incorporated it into a Collective. For the opening, all actors were underneath it. As the lights came up, a chant was heard as the actors began to move. Finally, the actors picked up the edges of the chute and waved it as they moved in a circle, each with a line to speak related to the theme. The lines came from the writings done after the sharing circle. The parachute was then used in other contexts throughout the piece. It became a cape, a picnic blanket, a curtain to hide a monster from view and so on, until the end of the piece, when the actors again got underneath it as the lights faded to black.

In another piece I used lots of small hoops with long flowing silver tinsel. They were used creatively in various movement pieces throughout the Collage.

Entice the senses: Either the leader, or all group members, could bring in things that remind them of the theme, as a way to set the stage for the creative work. This might be songs, poems, music, posters, paintings or images from magazines. The images would be put up around the room to act as inspiration during the work. The music could be played to set the mood during the exercises. The poems or other published pieces could be shared aloud to act as a starting point for the group's own creative responses, which could become part of the final piece.

TIMS

Once the group has explored the theme, they are ready to begin the creative work of developing the material that will go into the final project. There are four classifications of exercises to explore, leading to a great variety of possible outcomes. Together they form the acronym **TIMS**.

- Tableaux
- Improvisation
- Movement
- Spoken word

Each group will do a variety of exercises from each section, then decide which ones they will keep in forming their own Collage Collective.

TABLEAUX

Tableaux can be defined as frozen moments in time. They can be used to great effect in Collectives, representing a visual illustration of the theme. Understanding the design elements of tableaux will ensure that they are used for maximum effect (see Tableaux). Although the exercises presented will ask group members to create tableaux spontaneously, they can still be studied later in the rehearsal process to ensure that they are conveying the appropriate message to the audience.

INDIVIDUAL TABLEAUX EXERCISES

Method: Two or three aspects of the theme are identified.

For example, the theme is "the future." Two aspects or categories of this theme that will be dealt with are Hopes and Fears. Students are asked to think of a situation that they could find themselves in, in relation to each category. They then take a mental photograph of this situation. They pose in a tableau of themselves in this photo and describe the photo to the group. The director listens and picks one short phrase from this description to become the title for the tableau. For example, a student creates a tableau under the category Fear. In her tableau, she is doubled over as if in pain. She describes her photo, saying, "I am afraid that I will develop an incurable disease, like other members of my family. I can't move, can't get past the pain. The idea of suffering pain paralyzes me." The director chooses the phrase, "can't get past the pain," as the title of this tableau. Alternatively, individuals in each group do this exercise simultaneously and everyone chooses his or her own short phrase. They do not need to explain where the tableau or phrase came from. It's personal and doesn't need to be shared. The phrases are a reflection of the theme, and don't have to be understood literally by the audience. There are many ways to then use these tableaux and phrases. For example:

- The owners of each tableau can repeat the others', with each individual holding her own when the group reaches it.

- The actor can say his tableau title to another actor, using it as the first line of an improv. The improv ends when the pair reaches the second actor's title, which then becomes the first line of an improv between the second and third actors in the group. Finally, the last improv is performed between the last actor and the first actor who began the exercise. Going the other way through the actors will produce entirely new results. All improvs are loosely theme related, but are not related to the original tableaux that produced the phrase.

- The titles of the tableaux can be used as a litany or chant, with or without the tableaux.

- An actor can pose in her tableau, say its title, and have it imitated by the other members of the group, or the whole group can perform each tableau at once.

- Each actor can hold a significant prop in turn, as they name their tableaux, before passing the object to the next actor.

- Each actor finds a repetitive movement that takes him out of his tableau and back into it. This creates a movement piece that can be featured or used as background to something else.

- Each member of the group can repeat each individual tableau in canon (one at a time, in a row, creating a wave action). This may be repeated for each tableau, or only one or two tableaux might be used.

- The tableaux can be strung together, with or without the phrases, forming a movement pattern. This can be featured, or used as background action for a scene, poem, monologue or song.

GROUP TABLEAUX EXERCISES

Opening/Closing: A full group tableau could open and/or close the piece, creating a picture, a visual representation of the theme.

Background: When actors are not involved in a part of the piece, they could move back into their place in the tableau instead of leaving the stage. Ladders, boxes or other set pieces could be utilized to create levels, with the actors occupying specific spots.

Spontaneous: Entire group forms individual, but interconnected tableaux based on their own emotional responses to the theme. Tableau can be formed instantaneously, on the count of three. Repeat this several times and pick one for further study. Discuss the relationship of one person to another. Is there a suggestion of a character? Is there a suggestion of a scene? Could they be used as transitions between pieces? Could one actor break out for a solo?

By the numbers: Number each person in the group. There will be as many tableaux created as there are group members. Each group member has an opportunity to begin one tableau, based on a character that could be involved in a situation relating to the group's theme. The first person begins by freezing in place. The others add on, in number sequence, to what they believe is happening. Each person becomes a new character in the tableau. After each tableau, discuss what the scene was. Did it develop according to the idea of the person who started it, or did it take a turn as more group members were added? Repeat the exercise for each group member. Decide on two or three to develop further. There are many different ways to allow this development. For example:

- Tableau comes to life in pantomime, creating a scene without words.
- Tableau comes to life with dialogue. Rehearse until scene develops.
- Chose one tableau to work with. #1 says a phrase representing her character's point of view. #2 responds, then #3, etc. Once everyone has spoken:
  - □ All group members leave playing area. They all repeat their phrases as they slowly walk into the playing area and reform the tableau.
  - □ In the reverse, group members repeat their phrases as they slowly back away from the tableau and move out of the playing area.

- Group begins out of the playing area, then forms the tableau one at a time, either repeating their phrases as they move, or stating it once after they are in place.
- One phrase is "featured" while all other phrases are repeated softly in the background. This could be repeated for all of the phrases.
- An improvisation develops, based on the phrases, said in turn as the first lines of the improv. #1 unfreezes and repeats phrase. #2 follows, etc.

- Tableaux are repeated in a sequence, as a stand-alone piece, representing many aspects of the theme.
- The phrases could become part of a soundscape (see Spoken Word).
- One at a time, group members unfreeze, disengage from the group tableau and speak to the audience, in single words, a short monologue, or perhaps sing a song or recite a poem. When she is finished, she rejoins the tableaux and another person disengages to present a solo.

Fluid tableau: Start with one person, others add on, first person disengages and adds back in with a new attitude or role. Each person follows, the result being an ever-evolving narrative. Continue until each group member has frozen and reengaged two or three times. Step back and see the story that was created. It could be presented with musical background or a self-created soundscape. It could also be played in reverse action. It could be played forwards and backwards, ending at the beginning. Keep the frozen tableaux at each step of the story, as each picture creates its own narrative.

Positive/Negative: Create tableau based on worst-case (theme-related) scenario. Create a second tableau representing the best possible outcome of the scenario. To a count of ten, morph from one tableau to the other (and perhaps back again).

- Each actor repeats one word or very short phrase that represents what his/her character in the negative tableau is feeling. Repeat it while morphing into the positive tableau, with a more hopeful word or phrase.
- Start with the negative tableau, morph into the positive, then unfreeze and begin scene based on postures. Scene becomes negative and ends when actors are in negative postures. Or, start with positive scene and end in negative tableau.

Headlines: Create a tableau representing a front-page newspaper photograph on an article related to this theme (at moment of highest tension or crisis). What does the caption read? Rewind action to show what happened before photograph was taken. This could mean that a scene is begun that ends in the headline tableau, or it could literally be played backwards, in rewind. It could end with group members disengaging and moving into another segment of the Collective, or a new, beginning tableau could be established. The group could also choose to fast-forward, showing what happens after headline photograph is taken.

Proximity: Create a tableau that expresses each character's desire for proximity to the others. Use characters from one of the other exercises in this section. One person begins the tableau. The second person decides how close or far away his character would like to be from the first, and so on, until everyone is in place. The group discusses the picture they have created and decides whether to take it further, shifting their proximity to each other to reflect changing attitudes, desires or states of mind, within the character. Unlike other tableaux, with interesting body postures, this tableaux is one of stillness: people just stand or sit, looking at each other, or not, walking towards someone during the shift, or turning away.

Group mingle: The entire group mingles about in their playing area, using free-flow movement patterns. The leader shouts out a word. Everyone instantly freezes in an individual tableau representing that word. They could repeat the word as they freeze. As soon as they have done so, they resume their mingling, waiting for the next word. Once they are again working within their own small groups of five or six actors, they can decide how to adapt it for their own use. Or, if ultimately all of the groups will be joined into one large collective, this is one of the exercises that could be carried through for all participants.

Group mingle/scenes: This same group mingle could be used to provide a backdrop for two-hander scenes. The pair that is going to perform the next short scene finds itself downstage for the next freeze. They play their scene while everyone else freezes behind them. Once finished, they blend back into the group. The three-line improvs could be used here, or the first-line / last-line pair improvs from the Individual Tableaux.

IMPROVISATION

Improvisations are spontaneous dialogue and actions, which create a scene. Unlike the focused improvisations used to create stories by improv troupes, and as taught in the Improvisation chapter here and in the companion book, **STAGES: Creative Ideas for Teaching Drama**, the improvisations in Devised Theatre can play by their own rules. Some improvisations within the Collective could tell a story and have a dramatic arc, but others can be very short and not concern themselves with storylines, or even making much sense. They are creating an impression of the theme, not necessarily a narrative. They are playing with language; the specific words chosen can carry a lot of weight, but don't have to link with story.

Noun and verb: Each person in the group has two pieces of paper, writing a noun on one and a verb on the other, all relating to the theme. Two by two, pairs within the group randomly pick one noun and one verb and create a scene – 30 seconds to plan, then re-enact for the group. Once words have all been used, the group decides on two or three of the scenes to develop. They may lengthen one, combine two in some way, etc.

- Instead of developing the scenes, just the nouns and verbs themselves could become the scenes. As they are all theme related, they could be used for a non-linear scene, with participants repeating them in sequence, perhaps combined with stylized movements or repetitive stage patterns, based on a grid (see Monologue chapter for developing dialogues from single words). They could also form a chant or echo, to be used as background for another aspect of the piece.

Interview: One person in the group becomes a news reporter, interviewing one or two others in the group, who are in character, finding out about their lives and problems. This is a way to present a monologue on the theme, allowing the audience an in-depth look at one person's story as it relates to the issue.

Three-sentence improvs: #1 asks question, #2 responds, #1 ends it. #2 asks #3 a question, #3 responds, #2 ends it. #3 asks #4 a question, etc. All questions are done in character and are theme related. Continue around circle until all have asked a question. In performance, the participants are no longer in a circle, but share their work with the audience; either stretching out to form a staggered line or semi-circle, or moving from one "conversation" to another around the stage.

Split-focus scene: Approximately half of the group decides on a scenario related to the theme. The other half creates a contrasting scenario of their own. For example: The first half of the group creates an improv based on the scenario of homeless people on the street, begging for a handout because they are hungry. The other half improv a scene of people eating in a restaurant, enjoying an exquisite meal. The two groups take turns as they develop their scenes. Each freezes in a tableau while the other develops its scene a little further. In the end, the members of each group could find a way to connect, or interact, or not. It could also end with both in their own tableau. This provides the audience with a contrasting view of the issue and is interesting to see develop. It teaches the actors how to manage split focus on stage, ensuring that in all of their scenes, the audience's focus is appropriately directed (see: DIRECTING THE AUDIENCE'S GAZE, in Directing the Actors).

Colour commentary: All but one of the group members creates an improvisation. The other actor provides the colour commentary. In a light-hearted theme, this can be very funny. For a serious theme, this might be done more as a narrated, documentary style.

Entrances/exits: In combination with a group tableau, the improvised scene could be played like a tag/team improv, with various group members entering and exiting the scene, changing the scenario each time a new member is added or subtracted (see ADD A SCENE and SUBS IN, in SMALL GROUP IMPROVISATION).

MOVEMENT

There are many different ways to use movement as part of the Collective. While there is the possibility of movement in other areas, such as the fluid tableaux or in many of the improvisations, stand-alone movement pieces can speak to an audience in another way, quite apart from words spoken.

Choreographed dance piece: If there are dancers in the group, a piece might be choreographed using the chosen theme as a starting point. If, however, the group doesn't have dance training, movement can still be used very effectively (see CHOREOGRAPHY in the MOVEMENT chapter of the Classroom Training unit).

Contact improv: In contact improv style of postmodern dance, group members find ways of connecting physically, using their bodies to counterbalance, lift and support each other. Falling, rolling movements are also incorporated, working off of a partner's impulses while staying physically connected. Partners improvise movement segments which can be left as improvisations, or worked on and repeated, becoming set choreography. The form can be researched and might prove to be useful for some group members to explore.

Transitions: Short movement segments can be used to create bridges or transitions between various pieces of the Collage. Certain floor patterns or sets of movements (see MOVEMENT chapter) could be used to represent certain aspects of the theme, and brought back at appropriate times during the piece.

Movement patterns: Repetitive movement patterns may be used as transitions between pieces. It may be distracting to an audience to see actors randomly pacing about on the stage during or between segments, but stylized repetitive movements can act as one more cohesive element in the piece, drawing the eye and holding the attention. There are many ways to create these patterns. For example:

- Using the eight Laban Effort Actions (see CHARACTER), have each actor take on one of the characters, designating spots on the floor to move between. Use a few characters at a time to create specific sequences using this as a base. Several actors could take on the same Effort Action for one sequence, then another for a later sequence. Perhaps an improv develops between characters when they reach a designated spot.

- Create a square grid on the floor and explore ways of moving in straight lines, turning only at right angles, responding to the people you intersect with along your line, acknowledging them, or turning away to continue on an individual path, depending on the theme.

Movement metaphors: Express a metaphor for your theme in movement. For example: The theme is trust. All actors line up and fall back into the next actor's arms. The last actor starts to fall and realizing that there is no one there to catch him, says, "Hey!" and goes into the next piece. The theme is evolution. Actors begin strung out all along the edge of stage left. All take one step forward, with the actor downstage remaining in a prone position. The rest take another step across the stage, with the next actor remaining down on the floor in a crouched position. As each actor drops out of the line, she forms another tableau representing the evolutionary chain, from amoeba to man (on a cell phone).

Break out: The group creates a movement pattern, or free-form dance. On a prearranged signal, all freeze in tableaux, with only one person still animated, saying a word, a phrase or an entire monologue. This could be repeated for each group member, or done only once or twice.

Lines: If the group is large enough to form lines of a significant length, it could do so, changing the line formations in unison. It is important that everyone stop at exactly the same time. They could go into a line from downstage to upstage, across the stage, on a diagonal, in a circle, etc. If the groups are small, they may increase their linear look with outstretched arms, fingers touching each other. This might be a repeating motif to use as transitions between segments.

Musical pantomime: A pantomimed scene, discovered through improvisation may be set to music. A piece of music related to the theme could be used as the starting point to inspire a scene (see MUSICAL PANTOMIME in the MOVEMENT chapter).

Ideas for beginning movement exercises and choreography are covered in the Movement chapter, in Part I, Classroom Training.

SPOKEN WORD

While there are naturally occurring instances of spoken word involved in the exercises for tableaux and improvisation, there is also a place for spoken word that is presented on its own, not associated with actions. Having members of the group speak to the audience directly, either with their own voices or role-playing a character, can have a powerful impact. Words might be strung together as thoughts, or left to hang in the air as individuals. The effect is much like a piece of visual art that incorporates words that are written on a canvas, which can make a strong statement along with the image.

Sharing circle: A sharing circle may be created with group members seated on the floor. As a small object is passed around the circle, each person gives a sentence or two on what the theme means to her. The object can go around several times. Actors are free to pass or speak. Immediately following the circle, group members independently write a page about what they heard in the circle. They can include what they said and what others said. It can be in point form or by paragraphs. It could be done in the first person singular or third person. It could even be written as dialogue, with "he said," and "she said." The writings are collected and used in the scripting of the final piece. One sentence could be quoted, or a larger piece could become a monologue. It could be used as a dialogue between two or more actors, or each actor could speak one line at a time individually, to create a running narrative for a time, including the whole group. One word or phrase could be repeated, or used in canon, to create a soundscape. The possibilities are endless.

Word association: This exercise allows the group to spontaneously generate individual words that might be used in a Collage. They can either be spoken by individuals, or repeated as a group chant as a transition from one longer piece into another, to offer just two ways of using them in the final presentation. Each person in the group circle responds to the word given by the person next to him. The next person responds to that word. Begin with theme itself. After two rounds, increase to short phrases. Take five minutes to write down memorable words and phrases, to be used in the final presentation. Random words can be used as chants or repeated by individuals as transitions or in any other way the group may choose.

A common thread: A word or phrase that represents the theme can be used to unite the piece. It can be repeated often in different ways. It can be said in canon, in unison, or by individuals, and used as transitions between pieces or to punctuate scenes or ideas expressed throughout the piece.

Soundscapes: The spoken word in a Collage may not be words at all, but a soundscape created by members of the group. For example: It could start with one actor holding a long low note. A second joins in with short repetitive sounds in a midrange. A third creates an operatic aria that almost creates its own melody. It might expand to include the whole group, or be done by only some of the group members and used as a backdrop:

- Behind a scene or monologue, poem or a song done as a solo by another actor.

- With a movement piece done by the actors creating the sounds.

- As a transition from one segment to another.

- Drums or other instruments might be added at various times to mark a beat.
- Different instruments could represent different characters. Each sound supports a different character, as they go through a short pantomime piece together.
- Instead of vocals, a phrase from another exercise might be developed as a chant.

Monologues: Each member of the group could write a short monologue, as a character with some connection to the theme. They could choose characters that are victims, perpetrators of the problem, bystanders or anyone else that might have a story to tell that is thematically linked to the chosen theme. These monologues are very short, about 150 – 200 words each. Once they are written, the participants read them to each other. The group may choose to present them all, or just a few of them. Writers may perform their own work, or there may be some writers who are more comfortable having another group member perform their words. Two contrasting monologues may be performed together, broken up to become an intersecting, colliding, but not fully connected dialogue. For guidelines in writing monologues, see Monologues, in the Playwriting chapter at the end of this unit.

- Various group members could be involved in someone's monologue, repeating a word or phrase, interrupting it with another idea, asking a question, providing a soundscape or background movement, etc.

Poetry: Whether written by group members, or taken from published sources, poetry can be a powerful addition to a Collage Collective. Unlike Readers Theatre, where everything is static, and the voice alone conveys the message, in a Collage Collective, poetry can be staged in a very active way. It can also act as a voice-over for another element, such as a segment of movement. In other cases, the moment of stillness provided by a single voice, or choral group, might be just the break needed between two very active segments within the Collage.

Once the group has experienced a variety of these exercises, encourage experimentation to further develop some of the ideas that were started. Eventually, the various sequences and segments are set into an order that allows the piece as a whole to represent the chosen theme.

SAMPLE SCRIPT: Excerpt – opening of directed COLLAGE COLLECTIVE

WABADEEN

(phonetic spelling for Arabic word, meaning, "What's Next?")

Tableaux – actors on set made up of two ladders and several boxes and platforms.

Jenn:	Within me lives a purpose; a reason why I'm here. *(group echoes, "here")*
Inga:	Where? *(group echoes "where")*
Jenn:	And one day soon it will say to me...

(3-second beat)

Rachel:	Me, look at me! *(jumps off box)*
Liz:	Hi there, the world needs you. Are you ready?
Adelle:	Me, I'm not some girl who wants that ordinary dream.
Cheryl:	If there were ever a time to dare to make a difference, it is now.
Liz:	Not for any grand course, necessarily, but for something that tugs at your heart.
Melissa:	Something that's your dream.
Paul:	Our desires, hopes and dreams can change on the slightest whim.
Nicole:	Or be bred into us forever.
Joel:	We're all looking for something. *(begins pattern of repetitive stage crosses)*
Jenn:	We set goals. *(cross)*
Corinne:	I hope to fulfill my dream. *(cross)*
Gord:	I hope to graduate. *(cross)*
Nicole:	I want to lead a healthy life. *(cross)*
Inga:	Aren't you healthy now? *(cross)*
Adelle:	I desire to go up in a hot air balloon. *(cross)*
Liz:	I hope to sleep all day. *(cross)*

Rachel:	I desire world peace. *(all stop and sigh)*
Cheryl:	I desire clothes that will fit me.
Paul:	I hope I won't need dentures after all this money on braces.
Corinne:	*(cross DSC)* I hope for an unforgettable journey through life, full of fun, adventures and unbelievable happiness.

DESIRE TABLEAUX with Improvs.

Rachel tap dances on top of piano while Liz plays "dream" song.

| Gord: | *(cross DSC)* Wabadeen. *(group echoes "wabadeen")* |

And the piece continues...

This opening is rapid fire, allowing all of the participants at least one line as they introduce their theme. The lines all came out of the circle sharing exercise, which was transcribed by each individual right after the exercise. The director gathered all the transcriptions, and pulled out suitable quotes. The actors didn't necessarily speak the lines that they had shared in the circle. Once written, the words can be used in any way suitable and spoken by anyone. The rest of the piece contains the results of many of the tableaux and improvisation exercises listed above. There were some short improvisations and monologues that told a story, but the rest of the piece was more esoteric, evocative of the theme's mood; what might happen next in the lives of these young people.

PLAYWRITING

In addition to improvising scenes for a Collage Collective, there may be a time that you or your class will want to write a scene, or a play, collectively, or as solo playwrights. If the purpose is to create dialogue without a fully staged play, consider the option of writing a Radio Play, as outlined in the Voice chapter.

The following suggestions are based on notes that I took in a playwriting workshop with Tomson Highway, author of *The Rez Sisters* and *Dry Lips Oughta Move to Kapuskasing.* You will find agreement in many sources for what he suggests every play needs. The process for creating the piece as a group activity is uniquely his own.

Tomson says it is important to create with the right side of your brain, your creativity, not intellect. You will not move an audience with intellectual writing. There are certain things that every play needs:

Rhythm: Mesmerize an audience with the rhythm of the lines. Regular rhythms put the audience to sleep. A play needs variety in its rhythms. Understand classical music and you will understand how to pace dialogue in a play.

Characters: Create unforgettable, fascinating characters. Go for maximum impact, strong choices. Don't do anything halfway. The character is very sad, or very happy. It's the best day or the worst day, etc.

Story: Tell a story that is interesting and riveting. The story must have a spine, a through-line, and an arc that it follows. Every scene within it has its own spine. Every monologue within every scene has its own spine.

The SPINE of the play must be able to be expressed in three words:

SUBJECT – TRANSITIVE (action) VERB – OBJECT

Pronoun or proper noun – Something you can do (not just feel) – Tangible noun

For example: Tanya crushes the monster. Robert uncovers the treasure.

Objectives: Every character must have an agenda, an objective. The play ends when the main character meets his/her objective, or fails trying; completes or does not complete his/her agenda. Each character's agenda is different from the others. The spine of the play relates to the main character's agenda. There will be a character that will help the main character win her objective and another character that tries to stop her.

The first draft will be a story that you know very well. By the seventh draft, the real people you wrote about will no longer recognize themselves.

PROCESS

1. Go around the group, everyone telling a short, true story.
2. Leader chooses one that the group will work on and develop into a play.

3. Open phone book randomly, point with finger to find names of characters (first name, middle and last). Do the same for their parents, siblings; anyone they talk about and place action is set in. Talk about historical significance of the time they were born and grew up in. The phone book is part of the magic. You will make connections with what you find that you would never think of if only using your intellect. I would add that you could use the same process to find birthdays, with a multi-page calendar. Using this method I once created a character who was born on April 1, April Fools' Day. I would never have thought to make that up, but was able to use it in the story. You could also use an atlas for important places, a hand-drawn clock face for times, etc.

4. Write out the entire history of each character. This could be done in point form, as a group.

5. Find the main character's agenda, the spine of the play. Keep it clear, simple and straightforward.

6. Write a monologue about an important event for each decade of each character's life.

7. Write a monologue for each character's favourite sport, flower, gemstone, colour, animal, song, bird, food, anything.

8. Write a monologue for each character's worst nightmare and greatest fantasy.

9. Assign the writing of these monologues to all of the group members, with the goal of everyone writing a set number of monologues between each meeting. Individual writing could also take place simultaneously, as meeting time allows.

10. Read monologues around the table, at least one per person.

11. Combine monologues that work together, or present contrasting views and turn them into dialogues for scenes. Leave others as monologues. Create the rhythm of the piece by varying the lengths of monologues and dialogues. For example, a section of rapid-fire short dialogue could be followed by a lengthy monologue, which could be followed by a section of mid- and short-length lines of dialogue created from several intersecting monologues.

While this method of creating a play works wonderfully for a small group, it is also effective for a single playwright. The playwright follows the same process, writing the monologues for each character, then combining them. My play, *Cry After Midnight*, a three-character play based on the war in Afghanistan, and my experiences as a Canadian Forces' 'war artist' there, was written in this way. While the characters were never in a traditional dialogue with each other, at times their monologues intersected or collided, or mirrored each other's thoughts, but from their own perspectives. Overlapping dialogue at certain times heightened this effect.

RULES FOR MONOLOGUES

- ALWAYS use ONLY present tense verbs. It brings the audience a step closer to the material.

- Use verbs with strong actions. For example: crawl, fly, creep, walk, run, instead of comes.

- Make the date, day of the week and time of day specific for each monologue. Even the weather will affect the speaker. Decide why the time, etc. is important.

- Write from your own perspective, not the character's. This can be transferred to the character in future drafts. If you try to write as the character, it sounds artificial and contrived. Write from your own soul. This is very important. You will hear the difference.

- Don't have more than one or two ideas, topics or imagines per monologue. Don't make it too crowded. Make them very specific, not general. Too many topics in a monologue confuse the audience and they lose interest.

- Make extreme choices; don't do anything halfway. Love it or hate it; strong attitudes.

- For the most part, write positively. You usually lose an audience with negativity. It is more interesting to see a character that is excited about something than down on it. Negative attitudes tend to repel an audience. They don't want to listen. You don't want the action to recede. You want attitudes and verbs that take the action forward.

- Employ the senses: you see it, feel it, hear it and touch it. Let it build in intensity.

- Every monologue has a spine; a through-line.

- Keep it all very simple. Sometimes you don't have to say every word. You can let the pause do the work rather than spelling it all out. For example: "Her hair..." rather than, "I love her hair." Overwriting only encourages overacting; theatrics.

- Don't tell what you can show. For example: Describing what you love about something shows that you love it. You don't have to say you love it.

After writing the first draft of a monologue, highlight all the verbs:

- Are they all transitive verbs; strong actions rather than just states of being?
- Do the verbs themselves have a spine, a through-line? Do you get a sense of the story by just reading them in order?
- Do they build in intensity; create a dramatic arc?

I would add the following tips when writing a monologue:

- A monologue is character driven. It is written from a character's point of view (your own, initially). It is a personal story, not a neutral retelling of an event.
- It works well to imagine another character that (you) this character is speaking to. The writer can imagine the reaction of the other character to things said and allow these reactions to push the narrative further.
- The monologue should be about something that allows for shifts and discoveries, so that it isn't played all on one level.
- It may be useful to decide whether the character will project an air of vulnerability or strength. Perhaps there could be a shift from one to the other.

SCENES

There may be times when students will take an improvised scene and script it for inclusion in a piece of devised theatre. Improvising the scene initially is a very accessible process for new writers. The following points should be considered when editing a scene.

- The scene should have a beginning, middle and end. This doesn't mean that everything is resolved at the end, but it has a spine and an arc.
- Each character must have an objective, something that she wants from the other character, a reason for remaining in the scene. Objectives should be phrased as a positive, rather than a negative. "I want...", rather than, "I don't want..." These objectives should be fairly concrete, phrased as an action, rather than an emotion. "I want...", rather than, "I feel...". There will be obstacles standing in the way of what they

want, and tactics or strategies they employ to win their objectives.

- Conflict is much more interesting to play and to watch than harmony. The objective of one character should not mesh easily with that of other characters.

- Consideration should be given to status. Are these characters of equal or different status? Are they both comfortable with the status they have in relation to the other characters or is the struggle for status part of the conflict? What is a character trying to win?

- Encourage students to base their stories on people that they know, rather than characters from movies or television that are already the result of someone else's imagination.

- The point of a scene (or play) is to ask questions of the audience, not to make statements. Let the audience answer the questions. If your scene has a message for the audience, find a way of introducing it that does not preach.

- You can use humour in tragedies, but remain appropriate with your subject matter. Know the difference between having characters find hope through laughter in a difficult situation, and making fun of something.

COMEDY

Writing comedy can be difficult to do purposefully. We know that in a comedy, there is a happy ending. In a tragedy, there is a sad ending. But how do we write comedy?

For definitions of comedy, we need look no further than Homer Simpson of the long-running animated comedy series *The Simpsons*. Homer occasionally comes out with his definitions of comedy, which are based on long-held universal beliefs.

- It's funny because it's true.
- It's funny because it didn't happen to me.

Generally, we laugh at things we recognize; things we relate to that have happened or could happen to us, especially things that come out of our anxieties. The second definition may seem more problematic. Can we laugh at the misfortune of others? When does that cross the line? It is actually quite easy to define. We can laugh at the misfortune of others only when we see that there is no real pain involved. Sometimes we laugh at someone who slips and falls. It is quite an automatic response, as it can look comical to see someone go down, with arms and legs flailing. If the person falling immediately shows us that he is not physically injured, it will remain funny. However, if the person is physically injured, the laughter must stop. The difference between tragedy and comedy is the pain. In comedy, outrageous things can happen, events that you might well think could kill someone. However, the comic character recovers from the injury very quickly. Often, the character will have nothing hurt but his pride. When the audience sees no other effect of the injury, it stays in the realm of comedy.

THIRD TIME LUCKY

This exercise can act as a way into writing comedy. It gives the scene a structure and teaches students about the "comedic repetition of three" rule. It also deals with one of the fundamentals of comedy; the element of surprise. The audience is lulled into expecting more of the same when something changes, delivering the punch line.

Method: In pairs or small groups, have students prepare a scene in which an event happens repetitively. A situation is set up that is familiar to the audience. Everything is predictable on the first two repetitions. On the third repetition, something surprising happens. It may be helpful to give them one scenario to play, as a practice, before they develop their own. The samples are quite obvious, to be used as a starting point. In developing their own plays, they might use more subtlety in their situations and humour.

Sample activities:

- A pop machine that works fine (or not) twice, with something different happening with the third person that tries to buy a pop
- A water cooler or coffee machine in an office that malfunctions on the third usage
- Store clerks stacking shelves successfully twice, before a disaster occurs
- A fortune teller that gives two people predictable readings, before being surprised by the third customer
- Three customers in a coffee shop or ice cream stand, with the third one receiving something unexpected

Variation #1. In a longer scene, or collection of scenes, the results of this exercise could become a running gag, brought back three times, with an ever-increasing payoff each time. This would bring in another concept of comedy: the audience's expectation of a laugh. They laughed the first time the scene was played, so expect them to laugh again when they see the same set-up recur. This will increase their enjoyment of the humour.

SAMPLE SCRIPT LAYOUTS

Here are two different examples of how a script could be set up.

1. The following example is generally used in published scripts, as it takes up less space, saving on total pages.

The Name of the Play is in the header with the page #

The stage directions are italicized, and set to the left margin. Included would be anything the actors needed to know about their opening positions. They might also include a description of the set; so another group could use the script to perform the piece again.

ONE: The lines spoken by a character are set on a short tab off of the character's name, which is on the left margin. Subsequent lines by the same character (*and any actions ONE performs*) are set off the left margin with an even smaller tab.

TWO: The second character's lines follow, with one blank line spacing them from the first character's lines. (*any action done by a character in relationship to his/her lines is put in parentheses and italicized, without a capital letter beginning the instruction or punctuation ending it*)

THREE: All dialogues continues in this way. (*then another action takes place by the third character. If another instruction is included, it follows in a full sentence with a Capital letter and punctuation.*) Then the character's next line follows.

If some action is taken by other than the last character to speak, for example, by ONE, it is set apart from the text, in italics and full sentences, but no parentheses.

TWO: And so the script continues.

ONE: Characters speak and interact with each other, as the script dictates.

2. Generally used in working scripts, this layout makes it easy for actors to see when they speak, and what is coming up next.

The Name of the Play is centered on the page

> *The stage directions are italicized, and tabbed away from the left margin. Included would be anything the actors needed to know about their opening positions. They might also include a description of the set; so another group could use the script to perform the piece again.*

ONE

The lines first spoken by a character are set on the left margin, with no tab, under the name of the character, which is in caps and centered on the line.

TWO

(*if TWO does something before speaking, it looks like this*) The second character's lines follow, with one blank line spacing them from the first character's lines. (*any action done by this character is put in parentheses and italicized, without a capital letter beginning the instruction or punctuation ending it*) If the character continues to speak, it is included in the same paragraph.

THREE

All dialogues continue in this way. (*an action takes place by the third character. If another instruction is included, it follows the first in a full sentence with a Capital letter and punctuation.*) Then the character's next line follows.

> *If some action is taken by other than the last character to speak, it is set apart from the text, tabbed over from the left margin, in italics and full sentences, but no parentheses. If TWO or some other characters are involved, their names are entered in CAPS.*

TWO

And so the script continues.

ONE

Characters speak and interact with each other, as the script dictates.

GLOSSARY

STAGE POSITIONS

A stage can be divided in areas, like a grid, so that everyone can learn their names and identify them instantly.

The front of the stage, nearest the audience, is called downstage. In the early days of theatre, rather than have the audience on raised seating, the stage itself was tilted, or raked, towards the audience, so they would be able to see what was going on at the back of the stage, or literally, the upstage area. The front of the stage, nearest the audience, was literally tilted down, and so was called the downstage area. The sides of the stage are labeled according to the actor's right and left, not the director's. On a large stage, the positions would look like this:

UR	UCR	UC	UCL	UL
R	CR	C	CL	L
DR	DCR	DC	DCL	DL

LEGEND:

    C = Center
    L = Left
    R = Right
    D = Down
    U = Up

These are the abbreviations of the terms. Each of them could also have the word STAGE in the middle, as in, DL = DSL (downstage left) and L, could be expressed as SL (stage left).

If the stage is very small the Center Left and Center Right areas can be eliminated, leaving only nine stage areas in total.

UR	UC	UL
R	C	L
DR	DC	DL

TYPES OF THEATRE STAGES

Black Box: A room, usually painted black, converted into a theatre, with stage and seating areas, usually not permanent. Curtains and lights are rigged for use.

Found or Created Stage: An unconventional space that is converted to stage a production, usually on a temporary basis for the run of a play.

Promenade Theatre: There is no actual permanent stage or seating. The audience travels with the action of the play, led from one staging area to another.

Proscenium: The most common configuration. Stage opening is framed by the proscenium arch, through which the audience views the stage. The audience is seated in front of the arch. It may have an apron, which is an extension to the stage, which juts out into the audience past the front curtain.

Theatre in the Round: The audience is seated all around the stage. Entrances and exits are made through gaps in the seating areas. It is sometimes also called an Arena stage.

Thrust Stage: The audience is seated on three sides of the stage. It has a backstage area behind the upstage wall.

Traverse Stage: Quite uncommon in modern theatres, it is also known as the Alley or Corridor stage. The audience is seated on two (opposite) sides of the stage, facing each other. A modern adaptation is the fashion show catwalk.

STAGE AND ACTING TERMS

Ad-lib: To improvise action or dialogue within a scene.

Auditorium: The part of the theatre that seats the audience.

Backdrop: A curtain hung upstage, behind any scenery or set pieces, providing the back wall of the stage set. It may be painted to represent some part of the set. Frequently, the backdrop is replaced by a cyclorama.

Backstage: The areas of the stage that are not seen by the audience.

Blackout: To cut out the lights quickly, leaving the stage in darkness.

Blocking:

1. The collective movements of the actors in the play as a whole.
2. Obstructing the audience's view of something on the stage.

Border: A short length of curtain hung across the stage, above the playing area, to mask the loft from the audience's view.

Counter cross:

1. A shifting of position by one actor, when another actor crosses his path, done to minimize the amount of time the front actor is blocking him from the audience's view.
2. The shifting of more than one actor in order to balance the stage picture.

Cue:

1. The last words of a dialogue, or an action of one actor, which signals the action or dialogue of another actor.
2. A technical change in sound or lighting.

Cyc or cyclorama: A background curtain around the back of the playing area on stage. It could be black, to mask the backstage area, or white, to be coloured by the lighting.

Drop: A length of fabric, usually canvas, hung from the grid, attached top and bottom to battens.

Exit or exeunt: The word for leaving the stage.

Flat: A frame, made of wood, covered with canvas fabric and used a backdrop in a box set.

Fly loft: The area above the stage, where scenery is hung, masked from the audience.

Fly: To lower and raise scenery to the stage level.

Fresnel: A stage light that results in a soft-edged beam of light, generally used to create a wash of light on the stage. Usually pronounced "fre-nel."

Gauze or scrim: A large curtain, made of heavy gauze fabric, which is semi-transparent when backlit and opaque when lit from the front.

Gibberish: A made-up language. It could use sounds resembling a specific language.

Give focus: To direct the audience's gaze. This can be done by:

- A strong stage position
- Lighting
- The gaze of other actors on stage

Green room: A backstage room used for the actors, to lounge or wait for entrances.

Legs: Lengths of cloth hung on each side of the stage to mask the backstage area.

Leko: A type of stage light, named for its brand, that results in a hard-edged circle of light. It is also called an Ellipsoidal Reflector Spotlight (ERS) or Profile Spot. It is the one generally used for Specials.

Monologue: A speech said by one character.

Motivated movement: Any movement by a character that has a reason or motivation.

Places: The call for actors and crew to find their opening positions for the start of a show.

Pre-set:

1. The set-up before the show, with everything in place and ready to go.
2. The lighting used on the stage as the audience enters the theatre.

Sightline: An imaginary line drawn from a position on the stage to the corner of the auditorium to define the portion of the stage that is visible to audience members seated on the sides of the theatre.

Special: A light that is used for a special effect, often focused on a specific spot on the stage, generally for an individual performer.

Stage cross or cross: Any movement of an actor from one area of the stage to another.

Stage picture: What the audience sees on the stage; the positions of the actors, sets and props.

Strike: The call from the stage manager to remove set pieces from the stage, or to remove the entire set.

Rigging: All the hardware used to lower, lift and secure the performance equipment on or above the stage.

Traveler: A front curtain that opens to the sides, rather than up and down.

Two-hander: A scene or play with two characters. Not to be confused with two-actor, which is a play with two acts.

Upstaging: To steal focus or attention from another actor at an inappropriate time. This can be done in two different ways:

- Making noises, faces (mugging), or performing actions while others should have focus.
- Standing upstage of an actor during a two-way dialogue, thereby forcing him to turn upstage in order to continue the conversation. His back is now presented to the audience and he is giving focus to the upstage actor, directing the audience's gaze there as well.

Wash: Sometimes called a general wash, as it is used to cover the stage in light. Often it will be in a specific colour, either warm—reds and yellows, or cold—blues and whites.

Wings: The backstage areas on the right and left of the playing area.

SUGGESTED READINGS

Adler, Stella, Howard Kissel, editor. *The Art of Acting*, New York, NY: Applause Books, 2005.

Ball, David. *Backwards & Forwards: A Technical Manual for Reading Plays.* Carbondale, Il: Southern Illinois University Press, 1983.

Barr, Tony. *Acting for the Camera.* New York, NY: HarperCollins, 1997.

Boal, Augusto. Charles McBride, translator. *Theatre of the Oppressed.* New York, NY: Theatre Communications Group, 1993.

_____. *Games for Actors and Non Actors.* New York, NY: Routledge, 2002.

Bogart, Anne, and Tina Landau. *The Viewpoints Book.* New York, NY: Theatre Communications Group, 2005.

Braverman, Danny. *Playing a Part: Drama and Citizenship.* Staffordshire, UK: Trentham Books, 2002.

Brook, Peter. *The Empty Space.* New York, NY: Touchstone, 1995.

Bruder, Melissa, and Michael Cohn, Madeleine Olnek, Nathaniel Pollack, Robert Previto, Scott Zigler. *A Practical Handbook for the Actor.* New York, NY: Vintage Books, 1986.

Carroll, John, M. Anderson and D. Cameron. *Real Players? Drama, Technology and Education.* Staffordshire, UK: Trentham Books, 2006.

Chekhov, Michael. *To the Actor.* New York, NY: Routledge, 2013.

Cohen, Robert. *Acting One/Acting Two.* New York, NY: McGraw-Hill, 2007.

Clurman, Harold. *On Directing.* New York, NY: Touchstone, 1997.

Chubbuck, Ivana. *The Power of the Actor: The Chubbuck Technique.* New York, NY: Gotham Books, 2004.

Flemming, Michael. *The Art of Drama Teaching.* Abingdon, UK: D. Fulton Publishers, 1997.

Gallagher, Kathleen. *Theatre of Urban: Youth and Schooling in Dangerous Times.* Toronto, ON: University of Toronto Press, 2007.

Grotowski, Jerzy. *Towards a Poor Theatre.* New York, NY: Theatre Arts Routledge, 2002.

Hagen, Uta. *Respect for the Actor.* Hoboken, NJ: Wiley, 2008.

_____. *A Challenge for the Actor.* New York, NY: Charles Scribner's Sons, 1991.

Halpern, Charna, and Del Close. *Truth in Comedy.* Colorado Springs, CO: Meriwether Publishing Limited, 2004.

Johnson, Margaret. *The Drama Teacher's Survival Guide; A Complete Tool Kit for Theatre Arts.* Colorado Springs, CO: Meriwether Publishing, 2007.

Lee, Dennis and Frank Newfeld, illustrator. *Alligator Pie.* Toronto, ON: Key Porter Kids, 2001.

Little, Jennifer. *Changing the Way We Think: Using Arts to Inspire, Empower and Change Your Community.* North Charleston, SC: 2011.

Mamet, David. *True and False: Heresy and Common Sense for the Actor.* New York, NY: Vintage Books, 1999.

Meisner, Sanford, and Dennis Longwell. *Sanford Meisner On Acting.* New York, NY: Vintage, 1987.

Miner, Sue, and Mark Brownell. *Break a Leg: An Actor's Guide to Theatrical Practices, Phrases and Superstitions.* Winnipeg, MB: J. Gordon Shillingford Publishing Inc., 2011.

Oddey, Alison. *Devising Theatre: A Practical and Theoretical Handbook.* New York, NY: Routledge, 1996.

Robinson, Davis. *The Physical Comedy Handbook.* Chicago, Ill: Heinemann Drama, 1999.

Rolfe, Bari. *Commedia del'arte: a scene study book*. Berkeley, CA: Personnabooks, 1992.

Rosenfeld, Carol. *Acting and Living in Discovery: A Notebook for the Actor*. Newburyport, MA: Focus Publishing/R.Pullins Co., 2013.

Shurtleff, Michael. *Audition: Everything an Actor Needs to Know to Get the Part*. New York, NY: Walker & Company, 2003.

Spolin, Viola. *Improvisation for the Theatre: A Handbook of Teaching and Directing Techniques*. 3rd ed. Evanston, Ill: Northwestern University Press, 1999.

_____. *Theatre Games for Rehearsal: A Director's Handbook*. Evanston, Ill: Northwest University Press, 1985.

_____. *Theatre Games for the Classroom: A Teacher's Handbook*. Evanston, Ill: Northwestern University Press, 1986.

Stanislavski, Constantin. *An Actor's Handbook,* Translation, edited, E. Reynolds, New York, NY: Theatre Arts Books, 1996.

_____. *An Actor Prepares*. New York, NY: Routledge, 1989.

_____. *Building a Character*. New York, NY: Routledge, 1989.

Swados, Elizabeth. *At Play: Teaching Teenagers Theatre*. New York, NY: 2006.

Turner, Victor. *From Ritual to Theatre: The Human Seriousness of Play*. New York, NY: Performing Arts Journal Publications, 1982.

Wangh, Stephen. *An Acrobat of the Heart: A Physical Approach to Acting Inspired by the Work of Jerzy Grotowski*. New York, NY: Vintage Books, 2000.

Weston, Judith. *Directing Actors: Creating Memorable Performances for Film & Television*. Studio City, CA: Michael Wiese Productions, 1999.

Wilcox, Janet. *Mastering Monologues and Acting Sides*. New York, NY: Allworth Press, 2011.